Aristotle's Children

ALSO BY RICHARD E. RUBENSTEIN

Rebels In Eden
Left Turn
Alchemists of Revolution
Comrade Valentine
When Jesus Became God

RICHARD E. RUBENSTEIN

Aristotle's Children

HOW CHRISTIANS, MUSLIMS, AND JEWS REDISCOVERED ANCIENT WISDOM AND ILLUMINATED THE DARK AGES

HARCOURT, INC.

Orlando   Austin   New York   San Diego   Toronto   London

www.HarcourtBooks.com

Illustrations by David Toohey

Library of Congress Cataloging-in-Publication Data
Rubenstein, Richard E.
Aristotle's children: how Christians, Muslims, and Jews rediscovered
ancient wisdom and illuminated the Dark Ages /Richard E. Rubenstein.—1st ed.
p.   cm.
Includes bibliographical references and index.
ISBN 0-15-100720-9
1. Scholasticism.   2. Aristotle—Influence.
3. Faith and reason—Christianity—History of doctrines.   I. Title.
B734.R79   2003
189'.4—dc21   2003006582

Text set in Fournier
Designed by Linda Lockowitz

Printed in the United States of America

First edition
A C E G I K J H F D B

For Susan

"Love calls us to the things of this world."

CONTENTS

FROM THE BEGINNING, *Aristotle's Children* has been a series of surprises. One maps out a book in advance, of course, just like planning for any other journey. But there are books that carry the author in unforeseen directions—journeys that end with the traveler gazing, wide-eyed, at a landscape that resembles nothing in any tourist guide.

I first came across the story of the Aristotelian Revolution while doing research on the causes of religious conflict. In the twelfth century, I learned, Christian churchmen working in formerly Muslim Spain rediscovered the bulk of Aristotle's writings, which had been lost to the West for almost a thousand years. No intellectual discovery before or after had anything like the impact of this remarkable find. Translated into Latin by multicultural teams of scholars, and distributed throughout Europe's new universities, the recovered documents triggered a century-long struggle that forever altered the way we think about nature, society, and even about God.

The story itself was the first surprise. What most astonished me was how little known it was, considering its high level of dramatic interest and great historical importance. The Aristotelian

Revolution transformed Western thinking and set our culture on a path of scientific inquiry that it has followed ever since the Middle Ages. The confrontation between faith and reason that turned the medieval universities into ideological battlegrounds continues to this day in societies around the globe. One could hardly imagine a more pertinent story for modern readers, yet few people outside a small circle of academic specialists seemed to know anything about it. This was a puzzle whose solution eluded me until I had written most of the book.

One clue was the growing uneasiness I felt as I plunged more deeply into research about life in the medieval universities and the Church's reaction to the Aristotelian challenge. The historical materials seemed to contradict much of what I had been taught to believe about the emergence of the modern world from medieval backwardness. I knew—or thought I knew—that the High Middle Ages in Europe was an era of passionate religious faith and the bloody Crusades, inquisitorial terror, and fierce doctrinal dogmatism. I knew—or thought I knew—that Aristotle was the Father of Science, a thinker who believed that human reason, not tradition, revelation, or sentiment, could uncover objective truths about the universe. Naturally, in bringing these volatile extremes together, I expected an explosion. The Aristotelian Revolution would no doubt be a drama like Galileo versus the Inquisition or Charles Darwin versus the Creationists: an earlier version of the modern morality play in which brave Reason suffers at the hands of villainous Superstition before triumphing in the sunny dawn of Science.

Wrong! The story I found myself telling was far more complex and interesting than this stock scenario. Yes, scientific thinking in the West *did* begin in the intellectual explosion that followed the rediscovery of Aristotle's writings. But European Christians did *not* split into "rationalist" and "fundamentalist" camps, as I had expected. In a way that violated all of my modernist preconceptions, the leading force for transformative change in Western thinking turned out to be the leadership of the Catholic Church—the very same leadership that was also conducting anti-Muslim Crusades and burning Christian heretics.

Rather than choose between the new learning and the old religion, the popes and scholars of the High Middle Ages tried to modernize the Church by reconciling faith and reason. This Herculean task generated one of the richest, most searching debates in Western history—a battle of innovative thinkers whose discussions ranged over a vast spectrum of disputed issues, from the nature of scientific knowledge and the basic structures of mind and matter to the hope of immortality, the problem of evil, the sources of moral value, and the basic criteria for living a good life. Meeting the great scholastics and reliving their stormy debates proved an unexpectedly moving and absorbing experience—so much so, that my friends and students claimed that I had "disappeared" into the Middle Ages. But it was not really an escape from the present, since the concerns of these medieval thinkers resonate so sonorously with ours.

The Aristotelian Revolution took place during a period of economic growth, political expansion, and cultural awakening unprecedented in Europe: a turbulent, creative, dangerous era that some call the "medieval renaissance." People then, as now, felt a great yearning for wholeness and meaning in a world suddenly grown both smaller and more unfamiliar. They were consumed by the desire to *understand*, and by the need to make their lives on earth count for something. Perhaps that is why memorable characters like Peter Abelard and Roger Bacon, Thomas Aquinas, William of Ockham, and Meister Eckhardt seem to speak to us so directly about matters of common concern. Like us, they were experiencing an unsettling sort of "globalization."

Their great passion was to integrate their understanding of the way things are and the way they should be. Their mission as Aristotelians and as Christians was to bring intellectual and moral order into a transforming world.

By the fourteenth century, despite these efforts, faith and reason were already headed toward the conflict-ridden separation that has characterized their relations ever since. What our story demonstrates, however, is that this condition is not eternal. The civilization that we call modern, with its split between the cultures of the heart and the head, its sanctification of power, "privatization" of religion, and commodification of values, emerged out of a very different past, and is in the process of evolving toward a very different future. Late in the writing process, it dawned on me that this might account for the studied indifference that has all but erased the Aristotelian Revolution from our historical memory. Such blank spots are often the result of the semiconscious neglect reserved for stories that run counter to generally accepted notions of who we are as a people, and how we got that way. Even though they relate to events that happened long, long ago, these contrary tales still have an unsettling capacity to "rock the boat."

So it is with the story told here. In reliving the Aristotelian Revolution, we understand that we are *not* just the children of Copernicus and Galileo, Adam Smith, and Thomas Jefferson, but Aristotle's children: the heirs of a medieval tradition that seems more intriguing and inspiring as the shortcomings of modernity become clearer. Of course, most of us would not return to the Middle Ages if we could. Few people today would embrace the assumptions and conclusions of the medieval scholastics. But the Aristotelians' quest for meaning is also ours, and we have much to learn from their vision of a science infused by ethics and a religion unafraid of reason. In this little-known but formative chapter of our history, we may detect hints of a more humane and integrated global future.

Aristotle's Children

The Medieval Star-Gate

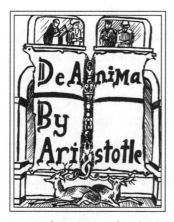

T HERE ARE FEW stories more appealing than tales of ancient knowledge long lost, then astonishingly found. In the classic version, an unsuspecting discoverer uncovers buried tablets while digging in a field, stumbles upon clay jars in a cave, or finds a dust-covered lamp or chest in the attic. Worthless junk, surely. On the verge of discarding it, however, the finder hesitates. What odd signs and symbols are these, etched in the metal, inscribed in stone, or inked on rolls of stiffened parchment? Perhaps the musty old thing has some value after all. The innocent discoverer has no idea, of course, that these arcane markings embody the voices of a vanished world. Someone more knowledgeable will have to recognize the relic for what it is: an intellectual treasure far more precious than gold or jewels. A source of ancient wisdom and power. Yes—a potent talisman capable of conjuring up the past, altering the present, and disclosing the path to the future.

The tale I am about to tell does not have this classic storybook form—there are many discoverers, not just one, and many discoveries as well—but in some ways it is more wonderful than the story of Aladdin's lamp or the search for the lost Ark of the Covenant. Make no mistake about it, this is a history not a fairytale. But it is not the sort of history to which the inhabitants of a scientific age are accustomed.

Could there be hidden in some long-forgotten storehouse a treasure trove of ancient knowledge—a body of learning so powerful and advanced that recovering it would revolutionize our thinking and transform our lives? From the standpoint of modern science, the notion is utter fantasy. We understand that scientific learning is cumulative, with each generation building on the work of its predecessors. We know a great deal more about the universe than our grandparents did, and their knowledge far outweighs that of their ancestors. Looking back, this implies a law of diminishing intellectual returns—a regression in knowledge that, projected back a millennium or two, leaves little room for the "secrets of the ancients." Moreover, the old documents we do discover, like the Dead Sea Scrolls and the Gnostic Gospels, do not contain revolutionary truths. As fascinating as they are, they do not threaten to overthrow our worldview, transform our science, or provide us with new models of social or political organization. Except in science fiction, one would not expect ancient writings to reveal a practical method of time travel, the secret of eternal youth, or even a cure for the common cold.

Of course not, seeing that "hard" scientific knowledge is cumulative. What one might expect to find in ancient manuscripts is noncumulative knowledge, "soft" learning involving issues of faith, ethics, folk wisdom, and personal philosophy. When it comes to deciding how to live and die, many people find the stories and sayings of the Bible, the Bhagavad Gita, the Koran, and other sacred books inspiring, although it is not at all certain how (or even whether) their truths can be proved. "Vanity of vanities, all is vanity." "Love thy neighbor as thyself." "God helps those who help themselves." Nowadays people call such thoughts "wisdom," although the ancients themselves would never think of separating ethical, religious, or philosophical knowledge from knowledge of the universe in general.[1] But we have been taught to make precisely this separation. The split between knowledge and wisdom, between the provable, apparently objective truths of science and the intuitive, subjective truths of religion and personal philosophy is a hallmark of what people now call the modern perspective. Ancient wisdom is fine in its place, says the modernist gospel, but when it comes to understanding how *Homo sapiens* and the rest of the universe are constructed, how they evolved, and how they operate, we will not find much of this sort of learning before the Age of Reason.

Yet the idea of lost knowledge haunts even the skeptical consciousness of a scientific age. Banished from respectable discourse, it reappears in the form of legends and folktales about secrets of the pyramids, chariots of the Gods, and powerful relics that guard their treasures against impure investigators. One of the most vivid versions of the myth is that recounted by science-fiction writer Arthur C. Clarke, which Stanley Kubrick brought to the screen in his classic movie *2001: A Space Odyssey*. In that film, modern scientists discover an ancient artifact—a black monolith—buried on the moon. Eventually they come to understand that the mysterious object is a bequest from an alien people, a gift planted on Luna eons ago by representatives of an advanced interstellar species. Although the object's discovery seems accidental, the astral visitors who buried it made sure that human beings would find it only when they were prepared to appreciate and use it—that is, ready to take the next step in their social evolution.

Unimaginably ancient (Clarke envisions a similar monolith stimulating the original transformation from hominid to man), its real function is that of a "star-gate": a portal to the interplanetary future.

Our story, as I said, is not fantasy or science fiction, but the discovery it describes is far more like Arthur Clarke's monolith than the Dead Sea Scrolls. Once upon a time in the West, in Spain, to be exact, a collection of documents that had lain in darkness for more than one thousand years was brought to light, and the effects of the discovery were truly revolutionary. Aristotle's books were the medieval Christians' star-gate. For Europeans of the High Middle Ages, the dramatic reappearance of the Greek philosopher's lost works was an event so unprecedented and of such immense impact as to be either miraculous or diabolical, depending on one's point of view. The knowledge contained in these manuscripts was "hard" as well as "soft," and it was remarkably comprehensive. Some three thousand pages of material ranging over the whole spectrum of learning from biology and physics to logic, psychology, ethics, and political science seemed to be a bequest from a superior civilization.

Or, I should say, from two superior civilizations. For Aristotle's books were not discovered written in Greek and stored in clay jars, but written in Arabic and housed in the libraries of the great universities at Baghdad, Cairo, Toledo, and Cordoba. After the fall of the Roman Empire and the collapse of order in Europe, the works of Aristotle and other Greek scientists became the intellectual property of the prosperous and enlightened Arab civilization that ruled the great southern crescent extending from Persia to Spain. As a result, when Western Europeans translated these works into Latin with the help of Muslim and Jewish scholars, they also translated the works of their leading Islamic and Jewish interpreters, world-class philosophers like Avicenna, Averroës, and Moses Maimonides.

The result was stunning. It was as if one were to find preserved in an antique vessel not just the works of some ancient Einstein but interpretations, applications, and updates of the material by Einstein himself and other modern physicists. Because of these commentaries, Aristotle's work turned up in immediately usable—and highly controversial—form. For medieval Christians, reading his books for the first time was like finding a recipe for interstellar travel or a cure for AIDS inscribed on some ancient papyrus. It was the sort of knowledge that is quite capable of overthrowing an existing worldview, revolutionizing science, and providing its readers with new models of human organization.

For this reason, the reappearance of Aristotelian ideas in Europe had a transformative effect totally unlike that of any later discovery. It did not cause the far-reaching changes taking place in European society in the late Middle Ages: the increases in food production and trade, the development of cities, the spread of learning, and the growth of popular religious movements. The usefulness of Aristotle's methods and concepts (like that of Clarke's star-gate) depended upon the achievement of a certain level of technical and economic progress, the development of a certain cultural momentum, by the receiving society. Given this momentum, however, the discoveries had a slingshot effect, accelerating the pace and deepening the quality of scientific and philosophical inquiry. In the Latin West, Aristotle's recovered work was the key to further developments that would turn Europe from a remote, provincial region into the very heartland of an expansive global civilization.

Imagine, more than four centuries before Francis Bacon and René Descartes proclaimed the Scientific Revolution, a recognizably modern perspective—rationalist, this-worldly, humanistic, and empirical—ignited cultural warfare throughout Western Europe, challenging traditional religious and social beliefs at their core. The struggle between faith and reason did not begin, as is so often supposed, with Copernicus's challenge to earth-centered cosmology or Galileo's trial by the Inquisition but with the controversy over Aristotle's ideas during the twelfth and thirteenth centuries.[2] For decades, specialists in medieval history have understood that the awakening of the West began during this "medieval renaissance." Many believe that the conflict among Christians over whether to accept or reject Aristotelian science marks a turning point—perhaps *the* turning point—in Western intellectual history.[3] But this understanding has not become part of our generally accepted cultural "story." On the contrary, we continue to tell the story of modernism as if it began with the sixteenth-century Renaissance, and with scientists like Copernicus, Galileo, and Isaac Newton.

Why? One reason involves the myth of cultural authenticity: the notion, common to many cultures, that a particular civilization developed on its own from original sources rather than being borrowed from or imposed by outsiders. "Our" culture is authentically native, the partisans of every nation insist, while "theirs" is merely derivative or imitative. For those anxious to establish the superiority of Western culture to all other traditions, the story of Europe's first intellectual revolution is something of an embarrassment. Not only was the chief transmitter of these advanced ideas a non-European civilization, it was the civilization that Christians long considered their nemesis: the Muslim empire that occupied the Holy Land, dominated the Mediterranean sea lanes, and challenged Europe militarily for almost a thousand years. Worse yet, as the Crusaders discovered, this "infidel" culture was clearly more advanced in significant respects than that of the Latin West. Not only had the Arabs and Jews acquired Aristotle's philosophy and natural science, they had also absorbed Euclid's mathematics, Ptolemy's astronomy and optics, Archimedes' engineering principles, the medical science of Hippocrates and Galen, and other classical treasures. In addition to translating these works, they had interpreted, applied, and improved upon them, as well as adding new sciences of their own, such as chemistry, algebra, and history.[4] Little wonder that the Arabs considered the Crusaders barbarian raiders, or that Europeans looked upon the Islamic world with that peculiar combination of fear and admiration, hatred and envy, that poorer, less "civilized" peoples often feel for those more prosperous and refined than themselves.

Cultural chauvinists may find it awkward to recall that Europe depended upon Muslim and Jewish scholars for the recovery of its classical heritage. But for many modernists, an even more acute source of embarrassment is the leading role played in this drama of discovery by the Roman Catholic Church. Today we tend to think of science and orthodox religion as inherently and perpetually in conflict. One of our favorite stories is "Galileo versus the Inquisition"—a morality play in which the courageous, imaginative man of reason confronts his dogmatic, black-robed persecutors. Yet, the Church-run universities of the Middle Ages were vehemently opposed to this sort of ignorant obscurantism. As Galileo himself recognized, their turbulent, "Aristotelianized" schools of arts and theology were the seedbeds of scientific thought.[5] Surprisingly (at least for those trained to believe that the age of faith was an age of darkness), the decisive contest between rationalist and traditionalist thinking was not fought out in a confrontation between the medieval Church and its opponents. It took place within the Church, where forces favoring the new Aristotelian learning did battle with those opposing it.

That struggle is the subject of this book. It is no exaggeration to say that its outcome largely determined the future of Western intellectual development. In medieval times, of course, the main issue in contention was not "science" versus "religion." What we now call science was part of a comprehensive worldview that included logic, ethics, metaphysics, aesthetics, and even theology—and everyone involved in the conflict was a committed Christian. The controversy was really about the extent to which European intellectuals would commit themselves to the quest for rational understanding, and how they could do so without losing their religious and cultural identity. Could Christian thinkers inspired by Aristotle make sense of the natural universe, including the realm of human motivations and relations? Could they use these same techniques of reasoning to explain the relationship of the created world to God? To many traditionalists, the project seemed as dangerous as it was ambitious. Aristotle was a pagan, and certain of his ideas clashed with established Christian doctrines. More important, the Aristotelian stance, with its unabashed admiration for the material world, its distaste for mystical explanations of natural phenomena, and its optimism about human nature, ran counter to centuries of otherworldly, ascetic Christian values and practices.

Could Christian thinkers follow the teachings of the Greek sage they called "the Philosopher" and follow Jesus Christ, too? For almost a century, the answer remained in doubt. Because of the threat they posed to established modes of thought, Aristotle's books of "natural philosophy" were originally considered too dangerous to be taught at European universities. Early in the thirteenth century they were banned, and some of their more wild-eyed proponents were burned as heretics. As late as 1277, the Church condemned a number of Aristotelian ideas being taught in the schools, including some propositions espoused by the century's greatest genius, Thomas Aquinas. In the end, however, the leaders of the Church allowed Christian thinking to be transformed by the new worldview. With irreversible social changes remaking European society, they realized that the Church would have to adapt to new currents of thought if it were to retain its position of intellectual and moral leadership. Farsighted popes and bishops therefore took the fateful step that Islamic leaders had rejected. By marrying Christian theology to Aristotelian science, they committed the West to an ethic of rational inquiry that would generate a succession of "scientific revolutions," as well as unforeseen upheavals in social and religious thought.[6]

As a result, Europe's first natural scientists were scholastic theologians, and its most innovative social thinkers were masters of arts in the new Catholic universities. For four centuries, European students—an elite destined for leading positions in the Church, the government, medicine, and law—were immersed in a curriculum that blended Aristotle's logic and natural philosophy with Christian education. Scientific activity (including the analytical treatment of ethics and politics) was legitimized by its association with religion, and theology—the application of reason to questions of faith—was considered the "queen of sciences." The Aristotelian movement had taken power . . . yet the marriage of faith and reason was never an easy one. Even before Thomas Aquinas wrote his synthetic masterwork, *Summa Theologica*, conservatives were denouncing it for being too Greek and radicals for being too Christian. In the fourteenth century, the brilliant Franciscan scholar William of Ockham, insisted that Aquinas had erred in trying to formulate a "natural theology," and that science and religion would both be better off if they separated. By the time a new scientific revolution rocked Europe in the age of Galileo, the divorce proceedings were well under way. Most of the "new men" of the seventeenth century recognized Aristotle not as an inspiration but as an enemy.

There were several reasons for this, but one, surely, is the degeneration of scholasticism. Once the source of creative speculation and rollicking, no-holds-barred debate, the universities now combined an arid orthodoxy in matters of doctrine with absurd theological hairsplitting. As the great Catholic humanist Erasmus

noted, the "scientific" theologians of the schools were now devoting themselves to questions like "Shall we be permitted to eat
and drink after the resurrection?" ("We're taking due precautions
against hunger and thirst while there's still time," he remarked
dryly.[7]) With the Church on the defensive against Protestant rebellion and the growth of secular power, Aristotle's followers had
become knee-jerk conservatives, slavishly defending their master's every conclusion, even in the face of newly discovered evidence to the contrary. Thus, when Galileo's telescope revealed
that the moon was pockmarked and that the planet Venus waxed
and waned like the moon, many scholars declared that there must
be something wrong with his lenses, since the Philosopher had
held that the heavenly bodies were perfect and unchangeable, and
that the earth, not the sun, stood at the center of the universe. As
Galileo remarked, Aristotle himself, with his great respect for evidence, would never have reached such a conclusion.[8]

Other thinkers of the postmedieval Renaissance were not as
kind as Galileo to their great intellectual ancestor. After Copernicus and his successors set the earth in motion and abolished most
of the distinctions between the laws governing earthly and heavenly behavior, Aristotle's ideas were frequently portrayed as rank
superstition—a relic of the dark, medieval past. But this was
never the case. Aristotle's cosmology was wrong, not "unscien-
tific." Like the rest of his system, it was based on principles,
highly controversial at first, that later became accepted pillars of
scientific method: for example, the ideas that the world our senses
show us is real, not just a shadow of reality; that humans using
their reason are capable of discovering general truths about this
world; that understanding phenomena means comprehending relationships of cause and effect; and that natural processes are developmental, revealing to skillful inquirers orderly patterns of
growth and change. Of course, the Philosopher's science was not
ours. His worldview contains many features that modern science

rejects, and omits one feature—mathematics—that scientists today insist on. But the dogmatism of his latter-day followers was not his. It was a senile manifestation of a system that, in its prime, revolutionized European thinking and gave it many of its boldest and most dynamic characteristics.

With the further progress of science, the growth of secular power, and the fragmentation of the Church, Aristotle's work lost its standing as the key to universal knowledge. Simultaneously, among European intellectuals, the divorce of faith and reason became final. Driven by a need to liberate their thinking from religious constraints, the apostles of the Enlightenment engineered a separation between subject and object, values and facts, religious beliefs and scientific knowledge, which still commands widespread acceptance. Or does it? During the past three decades, the conflict that first rocked Western society in the High Middle Ages has reappeared on a global scale. The most violent and dramatic struggles pit the zealous defenders of traditional religious beliefs and attitudes against their modernist and postmodernist opponents. But it is not only the "fundamentalists" who declare themselves dissatisfied with the split between scientific and religious thought. Theologians, scientists, and humanists of diverse backgrounds and views are again wrestling with the issues that made Europe's universities and churches an intellectual (and sometimes a physical) battleground in the twelfth and thirteenth centuries.

Can thinking men and women comprehend the mysteries of the universe and master their own unruly natures? Is scientific enterprise consistent with religious belief? Does God intervene in nature and in human affairs? Can human beings live an ethical life without him? The rediscovery of Aristotle's works brought these ancient questions to the center of Western consciousness, inspiring a struggle to harmonize faith and reason that has not yet ended.

Chapter One

"The Master of Those Who Know"

Aristotle Rediscovered

I T IS HARD NOT TO think of twelfth-century Spain as a scholar's paradise. The picture that comes to mind is that of a broad table, well lit by candles, on which are spread out dozens of manuscripts written in Syriac, Aramaic, Arabic, Hebrew, and Greek. Around the table, poring over the manuscripts, taking notes, or conversing animatedly, are bearded Jews, tonsured Christian monks, turbaned Muslims, and dark-haired Greeks. The setting is Toledo, a Spanish city long ruled by Islamic authorities but now under Christian control. The table occupies the center of a hall in the city's cathedral, whose archbishop, Raymund I, stands to one side, benevolently watching the polyglot scholars at their work. In his own hands, he holds a book written in Latin—apparently a Catholic missal or one of Saint Augustine's works. But close examination reveals its distinctly non-Christian authorship. The book that the archbishop holds so carefully, as if he were afraid it might once again disappear, is a new translation of *De Anima*—Aristotle's lost book on the soul.

How was this famous work—along with the rest of the Aristotelian corpus—rediscovered? The story really begins in the tenth century, when Christian knights launched the *Reconquista* (Reconquest)—a lengthy, on-again, off-again struggle to reclaim the Iberian Peninsula from the Muslims who had ruled it for more than three hundred years. The Christians would not drive the Muslims out of Spain altogether until the fall of Grenada in 1492, but by 1100, great centers of Islamic culture like Toledo and Lisbon were already under their control. The very length of this campaign, and the fact that the cities and peoples conquered were among the most civilized on earth, made it more "a work of co-penetration and synthesis" than a simple military crusade. One commentator justly calls it "a long-term, sensible, humane, even liberal process of fusion between different faiths and races, which does great honour to the people of medieval Spain and Portugal."[1]

In a way, the Reconquest resembled the "barbarian" takeover of Rome centuries earlier, for the society that the conquerors acquired was far more developed than their own. While Europe was just emerging from centuries of poverty and social strife, Muslim Spain—*al Andalus*, as the Arabs called it—was a land long enriched by international trade, brilliant artisanship, and a highly productive agriculture. The kingdom's rulers were literate men, heirs of the Roman tradition of rational-legal bureaucracy, and generous patrons of scholarship and the arts. Its world-famous poets anticipated and probably inspired the love songs of the troubadours. Its intellectuals were admired for their achievements in law, philosophy, mathematics, astronomy, and the natural sciences, as well as chemistry, metallurgy, and the practical arts. At a time when learning in Europe was confined to a few monasteries and church schools, the scholars of *al Andalus* taught in publicly supported universities and did research in well-stocked libraries. In an era when most Christian healers were still brewing herbs and casting spells, Muslim and Jewish physicians practiced something akin to scientific medicine.[2]

As in other Muslim kingdoms, the authorities had permitted these secular activities to flourish, so long as they kept their distance from the mosque. And they had encouraged non-Muslims—Jews, in particular—to play significant roles in the kingdom's politics, trade, and intellectual life, on the sole condition that they pay the "minorities tax" and recognize the Islamic majority's supremacy. As a result, Spain's Christian invaders found themselves mixing with well-established, highly cultured Muslim and Jewish communities. This situation was to have fateful consequences for the future development of European thinking, for behind Christendom's armed knights marched its clergy—at this point, Europe's only literate class—and what they found in Spain left them astonished and perplexed. Not only were cities like Toledo and Cordoba clean and well-ordered; not only was life softened and beautified by fountains, flowers, music, and an architecture as imaginative as Europe's was stolid; not only did the Arabs live at peace with a bewildering assortment of minority communities, but scholarship flourished as in some dream of ancient Athens or Alexandria. One can only imagine what it must have been like for dazzled Christian churchmen to talk with Muslim and Jewish scholars about philosophical and religious issues that their coreligionists had been exploring with great insight and sophistication for the last three hundred years.

There was a religious rationale, of course, for studying the philosophy and science of the Arabs. In order to defend the faith and convert the unconverted, one had to know their language and thinking. Still, defensive strategy alone cannot explain the Christians' fascination with Muslim culture. How had the former horsemen of the Arabian Peninsula managed to develop such remarkable competence in science and philosophy? What were the sources of their wisdom? It had long been rumored that they were in possession of ancient documents long lost to the Latin West—priceless treasures of esoteric or forgotten knowledge. But the reality was more fantastic than anyone had imagined. Almost as soon as they began to talk with local scholars, inquisitive Christians discovered that the Muslims and Jews had long ago translated virtually every important work of Greek learning (as well as monuments of ancient Persian and Indian culture) into Arabic. Not only that, they had commented extensively on Aristotle, Plato, and the Greek scientists, and reinterpreted classical thinking in the light of their own commitment to monotheism.

Clearly the Muslims were creative thinkers in their own right. Their cultural achievements were the pride of Moorish Spain. But the warrior-kings who, centuries earlier, had conquered the great centers of classical learning in Syria, Egypt, and Mesopotamia had given them a head start by acquiring their subjects' cultural treasures along with their lands. Al-Kindi, the ninth-century founder of Muslim philosophy, acknowledged his people's debt to the Greeks. Without them, he wrote, "it would have been impossible for us, despite all our zeal, during the whole of our lifetime, to assemble these principles of truth which form the basis of the final inferences of our research." He also described the Arab scholars' method, which was "first to record in complete quotations all that the Ancients have said on the subject, secondly to complete what the Ancients have not fully expressed, and this according to the usage of our Arabic language, the customs of our age, and our own ability."[3] This bold attempt to "complete" the work of the Greeks permitted al-Kindi and his successors to adapt classical ideas to the requirements of contemporary Muslim civilization. For the next three centuries, the Arab philosophy movement (*falsafah*) generated works of great originality by thinkers like al-Farabi, the founder of Muslim Neoplatonism; the Jewish mystic,

Ibn Gabirol (Avicebron, to Latin-speakers); the brilliant Persian, Ibn Sina (Avicenna); Moses Maimonides of Cordoba, the Jewish sage; and his fellow Cordoban, the boldest of all commentators on Aristotle, Ibn Rushd (Averroës).

All these authors' writings could be found in the libraries of Toledo, Lisbon, Segovia, and Cordoba . . . and so could their original sources. There, to their amazement, Spain's new masters found Arabic translations of books that Europeans had long talked about but never read—legendary works like Ptolemy's *Almagest,* the lost key to astronomy and astrology. In one library, Muslim physicians could be seen consulting Galen's *On the Art of Healing* and *On Anatomical Procedures,* the first scientific medical textbooks. In another, mathematicians perused Euclid's *Elements of Geometry* and Archimedes' treatises on mathematical engineering, unread in the West for the past seven hundred years. Most remarkably, the Christian scholar-priests discovered that their new subjects were in possession of the vast corpus of Aristotle's works—not just the few books on logic that a sixth-century scholar named Boethius had translated into Latin but the mother lode. Here, in Arabic translation, were the Greek sage's great essay on the philosophy of Being, *Metaphysics,* and his treatises on methods of reasoning and the divisions of knowledge. Here were his scientific masterpieces: *Physics, On the Heavens, History of Animals,* and *On Generation and Corruption.* And here (one can imagine Archbishop Raymund gasping with wonder as the manuscripts were placed in his hands) were Aristotle's world-famous treatise on the soul, *De Anima;* his *Nicomachean Ethics;* and his *Politics.* Even mystical vision was represented by *Theology of Aristotle* and *Book of Causes,* works thought to have been written by the Peripatetic master, but actually produced by later Neoplatonists.

Taken together, these books represent the most important documentary discovery (or "rediscovery") in Western intellectual history. One historian calls the recovery of Aristotle's works "a turning point in the history of Western thought...paralleled only by the later impact of Newtonian science and Darwinism."[4] If the spirit of inquiry in Europe had not already begun to flower, the discovery's true significance might not have been recognized. But by the mid-twelfth century, Christian thinkers were already displaying a new interest in natural processes, human reason, and the natural world's relationship to a supernaturally creative, powerful, just, and omniscient God. That is, they had already begun to ask the questions to which Aristotle and his Arab interpreters offered answers: How does the natural universe work? Did it have a beginning in time, or is it co-eternal with God? Does nature obey certain laws? If so, how can humans exercise free will? What does it mean to say that our individual souls are immortal? The unexpected, almost miraculous appearance of ancient books and more recent commentaries addressing all these concerns caused an immediate sensation. All that was needed for the West to have access to this vast storehouse of learning was that its contents be translated into Latin.

Nowadays when people think about the response of the Catholic Church to new knowledge, they often recall Rome's hostility to free inquiry and its willingness to suppress unpalatable truths. But the travails of scientific pioneers such as Giordano Bruno and Galileo have obscured an earlier, brighter image: that of Archbishop Raymund of Toledo, one of the unrecognized heroes of Western culture, who did more than any man to make the treasures of Greek philosophy and science available to the Latin world, and who opened the door to advanced Arab and Jewish ideas as well. Little is known of Raymund's career and personality, but all agree that it was his idea to create a translation center in Toledo and to recruit the best scholars available to work there, whether they be Christian, Jew, Muslim, Latin, Greek, or Slav.

Moreover, this work would be carried out without censorship. There would be no attempt by Raymund and his colleagues to distinguish between potentially dangerous and inoffensive books, or to substitute orthodox language for non-Christian words or phrases. Very likely, the archbishop's sunny faith did not recognize the possibility that the truths enunciated by Aristotle, Euclid, or the inspired philosophers of other religions could be incompatible with the truths expressed by the Apostles of Christ and the Church Fathers. God, after all, was Truth itself... and all of Spain's three faiths agreed that God was One.

Spain's three faiths, in fact, supplied the new translation center with its first personnel. One key figure was an archdeacon of the cathedral named Domingo Gundisalvo, a talented linguist with philosophical interests of his own. Gundisalvo was very likely a "Mozarab"—a native Christian who had been permitted to practice his religion during the period of Muslim rule—although he may have been a converted Jew.[5] He had a close friend and colleague called Juan Avendeuth, a Jewish scholar who was an authority on Arabic language and literature. (Some believe that Avendeuth's correct name was Abraham Ibn Daud, and that he was the author of a well-known book called *The Sublime Faith*.[6]) When Raymund asked Gundisalvo to join him in establishing a workshop in Toledo to translate Arabic manuscripts into Latin, the archdeacon brought his Jewish colleague in on the project. There the two men developed a unique method of collaboration. Avendeuth translated the Arabic texts word for word into Castilian, leaving it to Gundisalvo to turn the Castilian into scholarly Latin.[7] Working together, the duo produced Latin versions of a large number of precious manuscripts, including Aristotle's treatise *On the Soul*—remarkably accurate translations, considering their method of production.[8]

In any case, the two collaborators did not work alone for long. As word of the discoveries spread, scholars throughout Europe were drawn toward Toledo like northern birds to the Spanish sun.[9] England supplied a large contingent, including Robert of Chester, Adelard of Bath (one of Europe's first empirical scientists), and Daniel of Morley, a Christian theologian strongly interested in astrology, which was then considered a science. From northern Italy came John of Brescia, Plato of Tivoli, and the incomparable Gerard of Cremona, who, among other accomplishments, produced Latin versions of Aristotle's major works of natural science, the mystical *Book of Causes,* Ptolemy's *Almagest,* Euclid's *Elements of Geometry,* al-Khwarizmi's *Algebra,* and twenty-four medical texts — in all, some seventy or eighty books. Flanders was well represented, as were France, the Balkans, and Germany. Distinguished Jewish scholars like Moses ben Samuel ibn Tibbon and John of Seville made shorter journeys from Provence and Spain, Greek savants arrived from the Byzantine Empire, and learned Arabs were gratefully welcomed. "It was from the example of Toledo," writes one historian, "that Europe first learnt to understand that learning knows no frontiers, that it is universal, global, and 'human,' and that it concerns mankind as a whole, without respect of race or religion."[10]

The translation center at Toledo remained in operation well into the thirteenth century, attracting world-class scholars like Michael Scot and Herman the German (Hermannus Alemannus), who produced definitive Latin versions of Aristotle's ethical and political works, as well as more recent masterpieces like Moses Maimonides' *Guide to the Perplexed* and the great commentaries on Aristotle by Averroës. At the same time, everywhere that Western Christians could mingle freely with Jews, Muslims, or Greeks, new centers sprang up. Provence, with its large Jewish population, was one such "open" region, specializing in translating Arabic texts first into Hebrew and then into Latin. Northern Italy, which (thanks to the Crusades) had developed a thriving trade with North Africa and the Byzantine Empire, was another.

The first important translations of Aristotle's works directly from Greek into Latin were made by James of Venice, who spent years in Constantinople working on the Aristotelian books that Europeans called the "New Logic."

The richest amalgam of cultures, however, was to be found in Sicily, a kingdom that had been part of the Greek-speaking Byzantine Empire before being conquered by the Arabs, and, more recently, by Latin-speaking adventurers from Normandy who had also extended their rule over England. In the twelfth century, the Norman ruler, Roger of Sicily, consolidated his hold over southern Italy and ruled his polyglot kingdom from Palermo, "where his court, with its black servants, its Saracen guards, its harem and its pleasure-domes became the scandal and the envy of Christendom."[11] Another reason for scandal, at least in some quarters, was the king's patronage of Byzantine Christian, Muslim, and Jewish scholars as well as Roman Catholics—an imitation of the Arab tradition of clustering scholars representing many cultures and religions around a "glittering" royal court. As a result of this tolerant policy, which encouraged Greek-speaking scholars to remain in the kingdom, Palermo soon became Europe's premier center for translating ancient manuscripts from Greek into Latin.[12] There was great interest among the scholars there in making scientific and medical books available to Latin-speakers, while in nearby Salerno, students and teachers from many lands (including a number of female students) were creating Europe's first medical school.[13] But Palermo also produced a flood of philosophical translations by such figures as Henricus Aristippus, the first translator of Plato's *Meno* and *Phaedo*; the Muslim nobleman and poet, Eugene the Emir; and Michael Scot, the brilliant English scholar whose specialities were Aristotle and astrology.

Scot's linguistic abilities were legendary. While in Toledo, he had made numerous translations from the Arabic, including Aristotle's *Metaphysics,* with the help of a Jewish scholar,[14] but he was also proficient in Greek, Hebrew, Syriac, Chaldean, and several other tongues. While traveling during the 1220s, he was summoned to meet Frederick II, the young emperor of Germany, who considered himself a man of destiny, and who was particularly interested in Scot's command of astrology—the "science" of prediction.[15] Greatly impressed by the Englishman's talent, Frederick invited him to come to work in Sicily, which he had just inherited from Norman relatives. As a result, Scot spent the rest of his life translating manuscripts, writing his own astrological treatises, and advising Europe's most colorful and controversial ruler: the man known to his admirers as "Stupor Mundus"—the Wonder of the World.

Frederick was a remarkable character—remarkable enough to inspire some of his hopeful and credulous subjects to consider him a messianic figure whose appearance betokened the approach of the End Times. His enemies, equally passionate, were more inclined to compare him to the Antichrist. To the horror of several popes, he dreamed of uniting all Italy and Germany (including the papal states) under his rule in a revived Roman Empire. A man of unbridled imagination, boundless energy, and legendary ruthlessness, he ruled the empire from his Sicilian court like a combination of Roman emperor and Muslim caliph, creating a new legal code, hunting down Christian heretics, enjoying (it was said) the attentions of numerous "wives," and plotting against the papacy. Such was his knowledge and appreciation of Muslim civilization that when ordered by the Vatican to go on Crusade in the Holy Land, he used his connections and diplomatic skill to negotiate the return of Jerusalem (temporarily) to Christian control.

Frederick never realized his dream of unifying Europe under his own "Holy Roman" banner. After he died, in fact, the extermination of his heirs became an obsession of the Vatican, and was finally completed late in the thirteenth century. But the translations produced by his scholars, along with those emanating from Spain, Italy, and Provence, would soon revolutionize Western thinking. After his demise, the effort to make all of Aristotle's work available to Latin-speakers was brought to completion by the greatest translator of the century, William of Moerbeke, a Dutch cleric who worked in Italy during the 1260s and who later became archbishop of Corinth in Greece. Working directly from Greek manuscripts, William provided new translations of scores of Aristotelian treatises, commentaries by other philosophers, and Greek and Arab scientific works, but the translations that excited the greatest interest among Europe's new intellectuals were those of Aristotle's *De Anima,* his little-known *Politics,* and his *Poetics.* One colleague who knew William in Italy and found his handiwork especially useful was a native of the Kingdom of Sicily originally trained at the University of Naples—a controversial scholar whose ideas were considered dangerously radical by many Christian traditionalists. The radical's Latinized name was Thomas Aquinas, and he was destined to become the spearhead of the Aristotelian Revolution.

But we have gotten far ahead of our story—more than one thousand years ahead, in fact. The tale really begins in Athens, with the arrival of an obscure young man from the provinces at Plato's famous Academy. Who was Aristotle of Stagira? How did he emerge from Plato's shadow to become the giant figure that the poet Dante called "the master of those who know"? What were the ideas that, rediscovered centuries later by Christian scholars in Toledo, would change the course of Western history? Our inquiry calls us back to a time when "civilization" meant the life of cities, and one city above all others symbolized the life of the mind. Athens, where men first dreamed of understanding the great universe outside them and the little universe within, drew Aristotle irresistibly into its orbit . . . as it must now draw us.

WHEN ARISTOTLE first arrived in Athens, Plato was out of town. The teenager may have been disappointed to find Eudoxus of Cnidus directing the affairs of the Academy in place of its famous founder, but he would not have been surprised to learn that Plato was on an urgent political mission to Syracuse. Only in recent times have philosophers been considered impractical, unworldly creatures spinning obscure conceptual webs far from the centers of power. For centuries, their duties included advising rulers how to govern wisely, and subjects when (and when not) to obey. A dangerous occupation, to be sure. Plato's mentor, Socrates, was condemned to death for teaching his students to question traditional sources of authority. In his old age, Aristotle would also become the target of a political prosecution. And Plato's current business in Syracuse—instructing the city's young "tyrant" in the arts of government—was no less risky. When the king became embroiled in a dispute with dissident aristocrats, Plato offered his services as a mediator. The mediation failed, and the philosopher was lucky to escape with his life.[16]

In Athens, meanwhile, Aristotle was running another sort of risk. We can imagine the young provincial entering the Academy for the first time, full of dreams and self-doubt. In Stagira, his hometown near the Macedonian border, he is accounted a genius, but this is Athens, and the Academy is home to the greatest thinkers of the Greek world. No known subject lies outside the intellectual reach of the Academicians. What they call philosophy includes astronomy as well as metaphysics, mathematics as well as ethics, and, while each scholar has his favorite interests, nobody would think of "specializing." The acting director, Eudoxus, a student of medicine and politics, has developed a system to account for the movements of the heavenly bodies by picturing them as attached to nested spheres that rotate, each at its own pace, around the fixed earth. Speusippus, Plato's nephew, writes on the theory of mathematical proportions and on the nature of knowledge, openly criticizes his uncle's theory of "Ideas," and has identified ten different modes of being. Xenocrates of Chalcedon, a young man in his twenties, is one of Plato's closest colleagues (and soon to be one of Aristotle's), although, unlike the master, he believes that the basic constituents of matter are elementary atomic particles. In fact, while Plato is clearly the school's most influential figure, Aristotle soon discovers that there is no orthodoxy to which he must conform. Some of his own interests—biology and psychology, for example—are not yet recognized as suitable subjects for analysis, but there is nothing to stop him from "theorizing" these subjects and making them his own.

Perhaps this is why, despite his differences with Plato, Aristotle remained at the Academy for twenty years, until the founder's death in 347 B.C.E. at the age of eighty. Plato's school was not like our modern colleges, with their examinations and grades, degrees and professorial ranks. It was more like a club whose aim was to train privileged young men to reason well (and, eventually, to govern well) by exposing them to the best conversation in Greece. Internally, the Academy was a meritocracy. After an initiation period, a student with Aristotle's talent would be treated as an equal by scholars many years his senior; eventually, he would be invited to lead discussions and to write treatises of his own. Socially, the institution's general tone and political leanings were aristocratic, reflecting distrust of the uneducated poor and contempt for the uneducated rich. As a physician's son—even one whose father had treated the king of Macedonia—Aristotle was not an aristocrat of the highest rank. Attending to patients was, after all, a form of manual labor. But he shared the general ethos of the Academy, and his remarkable gifts assured him recognition. Plato called him "the Reader" and "the brains" of the school,[17] remarking wryly, a propos of his audacious brilliance, that while some of the slower thinkers at the school needed the whip, his most precocious student required a bridle.[18]

It tells us a good deal about Aristotle to discover that he was the son of a doctor, and not just any doctor but one of the new breed of physicians who believed that the causes of illness were natural, and that sick people could be cured by natural means. Nicomachus, his father, was a member of the guild of Asclepius, the legendary demigod fathered by Apollo with a human woman. For ages past, when illness was attributed to the anger or indifference of the gods, the physician's role was that of a priest or magus who invoked the demigod's aid to heal the suffering patient. Thousands came to the Asclepian temples to sleep in special dormitories and dream healing dreams sent by their divine helper.[19] But around 400 B.C.E., something happened to change the nature of medical practice. One of Nicomachus's contemporaries was Hippocrates, who had the astonishing gall to accuse the magus-doctors of quackery. Writing about the "sacred disease" (epilepsy), he denounced the "witch-doctors, faith-healers, quacks and charlatans" who "pretend to be pious and to be particularly wise." Of course the gods existed—that was not the point—but by using them to explain epilepsy, the old-school physicians "were able to screen their own failure to give suitable treatment, and so called this a 'sacred' malady to conceal their ignorance of its nature."[20] Not only did the great physician offer his own explanation of the disease based on a theory of bodily "humors," but he proposed dissecting a goat to see if the theory could be verified.

No evidence of direct contact between Hippocrates and Nicomachus exists, but Aristotle's father was almost certainly one of the new voices in medicine. Why else would the high king of Macedonia have summoned him from Stagira to minister to the royal family at the Macedonian court? We know that King Amyntas's future grandson, Alexander (later to be dubbed "the Great"), was subject to seizures. If other members of the family were similarly afflicted, Amyntas might have felt the need for a doctor whose views were more advanced than those of the "quacks and charlatans" pilloried by Hippocrates. Nicomachus was qualified; he was available; and he had the requisite status for a position at court, since his wife, Phaestis, was a wealthy aristocrat from the powerful Greek city of Chalcis. It was not a long trip from Stagira to the high king's court at Pella. The physician and his wife made it in a few days, carrying their small son with them.[21]

King Amyntas also had a son: Philip of Macedon, the future conqueror and "protector" of most of the Greek city-states, who was a year or two older than Aristotle. According to one story, the boys were childhood playmates and best friends. Perhaps they were, since, years later, the Philosopher was happy to return to Pella to advise King Philip and, it is said, to tutor the teenaged Alexander. Another apocryphal tale suggests that, while serving the Macedonian king, Nicomachus taught Aristotle the rudiments of medicine and initiated him into the cult of Asclepius. Since the physician's art was customarily passed down from father to son, this story is also plausible. But whether or not the boy received formal medical instruction, there are indications in his later life of the same passion for logical non-supernatural explanations, the same practical bent and aptitude for meticulous observation, and the same craftsmanlike taste for getting his hands dirty that characterized his father's work. Along with this intense interest in the physical world, Aristotle seems to have absorbed some of his father's knowledge of human anatomy, natural remedies, and the life processes. The tendency to split the mind from the body, the realm of the spirit from that of matter, that played such a large role in the thinking of Plato and other "pure" philosophers never made much sense to the physician's son.

Aristotle seems to have had a happy childhood as well as a privileged one, at least until tragedy cut short his boyhood adventures at King Amyntas's court. When he was ten or eleven years old (the date is uncertain), Nicomachus died suddenly, followed shortly thereafter by his young wife. Very likely, both were victims of one of the plagues that periodically swept the region, or of some disease contracted by Nicomachus in the course of his profession. The disaster was followed almost immediately by a great stroke of good fortune, although the orphaned boy may not have immediately recognized it as such. His uncle, Proxenus, came up from Stagira to fetch him home, and he and his wife raised him for the next seven years with their own children as a beloved son.[22] What would have become of the precocious boy without these doting foster parents is impossible to say, but without them, it is hard to imagine him maintaining his sense of the natural world as a welcoming and comprehensible place. Nor would his unusual curiosity and talent for reasoning things out have been so quickly recognized and cultivated. Proxenus groomed Aristotle for advanced study, and, when he reached the age of eighteen, sent him to Athens to be educated at the Academy. Aristotle's gratitude to his foster family was lifelong. He would later adopt Proxenus's son as his own, and would order in his will that statues of his guardians be erected after his death.

If Aristotle had lived in our time, we would probably have an autobiography, or at least a reliable biography, to tell us how his thinking developed at the Academy, and at what point he became aware of profound differences separating him from his great mentor, Plato.[23] In the long march of centuries that followed both men's deaths, the separation between them became a gap, the gap a chasm, and the chasm an oceanic rift. In medieval times, the clash between Platonic "spirituality" and Aristotelian "material-ism" would cost a number of scholars their careers and several ideologues their lives. Viewed in the context of their own time, however, these differences seem as much a product of contrasting interests and temperaments as of conflicting beliefs. Aristotle was inspired, most of all, by nature and the life sciences. A man basi-cally at home in the world, he felt himself to be part of a living, integrated, self-sufficient universe—a place whose basic princi-ples could be understood by reasoning from the data presented by sense impressions. Reality, for him, was composed of particular substances—the man, Plato, for example—each an inseparable and unique fusion of matter with form, and each in the process of realizing its natural potential. In Aristotle's universe, what you see and reason about is pretty much what you get. If the Philoso-pher were living today, he might well add, in the words of lyricist Ira Gershwin, "Who could ask for anything more?"[24]

Plato, on the other hand, asked for a great deal more. The studies that especially inspired him were mathematics and art—activities (as he saw it) that focus not on the ephemera of the senses or the depressing processes of growth and decay, but on unchanging concepts no less real for being abstract, like the line, the circle, and the square root. For him, nonmathematical con-cepts like Beauty, Goodness, and Justice shared this same reality. Some might call them mere abstractions, but Plato believed them to be "really real": timeless realities that bear the same relation-ship to the things of the sensory world that a perfect geometrical figure, a sphere, say, bears to an imperfect approximation like an orange. How can we recognize an orange as spherical, Plato won-dered, without having somewhere acquired the idea of a perfect Sphere? How do we know that a government is unjust without possessing some notion of genuine Justice? But if there are no perfect spheres in nature or genuinely just states in the known world—and there are not—where can these ideas come from other than some place outside nature and society: a realm of eternal Forms or Ideas? And how could such Ideas enter our minds unless those minds, or some part of them, inhabited that same realm once upon a time? Indeed, compared with the calm beauty, exquisite precision, and illuminating power of the Ideas, the world of everyday experience seems chaotic, untrustworthy, and, in the end, unreal, like a bad copy of an inimitable masterpiece.

Plato did not hate the world, but it reminded him of a much better place. What evoked joy and wonder in the old man was the conviction that behind the façade of deceptive sense impressions and turbulent emotions was a realm of pure thought that gave mundane experience whatever intelligibility and value it had. That is why he saw art as a window to eternity, and why he pictured God as an artisan. What most pleased and excited Aristotle, on the other hand, was his conviction that the "real world" perceived by the senses—our only home, however much one might wish for another—contains within itself the sources of intelligibility and value. He agreed with Plato that surface appearances are deceptive, that the real nature or structure of things is hidden, and that wisdom means uncovering these underlying realities. But he denied the existence of a world of absolute intelligibilities separate from the natural world. In his view, ideas cannot exist without the input of the senses, nor are the things of this world mere shadows or approximations of eternal concepts. On the contrary, they embody concepts. To Aristotle, that is the miracle: that apparently dumb, "thingy" reality can speak to human beings, and that humans using their powers of reason can apprehend the principles inherent in things.

Of course, the teacher and the student had a great deal in common. Both men, for example, opposed the atomists, who believed that reality could be reduced to the mechanical interaction of material particles. Neither had any use for the skeptics, who believed that no certain knowledge of any sort was possible, or the religious traditionalists, who considered it impious to inquire into sacred matters. Rationalist to the core, neither philosopher doubted (as do some of their modern successors) that a depth analysis of experience would reveal fundamental principles of order intelligible to reason, or that these structural realities were really "out there," and not just in people's minds. But their differences were undeniable. While Plato heard *through* the static of imperfection and illusion the immortal music of the gods, Aristotle perceived orderly rhythms and melodies *within* the same apparent cacophony. One can understand why, at a later date, pious Christians with their hopes fixed on a better, realer world than this one would consider Plato's approach so appealing. "For now we see in a mirror dimly, but then face to face."[25] One can also see why those enraptured by Creation would tend to favor Aristotle.

Considering Aristotle's originality and independence of mind, one might expect him to have broken at some point with his old teacher, but this never happened. In his own lectures and writings, he criticized many of Plato's ideas, but he was never disloyal to him, as some of his enemies later alleged. The glowing eulogy that he wrote for Plato's funeral rites bespeaks his high regard for his mentor's character. Plato, he wrote, was the first man to demonstrate, "by his own life and by the methods of his words, how to be happy is to be good."[26] While the old man lived, Aristotle could claim, with much justification, to be a loyal Academician with ideas of his own—a "Left Platonist," so to speak, whose attempt to bring his teacher's thinking down to earth was true to the best elements of the master's thought.[27] Other scholars at the Academy disagreed, seeing in his ideas the potential overthrow of Platonism by a belligerently earthbound naturalism.

The real battle of ideas would begin with the death of the Academy's founder and the struggle over his intellectual legacy.

WHEN PLATO DIED at the age of eighty, his prize student might have stepped into his shoes. At thirty-seven, Aristotle was a bit young for director of the Academy, but he was already recognized as one of Greece's most brilliant philosophers. No matter: the Academy's elders chose Speusippus instead, and Aristotle left Athens shortly thereafter to teach in Atarneus, a small Greek colony on the coast of Asia Minor.

We do not know why he left so abruptly. Speusippus was the older, better-established man, and the fact that he was Plato's nephew may also have helped advance his candidacy, but being passed over for the directorship must have stung. As important as any injury to his pride, however, was Aristotle's discomfort with the philosophical perspective espoused by the new director. A talented mathematician with a special interest in geometrical proportions, Speusippus went considerably further than Plato had gone in declaring that the universe was governed by numbers, and that the only sure knowledge was the knowledge of mathematical relationships. Aristotle, on the other hand, insisted that doing equations was only one way among others of describing the natural world, and that mathematics should not be permitted to swallow up the rest of philosophy.[28] In any event, Aristotle took the mathematician's appointment as a sign that it was time to strike out on his own. With his good friend, Xenocrates of Chalcedon, he set out across the Aegean Sea for Asia Minor.

Politics in a larger sense may also have played a role in convincing the Philosopher to leave his adopted city. In the same year that Plato died, Philip of Macedon attacked and captured the northern city of Olynthus, initiating the process that would soon make him master of all Greece. In Athens, where the shock was tangible, the orator Demosthenes, leader of the powerful anti-Macedonian party, lost no time in rallying the frightened citizens to defend (at least verbally) their city's threatened independence. So far as we know, Aristotle was not a direct target of the orator's wrath, but he was certainly vulnerable. He was not an Athenian citizen, and his family's Macedonian connections were well known. For the moment, these connections were embarrassing; later on, his star would rise with that of Alexander the Great. Meanwhile, a period of self-exile from Athens was exactly what he needed. When he left the Academy, Aristotle was a thinker with ideas of his own, but still standing in Plato's enormous shadow, a bachelor, and a public man with disadvantageous political associations. He would return happily married, philosophically independent, and politically influential—a leader ready to establish his own "Academy," the Lyceum, and guide it to the heights of philosophical and scientific achievement.

All this began with a friendship—one that, much later, would prove unexpectedly dangerous to Aristotle and his family. Hermias, the "tyrant" of Atarneus, had been Aristotle's schoolmate at the Academy. After learning that his old chum would not succeed Plato as director, Hermias invited him to come to his court to lead a small Platonic circle that had been established there and to establish a school of philosophy. The Philosopher was glad to make a fresh start outside Athens. Free of the pressures of the Academy and delighted by the teeming marine life of the eastern Aegean, he plunged into biological research. Not only that, he soon discovered the joys of family life. Hermias gave him his niece, Pythias, in marriage; the couple had a daughter whom they named for her mother; and Aristotle lived contentedly in Atarneus with his new family, surrounded by good companions and admiring students. This period of calm hiatus seems to have defined many of the values that would later inform his human-centered, this-worldly ethics and politics. To Aristotle, the good life always meant living happily in the present world rather than renouncing temporal pleasures for the sake of eternal bliss. Moderation, as opposed to extremes of asceticism or sensuality, was his watchword. Friendship, family life, political participation, and study ("contemplation") were the keys to genuine happiness—a view that may seem quite conventional now, but one that caused great consternation when his ethical works were rediscovered centuries later by Christians with their hopes fixed on heaven.

Aristotle's Aegean idyll climaxed in 344, when his best student, Theophrastus, a native of the nearby island of Lesbos, persuaded him to spend a year doing research in the island's capital, a place of legendary beauty. Then, suddenly, the interregnum was at an end. His friend Xenocrates returned to Athens, summoned by Speusippus, who had announced his intention to retire as director of the Academy. A year later, after a very close election, he would become the institution's third leader. Aristotle, meanwhile, headed for Macedonia to join the court of King Philip. In fact, his recall from the eastern Aegean was very likely orchestrated by Philip. An old story has it that the king wanted him to tutor his thirteen-year-old son, Alexander, but Philip probably had more urgent reasons for ending the Philosopher's sabbatical. Aristotle had already begun to collect the constitutions of the Greek world's city-states and to write on political matters, including the question of empire. He knew the state of mind of the Greeks and had just spent three years in Asia Minor. On the verge of a series of ambitious military campaigns, dreaming of a push eastward against the increasingly aggressive Persians, Philip no doubt sought advice from his boyhood friend. Other kings had court philosophers, why not he? Moreover, it would reassure him to have Aristotle at court while young Alexander acted as regent in his absence.

With Macedonian power ascending, one had to choose sides, and Aristotle would not have hesitated to cast his lot, as his father had, with Philip and Alexander. Family connections were only part of the reason. There was something in the Macedonian urge to stabilize Greece and to create a new world order that resonated with his own philosophical ambitions. Aristotle was nothing if not a universalist. He always sought to discover the principles governing man as man, nature as nature, being as being. Was he not, in fact, philosophy's own Alexander the Great, bringing vast, unmapped regions of inquiry under the sway of universal reason? It is hardly coincidental that this expansive, all-ordering worldview was created during the heyday of Greek imperialism and had its greatest impact, centuries later, in the expanding empires of Islam and late-medieval Europe.

Aristotle spent seven years at Philip's court while Alexander grew to manhood. Meanwhile, Philip forced the Greeks to accept Macedonian leadership, and competition between the resurgent Hellenes and their old Persian adversaries escalated to the pitch of war. In 341, Atarneus fell to King Darius's revamped Persian army. Aristotle's old friend and patron, Hermias, was tortured to death by the conquerors, and the philosopher responded with a passionate elegy in which he compared his lost comrade to a god—an impolitic verse, as it later turned out. Five years later, Philip was murdered, apparently in an attempted coup. Alexander became king, and Aristotle returned to Athens to establish his own school of philosophy. But the Macedonian connection did not end there. When the young monarch embarked on his campaign to subdue Asia, he took Aristotle's nephew Callisthenes with him as the expedition's official historian. And, if the story is accurate, Alexander ordered his navigators and soldiers to collect interesting biological specimens to send back to his old teacher at the Lyceum, the academy Aristotle had founded (with Macedonian financial support) just outside Athens.

Now the Philosopher entered upon the most satisfying and productive period of his life. One tragedy marred the otherwise happy return to Athens: the illness and death of his young wife, Pythias. Not long afterward, on a trip to Stagira, he met his future life-partner, a woman named Herpyllis. Although he does not appear to have married her, Aristotle was devoted to his new companion and had a son with her called Nicomachus, a name he would later immortalize in a book dedicated to the boy called the *Nicomachean Ethics*. Meanwhile, he set about establishing the Lyceum's plan of study—a curriculum considerably more extensive and scientifically oriented than that offered by the Academy—and teaching its first courses. His habit of walking the garden path of his academy in the mornings, discussing difficult philosophical questions with his students, gave his school and philosophy the nickname "Peripatetic." In the afternoons, he gave lectures on more accessible or practical subjects to large crowds of listeners. And he wrote—oh, how he wrote! The fifty or so treatises now called "the works of Aristotle" represent less than one third of his total output. Surprisingly, none of these extant writings was meant for publication in the form that has come down to us. Most are probably working drafts of his lectures that were preserved in his library, then privately copied, and finally reorganized two centuries later by the Roman scholar Andronicus.[29] This would account for their dry, methodical tone, as well as the absence of Platonic-style dialogues. Cicero, who praised the eloquence of Aristotle's dialogues, must have been referring to works lost some time after his own death, most likely during the early Christian era.

Eloquent or not, the scope of these works is astonishing, even if one remembers that, prior to modern times, the field of philosophy embraced what we would now call "hard" science (physics, mathematics, biology, physiology, meteorology, and astronomy), as well as social science (politics and psychology), humane studies (rhetoric, literature, religion), and a full range of philosophical topics (metaphysics, epistemology, logic, ethics, and so forth). Aristotle wrote treatises on all these topics.[30] In fact, it is hard to think of a subject that he did not write on, save for those that did not yet exist, and there were several topics not yet conceived of or systematized—deductive logic, for example—which he virtually invented. More than a millennium later, this dizzying omnicompetence would earn him the reputation among the common folk of a "magus," or cross between a sage and a magician. The Jews of medieval times had a legend that in his old age Aristotle had converted to Judaism, since anyone *that* wise must finally have recognized the true faith of Israel.[31] And in *The Divine Comedy,* the poet Dante calls him, quite simply, "the master of those who know."[32]

For thirteen years, lecturing and writing from his base at the Lyceum, Aristotle dominated the world of Greek philosophy. Of course, he had enemies as well as admirers. One detractor gives us the only physical description that survives. He describes the Philosopher as a skinny, unprepossessing fellow with narrow close-set eyes, bald, no beard (the usual badge of philosophical depth), a speech impediment, and gaudy taste in clothes. This contemptuous put-down may reflect the hereditary aristocrat's distaste for a *nouveau arrivé,* or the animus toward his school felt by those loyal to older institutions like Plato's Academy. But something more may have been involved. There were weaknesses in Aristotle's political position that might have put a less preoccupied and productive scholar on his guard. The Lyceum's chief patron, Antipater, was Alexander's top representative in Athens, appointed to keep the untrustworthy Athenians in line while his sovereign proceeded to conquer the world. Aristotle made no secret of his friendship with the official, but if Alexander's campaign faltered, the relationship could prove to be a dangerous liability.

In 326, the first of a series of disturbing reports reached Athens. After an exhausting campaign in the Hindu Kush mountains, Alexander had been forced to return to Persia to regroup his forces and consolidate his hold on that empire. Whether driven by rational considerations or megalomania, the king had begun to behave bizarrely, insisting that his men marry Persian women in order to found a new multicultural race, and demanding, as proof of their loyalty, that they acknowledge him as a god. These reports may have worried Aristotle, but one must have horrified him. A few men, including his nephew Callisthenes, had bravely but recklessly declined to recognize their general's divinity. In response, an overwrought Alexander had all of them tried for treason and summarily executed.

Three years later, the Philosopher found himself in serious trouble as well. This was not because Alexander sought his downfall, but because the god-king died unexpectedly in Persia, probably after contracting typhoid fever. Many Athenians rejoiced at the news. They bitterly resented their domination by Macedonian "protectors," and Antipater, although not considered an exceptionally cruel or irrational ruler, quickly became their prime target. Once again, Aristotle's connection to Macedonian power proved double-edged. Several years earlier, he had used his influence with Antipater to gain some important concessions for Athens, as a result of which the Athenians had voted to honor him and Callisthenes at Delphi. But confirmation of Alexander's death triggered a massive rebellion in the city. The anti-Macedonian party overthrew Antipater, expelled him, and established a new government. Aristotle discovered that the new regime was preparing to indict him for impiety on the ground that the elegy he had written twenty years earlier for his martyred friend Hermias was idolatrous, since it had praised the dead ruler's "godlike" qualities. With Socrates' fate in mind, he reportedly vowed that he

would not let Athens commit "a second crime against philosophy."[33] Then he fled for his life to the city of Chalcis, where his
mother had left him some property.

This ancient city was to be Aristotle's last residence. He lived
there for one year before dying at the age of sixty-two of a disease that had apparently troubled him for some time. Although a
letter of his to Antipater suggests that he felt lonely in exile, there
is no evidence to support the rumor that he committed suicide.
His state of mind is best revealed by his response to the news that
Athenian politicians had rescinded the honor conferred upon him
eight years earlier: "As for the honor which was voted me at Delphi and of which I have now been stripped, I am neither greatly
concerned nor greatly unconcerned."[34] This sort of balance is exactly what one would expect of a philosopher who had insisted
that virtue was a golden mean, and that the evanescent joys of the
world, although by no means sinful, were of little account compared with the lasting satisfactions of study. Even so, it was a sad
end to a remarkable career. One wonders what comfort Aristotle
might have felt in his last days if he had known that these doctrines, like virtually all the ideas associated with his name, would
be stated and restated, glossed, debated, and acted upon for more
than two thousand years after his death.

THE GREEK HISTORIAN Strabo tells a good story about the fate of
Aristotle's manuscripts.

When the Philosopher died, the story goes, he left all his writings to his best friend and brightest student, Theophrastus, who
had succeeded him as director of the Lyceum.[35] Twenty-five years
later, after a distinguished career as an administrator, teacher, and
writer, Theophrastus passed away, bequeathing his personal library, including Aristotle's manuscripts, to his nephew Neleus,
who lived in Skepsis, a Greek colony in Asia Minor. Since the mil-

itary rulers who had divided Alexander's empire between them were in the habit of confiscating books and anything else of value that they could lay their hands on, Neleus hid the manuscripts in a cellar. There they lay for more than two centuries, while across the Aegean Sea, Athens was raided by Celtic "barbarians," the Lyceum's reputation declined, and Aristotle's star grew dim. Around 70 B.C.E., however, the hundreds of tattered parchments secreted in Neleus's cellar were rediscovered by accident. The entire collection was brought to Athens, where a few Peripatetic philosophers still lectured, although to greatly diminished audiences. They passed the manuscripts on to Andronicus of Rhodes, a distinguished colleague who practiced in Rome, the new center of learning and power. Over the course of several years, Andronicus patched the writings together, classifying and collating (and, perhaps, editing) them. Copies were made and distributed. Once again, Aristotle's voice rang out across the Mediterranean world, and during the next two centuries, his philosophy enjoyed the first of its many revivals.

Andronicus of Rhodes did exist, and he did publish Aristotle's books. It is anyone's guess how true the rest of this story is. Since the Lyceum remained continuously in existence from the Philosopher's death until sometime in the third century C.E., the tale undoubtedly exaggerates the extent to which his ideas were first lost and then (miraculously) found. But it points to a truth still not well understood. There is something about these works, or about their conjunction with certain moments in human history, that makes them seem almost indestructible. Time and again, they fade from sight in one civilization only to reappear centuries later in another, often with the most extraordinary impact. "Lost" in Greece, they are later "found" in Rome. Neglected by Byzantine Christians, they inspire a great burst of philosophical creativity in the Islamic world. Unread for centuries in the

Latin West, their rediscovery in medieval Spain triggers an intellectual revolution in Europe. The enduring power of this work is
all the more remarkable when one considers that Aristotle's most
influential books are difficult to follow, do not tell stories like those
of Homer or the Bible, and have none of the literary appeal of
classical poetry or Plato's dialogues. The eighteenth-century poet
Thomas Gray is said to have compared the activity of reading
them to eating hay.[36] Yet their straightforward pedagogical style
provides a clue to their capacity to excite and inspire—and often
to antagonize—readers separated by eons in time and in culture.

What is most striking about Aristotle's writing is its reasonableness. Whether the subject is as cold as syllogistic logic or as
controversial as politics, his tone is one of calm, focused objectiv-
ity. In some writers, this sort of impersonality feels arrogant or
haughty. Aristotle's writing, though, is remarkably free of egoism,
rancor, or self-congratulation. There are even occasions on which
he is not sure how to answer a question and admits it! His usual
method is to frame an issue, defining its key terms; to acknowledge
other views and describe them fairly; and then to present his own
ideas, showing that they are logically coherent and consistent with
the available evidence. There is nothing in this form of argument
that commands belief. Aristotle does not say, "God spake unto me
and told me." He does not overwhelm the reader rhetorically, as
Plato does by making Socrates the fount of all wisdom and having
his dialogic opponents admit the truth of his remarks. The tone
of these presentations is that of a well-educated, thoughtful man
(in Greek terms, an aristocrat) addressing others who are as well-
educated and thoughtful as himself.

Aristotle is the lecturer and the reader is his student; yet he
never talks down to his readers or appeals to their emotions or
self-interest. He does not have to. Beneath the learned conversa-
tional style lies a bedrock assumption that would one day be con-

sidered highly controversial: the notion that human beings are, above all, thinking creatures, rational beings who, having discovered the truth, will accept it, and, having accepted it, will act upon it. He was aware, of course, that some people are better at reasoning than others. In his political writing he goes so far as to suggest that those capable only of following instructions are natural slaves.[37] No democrat, he—yet in his ethical and psychological works, Aristotle describes the power of thought as a gift belonging to humans as a species.[38] Everywhere people shine the beacon of their intelligence, they discover principles of orderly change— intelligible patterns that reveal how things are made and how they operate, how they originate and pass away, and how certain causes produce certain effects. Despite their limitations, people are capable of improving themselves morally, creating more stable and just communities, and living happy, useful lives. Not everyone is capable of doing advanced analysis, but to be human is to be self-conscious, to imagine, and to learn.

Reading Aristotle, one loses the sense of "all-too-human" inferiority inculcated by most of the old religions and many modern sciences. For one thing, he does not believe that sense perceptions are inherently misleading. On the contrary, they provide us with the evidence that permits us to reason with each other on the basis of common experience. Take a question of great interest to ancient geographers and navigators, as it would be much later to Renaissance explorers like Christopher Columbus: the shape of the earth. Simply looking across a field or out to sea, we would conclude that the earth is flat. Yet it would be improper to generalize from this impression that the entire earth is flat. Since we can only see so far, a curvature imperceptible to our short-range vision might be apparent from outer space. But Aristotle points out that we do have a way of "seeing" the earth as it might appear from outer space. When there is an eclipse of the moon, the earth is interposed between the sun and the moon, and the shadow thrown by the earth on the moon is always curved. Therefore, we know that the earth is spherical—and not only that, we know that it is not nearly as large as the stars. By measuring how much the position of the stars seems to shift as we travel on the earth, we can calculate that the earth is only about twenty thousand miles in circumference.[39]

People are not prevented by sensory data from understanding the universe, Aristotle insists. On the contrary, "common sense" experience is what makes consensual understanding possible. Nor are we naturally so passionate, so self-centered, or so fallen in sin that our conclusions are incurably subjective and biased. Mere opinion can be either true or false, but true knowledge, in Aristotle's view, connects us with realities that exist objectively as well as in our minds.[40] What gives him such confidence in the power of reason? The answer lies not so much in his glorification of the mind as in his conviction that the universe itself is meaningful. To know, Aristotle maintains, is to understand the causes of things.[41] This sort of understanding is possible not just because humans are naturally smart, but because in a sense the universe is "smart," too. There is a deep correspondence between the way the world works and the way we work. We have our reason, which makes it possible for us to think logical, purposive, patterned thoughts, but the universe has its own logic and purposes. If it did not—if the world inside and outside us were not intelligible—our thoughts would disappear into that void like light lost in pure darkness.

Unlike the Jews, Muslims, and Christians who would one day seize on this insight as proof of the existence of a supernatural Creator, Aristotle held that the natural universe, although meaningful, is self-sufficient. And, unlike the secularists who would one day deny that it has any intrinsic meaning at all, he asserted that it is full of purpose. Everything that exists, he taught, strives to fulfill itself—to realize (or, in his language, to "actualize") its inherent potential. This great law makes nature comprehensible and invites us to fulfill our own destiny by learning to comprehend it. Wisdom is the knowledge of causes, but, consistent with Aristotle's emphasis on a developing universe, his definition of "cause" is broader than ours. It includes not only a thing's "efficient" cause—the preceding event or condition that ordinarily produces it—but its "material," "formal," and "final" causes— the stuff the thing is made of, the patterned way in which that material is transformed, and the purposes that guide its transformation.[42] So, if we want to understand a particular person fully as a natural creature, we must know not only that she is the product of the sexual union of her parents but also that she is a fleshly creature animated by a soul—an individual whose natural aims are to preserve herself, continue her species, and become a self-conscious being.

Aristotle was aware, of course, that words like "purpose" and "striving" ordinarily refer to human motives and behavior, and he was not so benighted as to think that trees or rocks think or act as humans do.[43] But the opposite notion, that the universe is totally unlike us, that it is chaotic matter on which we impose a purely subjective mental order, he would have thought both arrogant (because it locates all meaning in the human mind) and despairing (because it deprives the nonhuman universe of meaning). The lynchpin of his thinking—the idea that connects the meaning inside people with the meaning outside them—is the presence of form in nature. Every natural substance, he declared, whether a tree, a star, or a person, is a compound of matter *and* form.[44] "Form," as he uses the word, means shape, but it also means that which makes a substance what it most truly is: the thing's internal structure and its animating force, the factor that realizes or actualizes a thing's potential to be the kind of thing that it is.

This is not as obscure as it may sound. It is what we mean when we look through a family photo album and announce that the bulge in mother's stomach, the squalling newborn, the child in school clothes, the groom in the wedding picture, and the old gent dandling his grandchild on a withered knee are the same individual. Form is a way of accounting for the fact that substances like a person, a tree, or a star have identity—that we are able to "think" them even though the object that presents itself to our senses may not be a grown person but an embryo, not a living tree but a fireplace log, not a star but a glimmering light in motion. According to Aristotle, the power to make sense of sense impressions in this way is reason, something divine. So powerful is reason, and so reasonable the universe, that we are able to grasp the form of everything that exists—even man, whose form is the soul. And, yes, even God, who is form and substance itself.

Like a scientist, Aristotle appeals to the ultimate authority of reason. Like a theologian, he insists that the universe is purposeful. Does he, then, believe in God? The answer is . . . yes and no. On the one hand, he asserts that there is a supreme being who is single, immaterial, unchangeable, eternal, and perfect. On the other, despite this deity's apparent resemblance to the Eternal One of the Abrahamic faiths, he (or it) is neither a creator nor a redeemer. He is not a transcendent being who exists outside the universe and who intervenes at will in the workings of nature and history. No. He is an "insider," a feature of the universe, unique, to be sure, but a feature still, like the heart or brain of a human being, or the engine (if one can imagine a conscious, immaterial engine) of a living machine. The God of the Bible and the Koran is the eternal ruler of a transient kingdom. He has no predetermined or knowable function, but acts freely as a sovereign lord. The Aristotelian God, by contrast, is the eternal resident of an equally eternal cosmos. He/it has a knowable function, which is to inspire everything in the universe to actualize itself as far as its nature permits. This task he carries out not actively but passively, by serving as a force of attraction (or, as Aristotle says, as an "object of desire and of thought"[45]). God is the great and necessary exception to the rule that every substance seeks to actualize itself. As pure actuality, the finished product, so to speak, he carries out his role simply by existing. The source of all movement and change, he changes not a whit. Conscious, but perfectly self-contained, he thinks only . . . of himself.

This conception of a detached, noninterventionist, essentially uncaring deity may seem strange to those raised in one of the Abrahamic religious traditions, but it is a logical (or, at least, not illogical) consequence of Aristotle's attempt to understand the universe on its own terms as a vast, intelligible reality comprehensible by reason. There is no place in his worldview for the supernatural, for multiple realities, or for any Platonic separation of the spiritual and material realms. It is a uni-verse that Aristotle wishes to explain: a unified reality that includes us and speaks to us; a place in which we can learn to live without cynicism or escapist illusions. When his works were rediscovered in the Middle Ages by Muslims, Jews, and Christians, one of the most difficult issues posed was whether one could accept his love of reason and his appreciation of the world without also accepting his "pagan" theology.

While Aristotle lived and taught, the key doctrines of human rationality and the intelligibility of the universe might be challenged or qualified, but they were not considered terribly controversial. In later ages, though, particularly at times when men and women were awakening to their ability to grasp and organize the world, these ideas provoked strong, often violent, reactions. Aristotle's writings were most likely to be "rediscovered" in eras of newborn confidence, when people who had formerly considered the universe impenetrable and their own natures ungovernable, or who had been too busy struggling to survive to imagine exercising dominion over nature and society, recognized themselves as rational beings—and as potential conquerors. The Philosopher's relationship to Greek imperialism, as suggested earlier, was not accidental. Nor is it surprising that Arab philosophers embraced his rationalist, universalist principles at the time they were bringing civilization and order to the Islamic world, or that European intellectuals rediscovered him just as the West embarked on an age of unprecedented cultural ferment and political expansion.

We will return soon enough to the rediscovery that transformed Western thinking and ushered in the modern world. For the moment, though, let us follow Aristotle's star as it declines in the Christianized Roman Empire and, through a strange combination of circumstances, rises in the Muslim East. The story of the manuscripts hidden and then found centuries later in Neleus's cave is a quaint tale—very likely a fiction, but not a shock to one's common sense. How the same manuscripts were carried eastward by Christian refugees fleeing their own Church is a far more surprising story, although it is not fictional at all.

CHAPTER TWO

The Murder of "Lady Philosophy"

HOW THE ANCIENT WISDOM WAS LOST,
AND HOW IT WAS FOUND AGAIN

FROM HIS HUSHED and curtained bedroom in the bishop's palace, Augustine could not hear the sounds of battle. Even those in the cathedral square heard very little, since the militia—what remained of it—had withdrawn inside the city's fortified walls to await the inevitable onslaught. From time to time, small detachments ventured forth to harass the enemy troops encamped just out of sight of the watchtower, or to forage for food in the ruined countryside, but few returned from these useless forays. The grainfields and orchards outside the walls had been stripped clean to feed the Vandal army, and the port that had made Hippo Regius one of North Africa's richest cities was blockaded by the Vandal fleet. Hippo was dying. Struggling for breath in his canopied bed, its bishop was dying, too. Augustine wondered whether he would still be alive when the forces that had besieged the city for more than two months finally hammered their way through its thinly defended gates.

The year was 430 C.E. The sick man grieved for his own town as he had grieved for Rome two decades earlier, when the Visigoths occupied and looted the Eternal City. Yet his own work gave him some solace. A few years before the barbarians swept from Spain across North Africa, he had published the last chapter of a book that had taken him fifteen years to complete. *The City of God* was the bishop's heroic attempt to make sense of the Roman Empire's catastrophic decline. Its essential message was that our life on earth, with its inevitable confusion and suffering, can only be understood aright from the standpoint of the truths revealed by God to his people. For pagans, the collapse of Roman power may seem "the story to end all stories." From a Christian perspective, it is a nanosecond in eternity—a minor scene in the cosmic drama that began with the Creation, and that will end with the return of Jesus Christ as mankind's judge and savior.

Rome fell, as ancient Babylon did, because of her people's sins. But the world of sin and death—the natural universe that seems so real to us—is a mere shadow of God's timeless kingdom, where all such evils are banished. To the eyes of faith, declared Augustine, the distinction that matters most is not that between Romans and barbarians, or even between Christians and pagans, but between "two communities of men, of which the one is predestined to reign eternally with God, and the other to suffer eternal punishment with the devil."[1] Only when Christ rules in glory can men and women realize their dreams of security, peace, love, and justice. Meanwhile, they must live, as it were, both in this world and the next, relying on the Church as the essential link between them. The business of faithful Christians, he concluded, is to inhabit the world knowing that it is fallen: to pray for the grace needed to resist the devil's snares, accept the discipline and solace offered by Mother Church, and hope for their initiation into the society of immortal saints.

Except for the Bible and Augustine's own autobiographical *Confessions,* no other piece of writing would influence Western thinking so strongly over the course of the next seven centuries. Steeped in Scripture and the traditions of the Church, *The City of God* was, of course, a Christian document. Yet few of its later readers understood how powerfully it was shaped by Greek ideas, or that it embodied a choice of philosophical perspectives. In fact, *The City of God* represented a decisive rejection of Aristotle's worldview in favor of that of Plato and the Neoplatonists. Because the bishop's writing was so passionate and insightful, and because his Platonized Christianity made such good sense in the context of post-Roman society, Western Christians came to believe that it was the only possible version of the true faith—that Augustine's doctrine *was* Christianity, period. They did not recognize that there might be other defensible versions that he had decided to reject.

To comprehend this choice, it helps to recognize that, in some periods of history, Plato's ideas and attitudes make obvious sense to thinking people, while in others, Aristotle's vision of the world seems far more realistic and inspiring. In Aristotelian epochs, economic growth, political expansion, and cultural optimism color the intellectual atmosphere. People feel connected to each other and to the natural world. Confident that they can direct their emotions instead of being dominated by them, they are generally comfortable with their humanity. Proud of their ability to understand how things work, they believe that they can make use of nature and improve society. The natural world seems to them vast and harmonious, populated by highly individualized people and things, but integrated, purposeful, and beautiful. Aristotelian thinkers know that they will die as all nature's creatures do, but the environment that nurtures them seems immortal, and this gives meaning to their lives. Curiosity and sociability are their characteristic virtues, egoism and complacency their most common vices.

Platonic eras, by contrast, are filled with discomfort and longing. The source of this discomfort is a sense of contradiction dramatized by personal and social conflicts that seem all but unresolvable. Society is fractured, its potential integrity disrupted by violent strife, and this brokenness is mirrored in the souls of individuals. People feel divided against themselves—not ruled by reason but driven by uncontrollable instincts and desires. The universe as a whole may not be evil, but it is far from what it should be—far, indeed, from what, in some other dimension, it truly is. Latter-day Platonists are haunted by a sense that the world people call real is, at least in part, illusory . . . and this is also the source of their longing. They believe that a better and truer self, society, and universe await them on the other side of some necessary transformation. Earthly life is therefore a pilgrimage, a stern quest whose pursuit generates the virtues of selflessness, endurance, and imagination. The characteristic Neoplatonic vices (the dark side of its virtues) are self-hatred, intolerance, and fanaticism.

In Christianity's early years, it was not clear which mode of thought and feeling the leaders of the young Church would find most congenial. Around 200 C.E., the famous Christian apologist, Tertullian, staked out a position that rejected all classical philosophy as inherently anti-Christian and productive of heresy. "Heretics and philosophers handle the same subject-matter," he observed darkly. "Both treat of the same topics—Whence came evil? And why? Whence came man? And how?" The irascible Latin Father was particularly wroth with "wretched Aristotle, who taught [the heretics] dialectic, that art of building up and demolishing, so protean in statement, so far-fetched in conjecture, so unyielding in controversy, so productive of disputes; self-stultifying, since it is ever handling questions but never settling anything."[2] His famous condemnation of philosophical speculation would echo even more stridently in centuries to come:

> What is there in common between Athens and Jerusalem? What between the Academy and the Church? What between heretics and Christians? ... Away with all projects for a 'Stoic,' a 'Platonic' or a 'dialectic' Christianity! After Christ Jesus we desire no subtle theories, no acute inquiries after the gospel.[3]

But this was only one side of the argument. A Greek-speaking archbishop, Clement of Alexandria, advanced a more tolerant view. "Philosophy was given to the Greeks immediately and pri- marily, until the Lord should call the Greeks," said Clement. "For philosophy was a 'schoolmaster' to bring the Greek mind to Christ, as the Law brought the Hebrews. Thus philosophy was a preparation, paving the way toward perfection in Christ."[4] Au- gustine agreed. Like Clement, he argued that just as God had given the Hebrews of the Exodus permission to "despoil the Egyptians" and take their treasures with them, the Church had permission to convert the treasures of Greek philosophy to its own use.[5] The question was: Which writings were genuine trea- sures and which were fool's gold?

By Augustine's time, the answer was becoming clear to most Christian thinkers. Tertullian may have been right to criticize "wretched Aristotle," but Augustine's own career was a testimony to the power of Platonist thinking. As he tells the story, he left his family's home in North Africa at the age of twenty-nine, and came to Rome to make his living as a teacher of rhetoric.[6] Recalling his classical education in Carthage, he remembered how proud he had been to master Aristotle's *Categories* without any help from his teachers.[7] At the time he came to Rome, the future bishop was neither a Christian nor a philosopher. He was, however, a deeply troubled young man. Like many other intellectuals of his time, he was haunted by a sense of his own unworthiness. Surpassingly brilliant, tormented by shameful desires, and deeply ambivalent about Roman civilization, he struggled desperately to make sense of a world that seemed split into diametrically opposed realms of holiness and maleficence, spiritual discipline and carnality, selflessness and insatiable willfulness.

Augustine's mother, Monica, a Christian convert, hoped that he would follow her into the Church, but in his early twenties, he had embraced Manicheism, a Persian religious import that postulated an eternal struggle between the forces of good and evil, each represented by its own deity.[8] During his first year in Rome—a time made miserable for him by the knowledge that he had left home to escape his mother—the ideas of the Manicheans seemed to him increasingly lifeless and shallow, but he could not discover more satisfying answers to the questions that plagued him. How could one worship the Manichean God—a weakling who was powerless to conquer Satan? But if God was all-powerful, as the Christians said, why had he created a universe wracked by sin and death? Restless and dissatisfied, Augustine became seriously ill and recovered; obtained a teaching job but detested it; and entered a period of moral crisis in which everything, even his loving, long-term relationship with a devoted mistress, seemed open to question. It was in this uneasy, questing state that he learned that he had been appointed professor of rhetoric in the imperial capital of Milan. This was the change he had been unconsciously awaiting.

Milan was not only the Roman army's headquarters but also the home of the West's most powerful churchman, Bishop Ambrose, a strong-willed, intelligent, violently intolerant man who did not hesitate to defend the rights of the Church, as he defined them, against all threats, whether emanating from unbelievers, heretics, or emperors of Rome. Philosophically, Ambrose was a Neoplatonist. He had nothing against dualism, so long as it was consistent with his own Church's belief in a single, omnipotent Creator and Redeemer. For him, as for others who drew Augustine into the Christian orbit, "the history of Platonism seemed to converge quite naturally on Christianity. Both pointed in the same direction. Both were radically other-worldly. Christ had said, '*My Kingdom is not of this world*'; Plato had said the same of his realm of Ideas. For Ambrose and his colleagues, the followers of Plato were the 'aristocrats of thought'."[9]

This tendency to split the world into natural and supernatural realms had some basis in Scripture, but it also reflected the reaction of the era's leading thinkers to the threats and disorders that increasingly troubled the Roman world.[10] The first burst of Neoplatonist philosophizing had coincided with the military reversals and civic demoralization of the third century C.E. By the fifth century, Rome had effectively become two empires, Latin and Greek; a period of imperial revival had ended; and Roman power was visibly crumbling in the West. Aristotle's vision of an integrated, coherent universe peopled by rational investigators seemed irrelevant to the material crises and spiritual needs of this troubled new age. As Christian thinkers drew ever-sharper distinctions between the violent, sensual, disorderly world of the present and God's eternal kingdom, Plato's philosophy seemed to provide a natural corollary to their faith. In certain of his dialogues— *Timaeus,* in particular—the great Athenian sounded uncannily like a Christian, so much so that a theory developed that, centuries before the birth of Christ, he had been visited by the Holy Spirit.[11]

In Milan, Augustine discovered parallels between Greek and Christian thought that he had not previously recognized. Not only did Plato affirm the existence of a Supreme Good—unitary, immaterial, perfect, and timeless—but he also gave precedence to spiritual over material values, argued for the immortality of the soul, and advocated a way of life aimed at refining human existence and opening the door to an experience of oneness with the Eternal. In the Neoplatonist books, Augustine said, "I found it stated, not of course in the same words but to precisely the same effect and with a number of different sorts of reasons, that: *In the beginning was the Word, and the Word was with God, and the Word was God.*"[12] In *Timaeus,* Plato had even suggested a sort of Trinity, consisting of the Divine Craftsman, the Ideas, and the World Spirit. But his most important contribution, from Augustine's point of view, was to insist that the world of appearances—the world of "facts" apprehended through sense impressions—is a kind of watered-down and distorted reality, a universe of imperfect copies rather than originals. The originals, of course, exist forever in what Plato called the realm of Ideas and Christians called the Kingdom of Heaven.

To this doctrine Neoplatonists like the great third-century philosopher Plotinus added the notion that the universe that proceeds originally from God yearns actively to return to him. Humans can therefore connect with the Absolute by meditating on the multiple things of this world and sensing their unitary, divine origins.[13] Augustine was greatly attracted by the mystical implications of this doctrine, which was to become vastly influential in the West when expressed in glowing terms by Dionysius, a Syrian mystic who flourished shortly after the bishop's death.[14] At the same time, however, he recognized there were serious differences between the Platonic and Christian worldviews. He understood that Plato's Divine Craftsman does not bring the entire universe into existence out of nothing, but works it up out of materials as ancient as himself. Nor does he intervene actively in history for the sake of man's salvation. At bottom, Plato's deity, called "the One" or "the Absolute" by the Neoplatonists, is no more personal a God than Aristotle's Unmoved Mover. For this reason, Neoplatonism had little to tell Augustine about the personal problem that most concerned him: the weakness of the human will, that soul-sickness that prevents us from doing the right thing even when we desperately want to. He would not become a Christian himself until his will was empowered by a shattering religious experience that owed very little to philosophical theories.[15]

Even so, the ideas of the Neoplatonists paved the way for Augustine's conversion, since they enabled him to accept the reality of immaterial things and permitted him to solve the philosophical problem that had originally driven him to become a Manichean: how a good God could have created an evil universe. He discovered, in short, that one could postulate a radical separation between heaven and earth without branding the created universe evil. Augustine adopted Plato's definition of evil as an absence of good—not something created by God, but a "privation of being," a sort of ethical black hole brought into the universe by man's misuse of his free will.[16] Wielding that doctrine against the Manicheans, Christians could show that sin and death are real, but only under certain conditions, while God's goodness is unconditioned and absolute. Plato's idea that there are degrees of reality was the key to the problem of evil. What God has created is wholly good. Evil, which exists only from an earthly perspective, is the voluntary choice of nonexistence over existence.

Platonism also supplied Augustine with a theory of knowledge that could be harmonized with the concept of man's fall. To the bishop and his successors, human knowledge was the result of a divine "illumination," not the product of unaided human reason. Aristotle had been wrong, therefore, to suppose that rational thought alone could unlock the secrets of the universe. Either God would enlighten us directly, or the truth would remain forever concealed. Augustine's own attitude toward reason was complex; he was, after all, the greatest thinker of his age. But the common interpretation of his viewpoint was simple. As one commentator puts it, "Whatever information God intended us to have about the physical world, He wrote in plain language; whatever is not immediately obvious, God does not intend us to know."[17]

In effect, this position wrote finis to the tradition of scientific inquiry that had been part of the classical worldview ever since Aristotle created the Lyceum's curriculum. It was not that science was illegitimate per se but that it was irrelevant, and possibly harmful, to men and women seeking salvation. As Augustine noted in *The City of God*, the Greek philosophers "made efforts to discover the hidden laws of nature.... And some of them by God's help, made great discoveries; but when left to themselves they were betrayed by human infirmity, and fell into mistakes."[18] The infirmity that most distressed him was pride. Proud of their ability to formulate geometrical theorems and predict eclipses, proud of their orderly cities and civilized social life, thinkers like Aristotle had ignored man's natural depravity and his absolute dependence upon God's grace. What good was knowledge of this world, Augustine asked, if it could not avert eternal damnation in the next?

Augustine of Hippo died in 430. He did not live to see his beloved city fall to the Vandals, but the Platonized Christianity that was his lifework long outlasted the invaders. For the next seven centuries, while Greek philosophy faded from memory, literate Christians ranked the works of the North African saint just below the Gospels themselves, rarely recognizing that they owed almost as much to Plato and Plotinus as to Saint Paul. Aristotle's work, meanwhile, vanished almost entirely from Western consciousness. In part, this was because there was as yet no Aristotelian Augustine to "baptize" his doctrines and to fuse them with those of Christianity. But the more important cause of this disappearance was the apparent irrelevance of his optimistic worldview, with its high regard for human reason and its focus on the things of this world, to the problems facing men and women in post-Roman Europe. As learning in Europe retreated behind monastery walls, the gaze of most Christians was directed upward, at the Heavenly City, or inward, at the state of their own souls. Exploring the wonders of nature and the possibilities of reorganizing the City of Man would have to await a more propitious time. And so, through centuries of travail, Plato lived on through Augustine, while Aristotle became a vague, disembodied legend—an ancient wizard, once very powerful, whose ideas were now all but forgotten.

THAT ANYTHING AT ALL remained of Aristotle's work in the West when Roman authority collapsed was largely the result of one man's effort. He was called Boethius—Marcus Anicius Severinus Boethius, to use the full panoply of names marking him as member of the Anici, one of Italy's ancient aristocratic families. His father had been consul of Rome, and if the world had been more predictable, he might have become an equally distinguished figure in the Roman state, perhaps even more powerful, considering his political and intellectual gifts. As it was, he left Rome to serve as prime minister to a barbarian king—an occupation full of intrigue, adventure, and opportunities for service, but not one designed to secure a long life or a peaceful retirement.

This tale begins a few years before his birth, in 476 C.E., the date accepted by most historians as marking the fall of the Roman Empire in the West. In that year, a skillful and ambitious general named Odoacer had himself acclaimed king of Italy by his troops. At the time, the Byzantine emperor Zeno governed Rome's Eastern domains from Constantinople, while Romulus Augustus nominally ruled the West from the imperial capital of Ravenna. I say "nominally" not only because Romulus was little more than a boy (he was known as Augustulus or "little Augustus") but also because Germanic tribes migrating unstoppably across the empire's northern and eastern frontiers had already divided the rest of western Europe between them.[19] By this time, the Vandals controlled North Africa and the Visigoths, Spain; France was divided among the Franks, Burgundians, and other tribes; and Italy was now at the mercy of the newest arrival, the Danubian Ostrogoths.

Odoacer's army was officially the army of Rome, but virtually all his soldiers were Ostrogoths like himself. In the fifth century, most of Rome's legions were composed of such outsiders, many of whom had been granted the status of allies and given lands in relatively underpopulated regions of the empire. Odoacer's troops, however, did not want to settle in the wilds of Gaul or Britain; they wanted land in Italy proper. When their demand for prize Italian land was refused (as Odoacer must have known it would be), the general led his army to Ravenna and took the city without a fight. Then, after sending "little Augustus" into exile with a nice pension, he made a crucial decision. Because of his foreign birth he could not be named emperor, but he might have convinced a Roman aristocrat to assume the office as a figurehead while he governed behind the throne. (This had been done before by other Gothic commanders.) Instead, he dispatched representatives of the Roman senate to Constantinople to inform the eastern emperor that there would be no successor to Augustulus, and that, legally speaking, Zeno was now the ruler of an undivided Roman Empire. In exchange, Odoacer asked to be recognized as the legitimate king of Italy.

Zeno accepted the imperial insignia but declined the gambit. While leaving Odoacer in peace, he refused to provide the "barbarian" with official recognition. This disdainful reticence, however, proved meaningless. Unless Zeno was prepared to move against the Ostrogoths—an impossibility, considering that he was beleaguered by other tribes in his own territory—Odoacer would remain indefinitely in power, and the Roman Empire west of the Balkans would become a legal fiction. This is precisely what happened. Odoacer ruled Italy until 493, when he was overthrown by an even cleverer and more ruthless Ostrogoth named Theodoric, accounted by some the most formidable Western leader from the fall of Rome until Charlemagne.[20] Theodoric's right to rule would later be recognized by Constantinople on the ground (erroneous, as it turned out) that he would make a reliable Western ally. Even before that time, however, his court had become a magnet for young Roman nobles who wished to play an important and civilizing role in the new Europe.

If anyone could be said to be a born administrator, the description fit the young Boethius. His wealthy guardian, Symmachus, who raised him from an early age after his parents' death, was a powerful figure in Roman politics as well as a devout Christian. Symmachus supervised the boy's early education and, when he was discovered to have scholarly talent, sent him to Athens to finish his studies at the Platonic Academy. Boethius's generation was one of the last to have that privilege. A few decades later, the school would be closed permanently by order of Emperor Justinian I on the grounds that the pagan philosophies taught there were inherently subversive of Christian belief. The young Roman's faith, however, was unshaken by exposure to the Academy's advanced ideas. In fact, it was probably there that he learned how to use the ideas of Plato and Aristotle to clarify certain confusing Christian doctrines. When he returned to Rome, Symmachus gave the graduate his daughter, Rusticana, in marriage. Shortly thereafter, armed with Christian beliefs, Greek philosophy, a new wife, and the family's flair for administration, Boethius came to Ravenna to pledge his service to King Theodoric.

One can easily understand the appeal of this mission to an ambitious young man in his twenties. Not only did Theodoric hold power with a firm grasp, but he was no more "barbaric" than the Roman aristocrats he placed in high administrative posts. The Ostrogoth king had been raised at court in Constantinople, where he had been held hostage by the current Byzantine emperor. (Royal families frequently kept the noble children of unreliable allies with them as a form of security for the observance of peace treaties—a pleasant form of captivity, so long as the peace lasted.) A great admirer of Roman government and Greek culture, he had reserved the highest offices in his realm for talented administrators like Boethius. "An able Goth wants to be like a Roman," he was fond of saying, "but only a poor Roman would want to be like a Goth."[21] At the same time, he insisted that no one but a Goth could hold high military rank. This division of labor was consistent with his long-term policy to establish himself diplomatically as a faithful vassal of the Eastern Roman emperor while creating, de facto, an empire of his own in the West.

In Boethius, Theodoric found an ideal servant to help implement this policy, since the young man's genius was for mediation—the interpretation of one culture to another. On the one hand, his job was to "Romanize" the Ostrogoth government. This meant training Gothic leaders to restrain their warlike impulses so that Theodoric's territories might be extended quietly, through negotiation and sound administration, rather than by military offensives that would alarm Constantinople. Facing east, on the other hand, his role was to translate Gothic interests and attitudes into terms that the imperial administrators could understand, while letting Theodoric know what he needed to do (or not do) to retain the Eastern emperor's trust.

These were delicate, dangerous tasks, but not impossible for a man of Boethius's gifts. A master of languages and what we would now call ethnography, he knew the tongues and customs of the Goths as well as the languages and ceremonies of the Byzantine court. Year after year, he made himself indispensable as an administrator and diplomat, gaining a succession of higher positions in Theodoric's government. The Ostrogoth ruler named Boethius consul when he was thirty, and in his early forties, he attained the highest office in the kingdom: Master of Offices—in modern terms, prime minister. Under his leadership, Theodoric's kingdom expanded eastward to include much of modern Yugoslavia and westward to absorb most of southern France. In the same year that Boethius became Master of Offices, his two sons were named consuls—a signal honor to him and his family.

The only other civilian official to attain anything approaching this preeminence was a younger Roman aristocrat, Cassiodorus, who served as Theodoric's chief speechwriter and propagandist, and who wrote *History of the Goths,* glorifying the Goths' cultural achievements.[22] Cassiodorus portrayed his master as an ideal Roman-style ruler, an image that Theodoric attempted to realize by governing liberally (for example, he did not persecute Catholics as the Vandals did in North Africa) and by patronizing Greco-Roman cultural projects. Boethius, far more talented as a scholar than Cassiodorus, took full advantage of the king's interest in promoting philosophy and literature. During the same years that he was rising to the pinnacle of power in the Ostrogothic kingdom, he produced a body of writing that was to be his most lasting monument.

Classical learning, Boethius could see very well, was disappearing in the western lands formerly governed by Rome. With the decline of the old educated aristocracy and a widening cultural rift dividing the Greek East from the Latin West, the sort of education he and Cassiodorus had enjoyed was becoming a rarity. The Goths were learning Latin, after a fashion, but the Latins were forgetting their Greek. Since all educated Romans had studied the writings of Plato, Aristotle, and other Greek thinkers in their original language, there had been no need to translate these works into Latin. The loss of literacy in Greek was therefore a potential catastrophe for Western society. It would mean the simultaneous loss of philosophy, mathematics, medicine, engineering, and science. Moreover, Christian thought would also be imperiled if the educated elite, at least, did not know the classics, since most of the Church Fathers had written in Greek, and even the Latin Fathers—Saint Augustine in particular—had been inspired by the ideas of the Neoplatonists. Stung by these dangers, Boethius set himself a Herculean task: "I will translate into Latin every work of Aristotle that comes into my hands, and all the dialogues of Plato."[23] In addition to translating these works, he promised he would translate key works of the Neoplatonists and attempt to prove that the two great philosophers were in agreement on most fundamental issues.

For a busy administrator and diplomat negotiating between two intrigue-ridden courts, these efforts were clearly quixotic. Even so, in little more than a decade, Boethius managed to translate the six books of Aristotelian logic known as the *Organon,* as well as treatises on logic by Cicero and the influential Neoplatonist philosopher Porphyry. He also wrote five commentaries of his own on Aristotle's works, a number of important essays using Greek philosophical techniques to defend Christian doctrines, and several short texts on subjects basic to the classical curriculum—arithmetic, music, and astronomy. Later, under most unusual circumstances, he added an original masterpiece: *The Consolation of Philosophy.*[24] Taken together, these writings would not fill one bookshelf in a modern public library. Yet for the next five centuries, as tribal migrations and raids, famines, plagues, and warlordism disrupted European society, the translations and essays of Boethius, along with two or three short summaries by other writers and a compendium of texts by Cassiodorus, would be all that the West would know of Greek philosophy. As a result, when learning revived in the Latin world half a millennium later, virtually every thinker's starting point was the logic of Aristotle as translated, interpreted, and applied by Boethius.

"Boethius was the last of the Roman philosophers, and the first of the scholastic theologians."[25] He is accorded the title "scholastic" not only because he commented on Aristotle and attempted to apply philosophical concepts and methods to the solution of theological questions, but because his attitude toward faith and reason became a model for European intellectuals of the future. As a devout Christian, he had no doubt that the truths proclaimed by faith were incontestable, and that reason alone could not encompass all of them. He noted, for example, that "the human mind is unable to understand the generation of the Son from the substance of the Father."[26] "We should of course press our inquiry only so far as the insight of man's reason is allowed to climb the height of heavenly knowledge," he wrote.[27] But it was equally clear to him that reason (that is, philosophy) could be used to clarify religious concepts as difficult as the Trinity and the Incarnation. A short article on the Trinity dedicated to his friend, John the Deacon (later, Pope John I), concludes with these words: "If these things are right and in accordance with the Faith, I pray you confirm me; or if you are in any point of another opinion, examine carefully what has been said, *and if possible reconcile faith and reason.*"[28]

"Reconcile faith and reason." The phrase is trickier than it seems, since it means explaining the truths of faith, to the extent possible, in terms that are applicable to other fields of thought. Boethius rejected the idea that most religious doctrines are inexplicable (or, as Mark Twain was to put it, that "Faith is believing what you know ain't so"[29]). But he was not at all interested in providing naturalistic reasons for supernatural events or divine ordinances—the sort of thing people do, for example, when they explain that the dietary laws of Leviticus were adopted for hygienic reasons. To him, using reason did not mean demystifying the truths of faith, but building conceptual bridges between the worlds of secular and religious knowledge. The truths of religion are not the same as those of philosophy or science, he insisted, but they are comparable. For this reason, one ought to be able to make most religious doctrines comprehensible without falling back on, "It's so because the Bible (or some other authority) says it's so."[30] In pursuit of this aim, he asked a series of startlingly bold questions: for example, to what extent the three Persons of the Trinity were "substances" in the Aristotelian sense comparable to individual entities in the known universe.[31] Later thinkers might not accept his answers, but they embraced the mission implicit in his questions: to make human sense of divine truths, to the extent possible.

By the early 520s, Boethius was at the apex of his powers both as a thinker and as a political figure. Then occurred a series of events that remain murky to this day, although their immediate consequences were all too clear.

A few years earlier, power had changed hands in Constantinople. The emperor Anastasius, a wise and moderate ruler, died and was replaced by Justin, an uneducated military man from the Balkans, whose fervently ambitious nephew, Justinian, dreamed of restoring Roman power from the Euphrates to the Atlantic. Anastasius had had no reason to oppose King Theodoric's accumulation of power in the West, but to Justin and Justinian, the Ostrogoth was an obstacle that would, sooner or later, have to be removed. Alarmed by the new regime's reported hostility, Theodoric dispatched the pope to be his ambassador to Constantinople, but before long, disturbing rumors began to reach him of a possible conspiracy between the pontiff and the emperor. Even worse, the king's agents informed him that elements of the old aristocracy in the Roman senate were plotting with Justin and the pope to undermine his power in Italy.[32] Could the Romans he had trusted and treated so well be preparing to rid themselves of the "barbarian" they secretly despised? Fearing a combination of Eastern and Western interests against him, the increasingly suspicious king ordered that the Romans he had appointed to high administrative posts be kept under close surveillance.

The atmosphere in Ravenna was thick with plots and counterplots, agents and double agents, genuine intelligence-gathering and false accusations brought to earn some cash or to settle old scores. In 523, one of Theodoric's spies intercepted compromising letters allegedly written by a Roman proconsul named Albinus to high officials in Constantinople. The letters seemed to confirm the king's worst suspicions. Without giving the proconsul a chance to explain, Theodoric had him arrested on a charge of treason and thrown into prison. Boethius, who knew both Albinus and the agent in the case, scented a conspiracy against the proconsul. Probably thinking that the king must accept his word after so many years of faithful service, he intervened in Albinus's defense, asserting that he had examined the supposedly subversive letters, and that they were clearly forgeries. By defending a fellow Roman, however, he brought suspicion upon himself.

Other evidence of alleged conspiracies involving Byzantine officials and Roman senators was brought to Theodoric's attention. Shortly afterward, at Verona, the enraged king "tried to shift on to the whole Senatorial order the charge of treason laid against Albinus, since he was eager to do away with them all."[33] Boethius stoutly defended the senate's innocence—but he greatly underestimated his old chief's panicky ferocity. Soon after the confrontation at Verona, three accusers (known scoundrels, according to Boethius) informed Theodoric that his Master of Offices had conspired with certain Roman senators against the kingdom. For good measure, they also accused Boethius of "sacrilege in canvassing for high office"—that is, using astrology to advance his career. Again letters were produced, blatant forgeries according to the accused man. But, like Albinus, he was not offered the chance to defend himself. In 524 Theodoric ordered him imprisoned at Pavia. The senate, no doubt to save its own members' skins, promptly issued a decree against him. His younger colleague and fellow scholar, Cassiodorus, somehow managed to avoid being swept up in the purge and was later named Master of Offices himself—a circumstance that some interpreted (without much evidence) as proof of his disloyalty to Boethius. Boethius's eldest son, however, was not so quick on his feet and was arrested several days later.

Was there a senatorial plot against Theodoric? Did it involve Boethius? It is impossible to say for certain, since there was never any public disclosure of the charges or trial of the accused men. Theodoric's fear of a Byzantine plan to destroy him was hardly paranoid. Shortly after his death, Justinian's armies would launch a brutal twenty-year war that finally eliminated the Ostrogoth kingdom, wrecking the Italian economy in the process. But if there was a conspiracy against Theodoric during his lifetime, Boethius was almost certainly ignorant of it. The book that he wrote in prison—"a golden volume," as the historian Edward Gibbon called it—does not seem the work of a guilty man. *The Consolation of Philosophy* is a meditation on the sudden change of fortune that hurled the author from the summit of power, fame, and wealth into the abyss. Alternating prose with poetry, it is written as a series of dialogues between the prisoner and Lady Philosophy, a beautiful Muse whose mission is to help Boethius regain his peace of mind despite the disaster that has befallen him. The Muse explains that what people call "fate" represents the workings of divine reason. Combining Neoplatonic with Aristotelian ideas, she then goes on to reconcile this belief with the apparent realities of worldly existence—unhappiness, evil, and injustice—and concludes by showing that God's foreknowledge is consistent with man's free will.

Fifteen centuries later, the book remains an astonishing performance: a brave and learned Christian man using the tools of classical philosophy to think his way out of a deep depression. Boethius must have hurried to complete it. A year or two after he entered prison—the exact date is unrecorded—the king spoke some words or gave a sign, and "the last Roman philosopher" was executed along with several other accused aristocrats. Shortly afterward, his son followed him into oblivion—or heaven, if their beliefs were vindicated.

Cassiodorus, the new Master of Offices, appears at the end of this story like the character who delivers the final speech in a Shakespearean tragedy. He preserves Boethius's translations and other writings, accumulates a collection of Greek and Roman manuscripts, and lobbies the pope to create a university in Rome on the model of the great universities in Alexandria and in Persian Nisibis. This would be the first university in the Latin West, but the pope has other things on his mind and nothing comes of the proposal. (As one commentator writes, the scheme's failure "was no accident; the prerequisite of political stability was lacking."[34]) Perhaps goaded by this reversal to do something to save the remnants of classical philosophy, Cassiodorus retires from public office at the age of fifty and moves to Vivarium, a town in southern Italy. It is an epochal move, since to house his library he founds an abbey that begins the monastic tradition of preserving and copying ancient manuscripts. Boethius rests in an unmarked grave, but his translations and commentaries on Aristotle's works, his textbooks, and his prison memoirs live on. For the next five centuries, they are copied and recopied by monks who hardly know what they are preserving, or why. Seeds sown in fallow soil, they will spring to life in due season.

IN THE WEST, Aristotle's work lay dormant while Europe endured half a millennium of endemic violence, poverty, and disorder. Little wonder that, during this seemingly endless winter, those seeking comfort and meaning would turn to the certitudes of faith rather than the conundrums of philosophy. The more surprising story takes place in the East, in the Greek-speaking lands long considered the Roman Empire's economic and cultural heartland. There, under autocratic Byzantine rule, the barbarians were held at bay and the Pax Romana survived. There trade flourished, supporting prosperous, densely populated cities like Alexandria, Constantinople, and Antioch. In these centers of learning where classically trained scholars continued to practice their arts, one might have expected a vigorous growth of philosophy and science. But this is precisely where intellectual history takes one of its strangest turns. One could call this tale "The Murder of Lady Philosophy."

The story begins, in fact, with the murder of a female philosopher. Hypatia was the daughter of a well-known Alexandrian mathematician who recognized that her talent far exceeded his, and who had encouraged her to develop her own interests in mathematics, astronomy, metaphysics, and ethics. By the year 415, she was a well-established and beloved figure—a Neoplatonist thinker famous throughout the East for her virtue and wisdom, and the best-known woman philosopher of her age. Hypatia ran a small school in her Alexandria home, where she lectured and conducted dialogues with students of good family who hoped to learn the art of reasoning well. Following the time-honored practice, she also walked the nearby streets in her philosopher's cloak, discussing philosophical issues with anyone who wished to question her. Although she remained a pagan, many of her students and friends in the predominantly Christian city were Christians. Her former students included at least two bishops, and her relations with Church leaders (many of whom were also Neoplatonists) were more than amicable . . . that is, until Cyril became the archbishop of Alexandria.

To comprehend Cyril, and to understand what happened to Hypatia, one has to cast one's mind back to the preceding century, when Alexandria was wracked by a theological conflict that ended by dividing the Christian community throughout the empire into two bitterly opposed camps. The issue in dispute was the relationship of Jesus Christ to God the Father, a doctrinal problem that, surprisingly, had remained unsettled for the past three hundred years.[35] Arius, an Alexandrian priest supported by many bishops and theologians in Syria and Palestine, spoke for those who believed that, while Jesus was divine, he was not identical with or equal to the Father. Athanasius, the archbishop of Alexandria, asserted, on the contrary, that Christ was both man and God, and that he was in no respect less than the Creator. Because the issues were very important to ordinary Christians (they involved attempts to reconcile Christ's divinity with traditional Eastern monotheism), and because various Roman emperors took sides in the dispute, the controversy was long-lasting and extremely violent. Regional rivalry also played a role, since the center of Arian theology was the city of Antioch, Alexandria's main competitor for cultural supremacy. Arianism within the empire was finally outlawed by the Council of Constantinople, convened by Emperor Theodosius I in 381.[36] The council declared that the Son was of the same essence as the Father, and that both were Persons of equal status, indissolubly united with the Holy Spirit as One God.

One might think that after this decision religious passions in the East would have cooled down a bit. Yet on the heels of the settlement, a wave of violent attacks against heretics, Jews, and pagans swept the region, with many assaults incited or winked at by bishops and perpetrated by zealous monks determined to "purify" their society. Half-consciously, the Mediterranean world was beginning its transformation from "a society in which Christianity was merely the dominant religion" to "a totally Christian society."[37] When monks in one Mesopotamian town burned a synagogue to the ground, the emperor ordered the local bishop to pay restitution for the crime out of church funds, but was dissuaded from enforcing his order by Bishop Ambrose of Milan, who threatened to withhold communion from anyone who aided the "enemies of Christ."[38] Theodosius was even less solicitous of the pagans, and issued a stream of orders outlawing their sacrifices and closing their temples. Again, contrary to his wishes, but beyond his control, mobs inspired by militant churchmen took matters into their own hands. In Alexandria, a crowd reportedly whipped to a frenzy by the fiery archbishop Theophilus attacked the Serapeum, an ancient temple with a world-famous library donated by Cleopatra, and utterly destroyed it.

The empire's remaining pagans were left vulnerable to attack by militants we would now call extreme "fundamentalists." Temple-burning became something of a popular sport in the East, and cultural treasures by the score disappeared in the flames lit by religious fanaticism. This situation still prevailed early in the fifth century, when the See of Alexandria was occupied by Archbishop Theophilus's nephew Cyril, a brilliant, passionate, and intolerant official "notorious for his love of quarreling, his violence, and his impetuousness."[39]

Perhaps because of Cyril's evangelical militancy, there was bad blood during his episcopate between the city's Jewish and

Christian communities. The Jewish community in Alexandria was very large—probably in excess of 200,000 people out of a total population of approximately one million—and very old. Jews had resided in Alexandria long before the destruction of the Temple in Jerusalem by the Romans. In the year 415, for reasons that remain obscure, the archbishop incited a large crowd of Christians to attack the Jewish quarter.[40] The result was the worst anti-Jewish riot in the city's history—what one historian calls "history's first large-scale pogrom," with synagogues sacked, property looted, and many residents murdered or mistreated.[41] The precise extent of the violence remains unknown, but the terror was sufficient to drive large numbers of Jews out of the city and to impel the prefect of Alexandria, an imperial official named Orestes, to intervene on their behalf. This intervention, however, was a trigger for more violence. When Orestes came to Cyril's cathedral to express the emperor's displeasure with the disorders and to demand the restoration of the victims' homes and properties, he was confronted by a large group of stone-throwing monks who had come from their mountain outside town to protect their beloved archbishop against imperial bullying. One stone-thrower, a monk named Ammonius, struck the prefect with a rock and injured him, whereupon Orestes had the monk arrested, tried summarily, and tortured to death. Cyril recovered Ammonius's body and treated the remains as the relics of a martyr.

Now we can return to Hypatia, for Orestes was known to be a friend of hers and had been a frequent visitor at her house. With or without Cyril's knowledge and consent, the word spread among the monks and local militants that the philosopher was conspiring with the prefect and the Jews to undermine the archbishop's authority and to pollute Christian Alexandria with her pagan ideas. The sequel was horribly predictable. Not long after Ammonius's death, while Hypatia was taking her evening walk, a gang of Christian men seized her and carried her off to a nearby church. There, they stripped off her clothes and tortured her to death, after which they dismembered her body and burned the pieces in a fire that they built in a place called Cinaron.[42] The savagery of the act, as well as its target, became the talk of the empire. Cyril vehemently denied any connection with the crime, but nobody was ever punished for it. Clearly the Byzantine realm was becoming a dangerous place for non-Christians and philosophers to live.

But Christians, too, were soon reembroiled in violent theological disputes—and, once again, we find Cyril at the center of the controversy. The struggle this time was not about Christ's identity as God—that issue had been settled at Constantinople—but about the relationship between the human and divine aspects of his person. What bothered and divided believers was this question: Is it correct to say that God himself was born of Mary, and that he suffered, died, and rose again? Or did Jesus have these experiences in his capacity as a human being, while the divine aspect of his person remained untouched by them? The theologians of Antioch believed that to say that God had had all these human experiences smacked of pagan notions of the birth and death of gods, and involved Christians in the worship of Jesus as a man. Those of Alexandria replied that to separate Christ's man-ness from his God-ness would be to split his personality and to revive the Arian heresy that considered him to be less than God. Though the Antiochene school had several leaders, it came to be identified in the public mind with Nestorius, the archbishop of Constantinople. The Alexandrian school had one principal leader, Cyril of Alexandria, who loathed Nestorius and devoted his final years to destroying him.

This fight, which was to become even more unmanageable than the Arian controversy, was not a repeat of the earlier struggle, but it resembled it in some ways. Once again, it was the Alexandrians, passionate, mystical, rigorous, and intolerant, who emphasized Christ's divine nature, while the more rationalist, worldly, and human-centered Antiochenes stressed his authentic manhood. Each side in the debate quoted "proof texts" from the Gospels and the words of the Church Fathers to support its position. But each side also used ideas drawn from classical philosophy to show that its own position was reasonable and the opposing position illogical or absurd. The Antiochenes, in particular, were inclined to use Aristotelian concepts to justify their conviction that Christ's divine nature must not be confused with his human nature. One of this group was Bishop Diodore of Tarsus, who, in addition to his purely religious work, also wrote treatises on "how hot the sun is" and commented on Aristotle's cosmology. Another was Theodore of Mopsuestia, a daring and innovative thinker who shocked traditionalists by denying that Old Testament books like the Song of Songs were allegories foretelling the coming of Christ. And a third was Nestorius of Constantinople, who triggered the controversy by criticizing the use of the term *Theotokos,* "God-bearer," to describe the Virgin Mary.

"God is not a baby two or three months old," Nestorius famously remarked, to the horror of those used to worshiping the baby Jesus.[43] Similarly, the Nestorians maintained, it was nonsensical and sacrilegious to say that the Creator of the universe emerged from Mary's womb and was tempted in the desert, that he increased in virtue, and that he died on the cross. God is unchangeable and impassible; he cannot be born or made to suffer, and, surely, he cannot die. These were the experiences of the man Jesus, who was "assumed" by God, sacrificed, and resurrected to free us from sin and grant us the hope of eternal life. Jesus Christ therefore has two natures, the Nestorians concluded: one human, the other divine. Both reason and faith dictate that these natures be recognized as separate and distinct. For if Jesus did not have his own mind and body, his thoughts and feelings as reported in the Gospels would be nothing but playacting. And if a real man had not died to redeem us from sin, how could his sacrifice and resurrection save us?

Alarmed by the humanistic tendencies of Antiochene theology, Cyril of Alexandria answered with a question of his own: "Have we, then, been baptized into a man, and shall we admit that this is true?"[44] The Alexandrian bishop had spotted two apparent weaknesses in the Nestorians' doctrine. Politically, many ordinary Christians wanted to worship Jesus Christ without worrying about the pagan implications (if any) of their belief. They adored the God-Man, and were not at all concerned that his birth, temptation, or agony on the cross could be attributed to God. Theologically, this attitude could be supported by insisting that since Christ was one person, the divine and human aspects of his personality must form a coherent whole. A person having two separate, unintegrated natures would be a pagan monstrosity, like a centaur. But if these natures were unified, how could one say that the man in Christ did this but the God did that? Furthermore, declared Cyril, if Jesus the man were not also God the Eternal, there would be nothing to give the Eucharist—the ritual consumption of his body and blood—its saving power.

To preserve Christ's humanity, the Nestorians had divided his person into two contrasting, possibly even conflicting halves. To preserve the unity of his person, Cyril would take the chance of subordinating the man in Christ to the God. Perhaps, if the Alexandrian archbishop had been more diplomatic and Nestorius a more astute politician, or if the emperor had been able to mediate between them, the two prelates might have found their way to some sort of doctrinal compromise. But Cyril was as adept at politics as he was uncompromising in matters of doctrine, and

Nestorius, perhaps the more subtle intellect, was no match for him in the complex court intrigues ("Byzantine," indeed) that characterized fifth-century politics. Thanks to Cyril's machinations, Theodosius II found himself caught in a crossfire between his powerful older sister, who disliked Nestorius, and his wife, who was one of the archbishop's most ardent admirers. With the emperor effectively neutralized, there was no chance of a negotiated settlement.

Cyril saw his chance. In 431, he convened a Church council at Ephesus in Asia Minor and packed it with his supporters. The Syrian bishops who favored Nestorius were several days late in arriving. In the interim, Cyril instructed the delegates already present to hear the case against Nestorius, after which they promptly excommunicated him for heresy and deposed him from office. When the Syrians, led by John of Antioch, finally arrived, they convened their own synod and condemned and deposed Cyril. These dueling councils thoroughly confused the emperor, who treated both synods as one, ratified all the condemnations, and put everyone under house arrest. Meanwhile, Cyril raised vast sums to bribe influential people at the palace, and Nestorius found the political ground disappearing from under his feet.[45] After several months, he found the dispute too frustrating and demeaning to continue and let it be known that he would not mind returning to his monastery at Antioch. The emperor granted his request and, under pressure from the Cyrillians at court, replaced him with a supporter of Cyril's.

Nestorius's career was effectively at an end. Later branded a heretic, exiled even from Antioch, he would end his life at a monastery deep in the Egyptian desert. Cyril seemed the winner, but in this controversy there would be no real winners. After the Alexandrian leader's death, his own movement split, with its more uncompromising "Monophysite" wing taking the position that

Christ had only one nature, and that nature divine. The great ecumenical Council of Chalcedon (in 451) attempted to settle the matter by declaring that Christ was "acknowledged in two natures, without confusion, without change, without division, without separation," the natures being "distinctive," but "combining in one person... not divided or separated into two persons."[46] The formula of "two natures in one person" was to become orthodox Catholic doctrine, but the Monophysites furiously rejected it as an insult to Christ and the struggle continued, punctuated by repeated imperial interventions, periods of persecution, and outbursts of mass violence. (One of these, the pro-Monophysite riot of 532 in Constantinople, destroyed the ancient cathedral of Sancta Sophia.) Even after the Arabs conquered most of the former Byzantine territories in the seventh century, the dispute among the surviving Christians continued, with first one side, then the other, gaining the upper hand. In one respect, at least, it never ended. The Copts of Egypt, the Jacobites of Syria, the Armenian Church, and the Ethiopians refused to accept the "two natures" formula and remain Monophysites to this day.

The principal effect of this long struggle on the empire's cultural life was to confirm the "murder" of Lady Philosophy. Despite the survival of Roman authority in Constantinople, the same shift from this-worldly to otherworldly concerns that marked post-Roman thinking in the West occurred in the East as well, although it took place more sporadically and slowly. While scholars in Alexandria and Constantinople continued to read Plato and Aristotle, "they commented endlessly on the learning inherited from the past, but almost never doubted this learning or tried to move beyond it."[47] To some extent, this petrifaction of philosophy can be attributed to the overcentralized administration of the Byzantine emperors, which destroyed the independent aristocratic elite.[48] But it was also the result of people's passionate interest in matters of faith and their inclination to use philosophy, if at all, as a stick with which to beat their theological opponents. In 529, Justinian closed the Platonic Academy in Athens for the reasons given three hundred years earlier by Tertullian—that philosophical speculation had become an aid to heretics and an inflamer of disputes among Christians. By that time, however, many of the empire's independent thinkers, both Christian and pagan, had already left for Mesopotamia and Persia, where scholars could pursue their researches without fear of meeting the fate of Hypatia or Nestorius.

How often have refugees fleeing a repressive regime carried the sparks of civilization with them in their well-thumbed books and manuscripts. So it was for the religious dissenters who sought sanctuary first in Edessa, a Mesopotamian city housing several famous schools, and then across the Persian border in Nisibis, whose university was considered the best in Asia. When Monophysites took power in a particular city or province, their Nestorian opponents went into exile, and when rulers like Emperor Justinian persecuted the Monophysites, their leading scholars headed east. The result was a transfer of culture similar, in some respects, to that caused by alternating waves of refugees from Nazi- and Communist-dominated lands in the twentieth century. The scholarly exiles found among strangers a freedom to inquire that had become obsolete in their own homelands. As a result, the works of Greek philosophy, science, and theology ignored, condemned, or simply preserved in Byzantium were actively interpreted and applied to current issues in Persia.[49]

This is how, in the seventh century, the Arabs inherited Aristotle and the treasures of Greek science. The Nestorians, who were famous linguists, had already translated much of Greek philosophy, as well as their own school's writings, into Syriac, the lingua franca spoken in Syria and Mesopotamia. Now they retranslated these materials into Persian for the use of their new hosts. When Muslim invaders seized control of the Fertile Crescent and Persia in the seventh century, they asked the Nestorians to help them translate the famous books of wisdom into Arabic . . . and the learned "heretics" were glad to comply. At around the same time, other Arab forces occupying Antioch, Damascus, and Alexandria procured translations of the philosophers' works from Syriac, Coptic, or directly from the Greek into Arabic—a task in which the Monophysites also participated.[50] Two centuries later, having absorbed all this new material, the Arabs and Persians were ready to produce their own Peripatetic philosophy, a blend of Platonic, Aristotelian, and Islamic ideas that they called *falsafah*. While Western Christians lost themselves in prayer and Eastern Christians in ritualized controversy, the cultural awakening that had not occurred in Byzantium became the glory of Islam.

IMAGINE YOURSELF a Christian scholar newly arrived in Toledo to work on one of Archbishop Raymund's translation teams. You will have read your Bible and missal, of course, the works of Saint Augustine, and a smattering of books by other writers like Boethius, Cassiodorus, and Saint Jerome. The only books by Aristotle you will have encountered are the six treatises on logic translated into Latin by Boethius, and the only dialogue of Plato, *Timaeus*. If you are very well read, you may also be familiar with the works of the ninth-century theologian, John the Scot, or the more recent essays of Saint Anselm of Canterbury. Interesting books, to be sure, some of them brilliant, but few will have challenged the basic framework of thought accepted by you and your ancestors for the past seven centuries. Your reading will have confirmed your understanding that the material world is an unstable, transient place full of dangers and temptations—an unpredictable environment whose operations and very existence are entirely dependent upon

God's mysterious will. You know—as everyone knows—that our brief life here on earth is merely a prelude to the afterlife; that we are inveterate sinners who can be saved, if at all, only by God's freely given grace; and that our ability to understand this fallen universe is limited by both the feebleness of our reason and the inherent deceptiveness of sense impressions. How can we be truly happy here? Aside from fleeting moments of joy, we cannot, since this realm of pain and illusion is not our true home.

This is what you know. Now imagine your confusion and dismay as you read, for the first time, Aristotle's *Physics, Metaphysics,* and *On the Soul,* the treatises on natural science, and the books on ethics, aesthetics, and politics. Clearly this Greek philosophy reflects assumptions and attitudes that are utterly alien to yours. Aristotle does not appear to be aware that the world of the senses is a place of suffering and unreality, or that there is a better, more real world to come. His universe is one, and he seems to feel entirely at home in it. His writings have nothing to say about God the Creator or the Redeemer, and pay little attention to our sinfulness or its consequences in the afterlife. In Aristotle's view (here the Christian might be tempted to cross himself), time and space exist eternally. Nature governs itself without divine interference, and human reason, far from being crippled, is perfectly adequate to secure man's knowledge, good behavior, and happiness. But if this is so—if the universe itself contains all that we need to understand and enjoy it—what need is there for Holy Scripture, the Church, or any other source of revealed truth and divine guidance? Of course, Aristotle talks about a deity of sorts that he calls the Unmoved Mover, but this abstract, passive creature has nothing to do with the God of Abraham, Isaac, and Jacob, the Lord who created the universe and begot us a Savior. From a Christian perspective, this worldview is godless—a very advanced form of paganism, but paganism nonetheless.

After reading such disturbing material, the pious scholar might consider casting it into the flames. (Fearful Church authorities did declare later on that some of Aristotle's works were too dangerous to be read by university students.) But he would not want to. For the Aristotelian corpus, troubling though it might be, represented the most comprehensive, accurate, well-integrated, and satisfying account of the natural world that medieval readers had ever encountered. Here one could discover a method of rational inquiry—the application of logical reasoning to observed facts—and the ways of spotting illogical ("sophistical") arguments. Here nature's mysterious secrets were disclosed: how fish sleep; why a thrown object continues in motion after it leaves the hand; how the Milky Way was formed. From such particulars, the reader could ascend with the Philosopher to breathtaking generalities such as the types of possible knowledge and classification of the sciences, the dynamics of natural change, and the nature of Being itself. Part of the work's appeal lay in its encyclopedic scope. Long known in Europe as a master of formal logic, Aristotle was now revealed as the master of all knowledge—a "magus" whose ideas would thenceforth become the starting point for almost all discussions of natural or social phenomena. Equally exciting was the idea that, although he might be authoritative, the Greek sage was not infallible. The Arab commentators had disagreed with him on certain points, and even dared to update and "correct" him. Why should Christian scholars be more diffident?

The first European scholars to confront the apparent clash between Aristotle's perspective and their own orthodox Christianity were the translators in Toledo. Scholars like Domingo Gundisalvo, Daniel of Morley, and Michael Scot understood that converting an ancient philosopher's map of reality into language understandable by those living in a different time and culture was far more than a mechanical task—that it really meant mediating between cultures.[51] The work of translation therefore carried over naturally into that of commenting on the newly translated material. The translators asked themselves what the concepts they were putting into Latin meant in terms of their own beliefs—whether or not they could be harmonized with traditional Christian doctrines—and if there were conflicts, how to deal with them. As unorthodox as it might seem, the Aristotelian world-picture was far too vivid and convincing to be written off as a pagan error. How, then, to explain its apparent divergence from traditional religious thinking?

Partly because of their mediating role, and partly because they were working with Muslims and Jews in a cultural milieu as diverse, tolerant, and cooperative as any Europe had ever seen, the commentators' tendency was to try to reconcile these competing worldviews. This is where the Arab philosophers proved invaluable. Centuries before Archbishop Raymund established his translation center, the masters of *falsafah* had summarized Aristotle's ideas and commented on them, criticized and modified them, and used them to solve a wide variety of theological and scientific problems. Like the Christians, they were serious monotheists, which meant that they had already recognized and dealt with certain aspects of Aristotelian thinking that priests and monks were bound to find disturbing. Their writings were to provide a crucial bridge between Aristotle's human-centered worldview and the God-centered vision of the universe long embraced by the People of the Book.

One solution to the problem of divergence had been developed with great skill by the eleventh-century Persian thinker Avicenna (Ibn Sina), an all-round genius whose works were among the first to be translated by the scholars at the Toledo center. Avicenna's method, in a word, was to spiritualize Aristotle at certain key points by reading Platonic ideas into his thinking. If the

Philosopher's this-worldly system could be "corrected" by incorporating in it the notion that the material universe is a reflection of eternal Spirit, it might be made acceptable to orthodox monotheists. This was a tricky business, first because Aristotle loathed the idea of a separate realm of Ideas existing outside the world of nature, and second because one who followed Plato too closely ran the risk of overspiritualizing the universe and denying God's creative intervention in history. Avicenna already had roused the ire of orthodox Muslims by describing the heavens and the earth as "emanations" of God rather than willful creations.[52] Nevertheless, following the Persian's lead, Gundisalvo and his colleagues set out to supply Aristotle's natural philosophy with the missing spiritual dimension.

An example is their revision of Aristotle's doctrine of the "four causes." The Philosopher had asserted that every natural substance can be completely understood by identifying its efficient, material, formal, and final causes: the circumstances that produced it, the material of which it was composed, its structural or developmental principles, and its purpose or place in the natural scheme of things. Gundisalvo declared the approach fundamentally sound . . . with one important reservation. Because Aristotle was pre-Christian, he talked only in terms of physical or "corporeal" causes. But Christians since Saint Augustine understood that the things of this fallen world mirror the realer realities of an eternal world beyond the time-bound realm of the senses. A Christian could therefore accept the doctrine of the four causes simply by recognizing that each corporeal cause has a spiritual counterpart. For example, the corporeal "efficient" cause of an animal is sexual procreation by its parents, but its spiritual efficient cause is God's creativity, which produces males and females able to procreate. The animal's corporeal "formal" cause is its genetic structure, but its spiritual formal cause is the "power lodged by God in the celestial regions to control generation and corruption, growth and age."[53] And so forth.

Similar "corrections" could be made in the case of other Aristotelian doctrines. Even the Philosopher's belief in the eternity of matter, apparently so at odds with the Scriptural doctrine of the creation of the universe from nothing, could be harmonized with orthodoxy if one understood that God created some material things (like unformed or "prime" matter) before time, other things (the celestial bodies) with time, and everything else during time.[54] The effect of all this was to portray the Greek sage as a Christian without portfolio, a transcendently wise philosopher whose view of the world could be made acceptable to the faithful merely by updating it and putting it in the proper supernatural context. This friendly misrepresentation had several momentous effects. To begin with, it bought the new worldview some time. By diverting attention from the philosophy's more subversive implications, it delayed the inevitable counterattack and initiated a germinative period during which educated Christians could absorb the vocabulary and fundamental concepts of Aristotle's thought. Equally important, it strengthened the assumption prevalent among some Christian thinkers that truth was One—that there could be no real contradiction between the conclusions of reason and the credos of faith. Nature, after all, was God's Creation. If one could discover fundamental truths about the natural universe, the result would be to reveal more of God's work to mankind. And whether the discoverer were a Christian or a pagan, an Augustine or an Aristotle, would make little difference.

Over a longer run, however, the disjunction between reason and revelation, Aristotelian natural philosophy and Christian faith, could not be papered over. Aristotle was neither Plato nor Saint Paul. Not only did he repudiate the idea of a world of Ideas separated from the natural universe but there were other aspects of his thinking that would prove difficult, perhaps even impossible, to "spiritualize" in a way helpful (or at least harmless) to orthodox Christians. For example: If the regular relations between causes and effects in nature are invariable natural laws, what room is left for God's freedom to make miracles? If the individual soul is wedded to the body, how can it survive the body's death? And if physical decay is inevitable when life passes from material entities, how can the same body be resurrected? Aristotle says that the good life—the life of reason and of ethical behavior—can be found on this earth. If so, what need is there for Heaven? Underlying all such questions is a larger one, which was to reappear in Europe at the end of the brief honeymoon mediated by the translators and Arab philosophers: Could Christian believers make sense of the universe, as Aristotle had attempted to do, and still remain believers?

In fact, the Muslim and Jewish philosophers had not answered this question to the satisfaction of their own religious authorities. For this reason (among others), the movement of *falsafah* was dying in the Islamic world just as it reached a takeoff point in Europe. The movement culminated in the work of the great Cordoban thinker Averroës (Ibn Rushd), who wrote thirty-eight commentaries on Aristotle, as well as books of his own, in an attempt to grapple with the serious differences between the Aristotelian and traditional religious perspectives. Although a faithful monotheist himself, Averroës insisted on "de-Platonizing" Aristotle—on reaffirming his focus on individual substances rather than timeless Ideas, and defending his contention that the natural universe is governed by natural laws, not by the whimsical or mysterious decisions of a miracle-making God.[55] Like his Jewish compatriot Maimonides, he argued that Aristotle's concept of God as a "self-thinking thought" might be defective, but that it was closer to the truth than notions based on literal readings of the Bible or Koran, which suggested that God must have a physical body, since he "sat" on a throne, "saw" that his Creation was good, and "heard" people's prayers.[56] An Aristotelian philosopher could be a convinced monotheist, but he could not believe in a simpleminded way in doctrines like divine miracles, the resurrection of the body, or the immortality of the individual soul.[57] Either these doctrines were true in a way that was unprovable by reason, or they were true in ways more complex than what was generally understood.

Not surprisingly, many orthodox Muslims had long viewed this sort of speculation with great suspicion. Around the beginning of the twelfth century, their instinctive aversion to Aristotle's worldview was given hard-edged expression by the mystical philosopher al-Ghazali, considered by some experts the most influential figure in Islamic intellectual history. According to al-Ghazali, for example, the very idea of cause and effect is a man-made illusion, since God, not nature, produces every effect, and since he is free to produce any effect he chooses.[58] His book attacking both Aristotle and Avicenna, *The Incoherence of the Philosophers*, "broke the back of rationalistic philosophy and in fact brought the career of philosophy . . . to an end in the Arabic part of the Islamic world."[59] A bit later, Muslim Spain saw a last resurgence of Aristotelian thinking in the remarkable works of Averroës and Maimonides, but after a fundamentalist North African regime conquered much of Spain, both philosophers found themselves in exile. From this time forward, gripped by what one commentator calls a "slavish traditionalism,"[60] the Muslim world turned definitively away from scientific inquiry. So did the Jewish world, which saw Maimonides' Aristotelian masterpiece, *The Guide to the Perplexed*, denounced as heretical by the same rabbis who applauded his legal and moral works.[61] In fact, the rabbis of Provence would later ask the Holy Inquisition to burn the book— a request they were happy to accommodate.[62]

The result of all this was a remarkable paradox. For all their brilliance and originality—or, perhaps, because of it—the great Arab philosophers came to occupy a relatively minor niche in Muslim society. Especially after al-Ghazali fired his devastating broadside at the practitioners of *falsafah*, conservative religious leaders, fearful that their teachings might confuse and mislead the faithful, kept them at a safe distance from the mosque. As a result, they talked mainly to each other, and their influence outside a small circle of intellectuals was in steady decline from the eleventh century on. Since philosophy in those days included much of what we call science, this did not bode well for the future of scientific inquiry in the Islamic world. In Europe, by contrast, Christian scholars wrestling with Aristotle's manuscripts—a relatively unsophisticated lot, compared with their Muslim and Jewish colleagues—unexpectedly found themselves in a position to transform and modernize their society's thinking.

In part, this leverage was a result of a new hunger in the West for knowledge and understanding: an unexpected and dramatic awakening. But—to modern eyes, most surprising—it was also a result of the scholars' intimate connection with the Roman Catholic Church. However much their ideas and interests might overlap, there was always this crucial difference between Christian and Arab intellectuals: while the Christians were part of the corporate Church and were bound by its rules of discipline, almost all the Arab *Faylasufs* were secular professionals supported by worldly patrons like the caliphs and provincial rulers. Many of them, indeed, were public officials; both Averroës and Maimonides were famous judges and court physicians. This meant, on the one hand, that they were freer than the Christians to follow the road of philosophical speculation even where it diverged from traditional religious thinking. On the other hand, though, this very freedom made them a danger in the eyes of the orthodox religious teachers, at least when they moved from fields like law and medicine to metaphysics, theology, and politics.

Hence, the paradox. While the world's most accomplished Aristotelian philosophers were isolated in their own Islamic lands, Christian scholars who had no knowledge of most of Aristotle's works before 1200 or so, and who could be punished for heresy if they philosophized too freely, had the chance to become the primary exponents of advanced philosophical ideas in Europe. This may be an example of what some have called the advantages of backwardness. Both Muslims and Jews liked to claim, with much justification, that in their civilization, religion was not simply an organization or "church" but a way of life. The Catholic Church, by contrast, was very much an organization. Because Europe had undergone such a long period of social chaos after the Roman empire collapsed, it was for centuries the Latin world's only unifying, civilizing agency. With its high degree of centralization, its vast number of priests and nuns in orders, its properties, its armies, and its monopoly of education, the Church was the dominant force in European intellectual culture—an institution without parallel in any other society. If Aristotelian thinkers were to "capture" it, European thinking would be transformed from the top down. A rationalist, scientific approach to nature and society would inevitably become part of the Western worldview.

But would the Church prove more hospitable to this sort of thinking than the mosque or the synagogue? If so, how much would be left of traditional Christianity, with its creative, redemptive, providential God, its faithful believers, and its hegemonic Church? These were the momentous questions facing a society now beginning to awaken as if from a long, deep sleep.

CHAPTER THREE

"His Books Have Wings"

PETER ABELARD AND THE
REVIVAL OF REASON

THERE HAD BEEN popular lecturers before at the cathedral schools of France, but never anyone like this. Even before the sun's first glow suffused the chill autumn fog, the students gathered in the street outside the monastery on Mont-Sainte-Genevieve, waiting for their hero to appear for his early-morning class. Those carrying breakfast loaves were persuaded to break off pieces for themselves and distribute the rest to hungry classmates. "This is my body"—the inevitable joke, as the loaf went from hand to hand, followed by a flask of rough wine: "This is my blood." Many students spoke in Latin, but some, gathered in collegial clusters, addressed each other in their native tongues: English, German, Flemish, Italian, Normand, or French. One can easily imagine them stamping their feet for warmth in the cobblestone street and gossiping about their legendary teacher.

Peter Abelard's students had much to gossip about. More than thirty years earlier, barely out of his teens, the young prodigy had landed in Paris like a thunderbolt, rattling the nerves and shaking the composure of more diffident or slower-witted folk. Shortly after arriving at the Cloister School of Notre Dame, he disagreed publicly with its teacher, the famous logician William of Champeaux; trounced him in debate; and left to found his own school, followed by many of William's best students. A few years later, Peter returned to the city to study with France's best-known theologian, Anselm of Laon, whose lectures he found appallingly boring. ("He had a remarkable command of words," Peter wrote later with typical asperity, "but their meaning was worthless and devoid of all sense."[1]) When he stopped attending classes, several of Anselm's faithful students challenged him to give his own lecture on a biblical topic that they would choose. Peter agreed on the spot. The topic they chose was an obscure prophecy of Ezekiel's that no previous commentator had been able to fathom. Abelard's interpretation of the passage was so ingenious and interesting that the students asked for more. His one lecture became three, each drawing a larger audience, until virtually the entire school was in attendance. After becoming a theologian in his own right, Peter would complete the triumph by publishing a highly acclaimed series of commentaries on Ezekiel.

Even his adversaries agreed that for sheer brilliance, Abelard had no peer in Europe. Wielding his copy of Aristotle's *Categories* like a sword, he helped make logic the most exciting subject in the medieval curriculum. His own ideas, while controversial, were invariably interesting, and opponents feared his biting wit almost as much as his skill at disputation. It was not just intellectual talent, however, but a certain tragic-heroic charisma that made him such an attractive figure to his students. The eldest son of a minor noble, he had chosen to become a scholar rather than a warrior, but he remained a knight in spirit—arrogant, impetuous, and thirsting for glory; always at war with some enemy, and never inclined to forgive a slight.[2] One recognizes in this reckless egoism, this impulse to push an advantage one step too far, a similarity to certain modern celebrities whose inclinations to live "on the edge" their youthful fans find so enthralling. For Abelard, it was not enough to defeat an opponent in debate; he must also humiliate the victim and make him a permanent enemy. Nor would he restrict his theorizing to safe topics of discussion. Most scholars of his time tiptoed gently around doctrines like the Holy Trinity and Original Sin, since it seemed virtually impossible to say anything new and interesting about them without falling into heresy. Abelard found this sort of challenge as irresistible as a glove thrown in his face.

Then, of course, there was the matter of Heloise. . . . The students waiting outside the church had just begun to discuss their teacher's notorious love affair, when a stir in the street announced his arrival. Abelard made his way slowly toward the monastery door, assisted by a corps of older boys who pushed a way for him through the crowd. Considering his enormous reputation, the philosopher was a surprisingly small man, but handsome, with a large head crowned by fine blond hair, and sharply defined Breton features. Even at a distance, he seemed to radiate intelligence, energy, and wit. He stopped for a moment to exchange greetings with some favorites, making a joke in Latin that provoked boisterous laughter, then was borne by his escorts through a side door of the monastery and into a large classroom. Somewhat more than one hundred young men jostling in behind him found places on the scholars' benches lined up on the floor of the room, while Abelard mounted to a desk on a raised platform. A number of students were turned away at the door, grumbling and vowing to return even earlier for next week's class.

"The question," said Abelard, immediately silencing the chatter, "is whether the Jews who killed Christ sinned by doing so."[3]

After a moment of shock, the murmuring began. The master was always unpredictable, but this question seemed dangerously eccentric. No one, not even he, dared question the Gospel accounts making the Jews primarily responsible for the Crucifixion. The "perfidious Jews" had rejected Christ, persecuted him, handed him over to the Romans, and refused to save him even when offered the chance to do so by Pontius Pilate. How could one possibly deny that conspiring to kill God constituted a sin?

The year was 1136. Archdeacon Gundisalvo and his Jewish colleague, Juan Avendeuth, had begun work on their translation projects in Toledo. Jews might be considered helpful collaborators in Spain, but elsewhere they were assumed to be the enemies of Christ, along with the Muslim occupiers of the Holy Land. The First Crusade to reclaim Palestine from the unbelievers had ended some forty years earlier with the capture of Jerusalem and the slaughter of its Muslim and Jewish inhabitants. Now Bernard, the powerful abbot of Clairvaux, was preaching a Second Crusade, and Europeans were again responding enthusiastically.

In an era of newly awakened piety and militant expansionism, Christians were affirming their common identity—a process that, for many, involved disaffirming the worth of outsiders, whether Muslims, Jews, or heretical Christians. The Jews were particularly unpopular these days, not only because they were infidels but because too many of them were getting rich. After centuries of stagnation, European commerce was reviving, and ready cash was in great demand. The feudal system, with its oaths of fidelity and religious sanctions, drove non-Christians off the land but permitted them to serve as moneylenders—a necessary but disreputable role in an expanding economy. Moreover, a long wave of inflation had exacerbated the financial needs of feudal landlords and rulers who frequently employed Jewish agents to squeeze their tenants for increased rents and taxes. In the popular mind, the image of Judas the betrayer, with his thirty pieces of silver, merged nicely with hatred of the "bloodsucking Jews." On their way to liberate Jerusalem in 1096, the Crusaders had stopped in Germany to massacre the local infidels, and mobs were now being stirred to violence in England and France by rumors that the Jews were sacrificing innocent Christian boys as part of a blasphemous false Eucharist.[4]

As if unaware of the stir his remarks had provoked, Abelard spoke again. "Let us analyze the problem of the Jews' sinfulness using the method of *Yes and No.*"

The lecturer referred to the method of reasoning described in his famous book *Sic et Non.*[5] In that work he had collected conflicting statements of the Church Fathers and arranged them in groups arguing for and against 158 different propositions: for example, "That faith is to be supported by human reason, *et contra*"; "That God is not single, *et contra*"; "That no one can be saved without baptisms of water, *et contra*"; "That it is lawful to kill a man, *et non.*" The purpose of the book was to show students a wide range of alternative arguments, to help them decide by close analysis which disagreements among the authorities were real and which were only apparent, and to encourage them to reconcile opposing positions. The compilation was basically a workbook, leaving it to students to do the required analysis and reconciliation, but Abelard's critics complained that his propositions were unduly provocative, and that his failure to harmonize the opposing statements himself emphasized the inconsistency of the authorities and brought them into disrepute. They also objected to the book's famous prologue, which seemed closer to the spirit of Aristotle than to that of the Church Fathers:

> I present here a collection of statements of the Holy Fathers in the order in which I have remembered them. The discrepancies which these texts seem to contain raise certain questions which should present a challenge to my young readers to summon up all their zeal to establish the truth and in doing so to gain in-

creased perspicacity. For the prime source of wisdom has been defined as continuous and penetrating inquiry. The most brilliant of all philosophers, Aristotle, encouraged his students to undertake this task with every ounce of their curiosity.... For by doubting we come to inquire, and by inquiring we perceive the truth.[6]

Of course, where the essentials of faith were concerned, Abelard was no doubter. He was certain that the Bible was the word of God, that the fundamental principles of Christian doctrine were valid, and that most of the apparently contradictory statements of the Fathers could be reconciled. But his logical methods had explosive implications, as the discussion of the Jews' sinfulness (*et non*) would show. On the "Yes" side, condemning the Israelites in no uncertain terms, were statements made by revered authorities such as Saint Augustine, who had declared that "the Lord Christ distinguished between His faithful ones and His Jewish enemies, as between light and darkness."[7] It was commonly held that the Jews' refusal to recognize Jesus as the Messiah and Son of God was a result of their deliberate obstinacy or "stiff-neckedness," and that their leaders' persecution of him was a product of pure malice. Abelard's students might well have asked themselves whether there was really anything here to debate. For if simple murder was a violation of God's law and an act evil in itself, how much more heinous must be the unthinkable act of deicide.

On the "No" side of the ledger, however—or at least not such a loud "Yes"—Abelard could cite two recent authorities, both opposed to indiscriminate violence against local Jewish communities. Anselm of Canterbury, the greatest theologian of the previous generation, had declared that the Jews' sin was venial not mortal, since, while blamefully stubborn, they had not recognized that the man they were persecuting was God. In a similar vein,

Bernard of Clairvaux preached against massacring those whose conversion, predicted by the Book of Revelation, would herald the End of Days. According to him, the Jews had been scattered throughout the world "so that by expiating their crime they may be everywhere the living witnesses of our redemption."[8] Bernard clearly believed that the Jews had committed a crime, although there were weighty reasons for not imposing a death sentence on their descendants. To Abelard, on the other hand, this sort of thinking made no sense. If the Jews were morally responsible for killing Christ, they were sinners deserving divine punishment as well as earthly suffering. But if they were not responsible, how could they be considered sinners at all? The master of Aristotelian logic could not resist drawing logical conclusions, even if—perhaps, especially if—their effect would be to outrage complacent conservatives.

Anselm had opened the door to rational reasoning with his reference to the Jews' ignorance, but he had not had the boldness to walk through it. What was the relationship between sin and ignorance? Previous thinkers had fudged the issue by defining sin as a weakness of the will or an impulse to do forbidden things. (Although Abelard did not name Saint Augustine as the author of these definitions, everyone understood whom he was attacking.) But all humans were prone to weaknesses of the mind as well as of the body. All were wracked at times by lust, anger, jealousy, rebelliousness, and other destructive impulses. These were the preconditions for sin, the lecturer argued, not sin itself. Were "evil" impulses sinful even if one resisted and conquered them? Could an act be sinful even if the actor believed it in good faith to be the will of God? Common sense and logic said "No." Sin was a matter of intention. It required "consent"—an act of the intellect as well as of the will. The sinner must understand that the act to which he consented was wrong. When the Jews gave Jesus up for crucifixion, they thought they were punishing a rebel against the authorities, not God's Son. Their understanding was nonexistent. They had no wrongful intention. Therefore, they committed no sin.[9]

Naturally, Abelard's analysis produced a storm of questions. Unlike many teachers who simply lectured to their students, Master Peter insisted that they participate in the give and take of disputation. But he was seldom at a loss for answers, and consistent answers at that.[10]

Q: Aren't some acts, like deicide, so heinous that they are sinful in themselves, no matter what a person intends?

A: No—sin is always intentional. Human authorities may decide to punish acts harmful to the social order without taking into account the actor's state of mind, but humans cannot see into each other's souls. God can, and he punishes souls, not bodies; sins, not antisocial acts.

Q: But if individual consent is needed to make an act sinful, what becomes of Original Sin? Don't we inherit our sinful natures from Adam and Eve through the act of procreation?

A: Not at all. The idea of hereditary sin makes no sense. Since we don't have Adam and Eve's intentions, we can't inherit their sin. But we can inherit their punishment, just as the descendants of a person whose property has been forfeited for some crime must do without the property.

Q: Yet Christians may escape this punishment. Christ died to pay Adam and Eve's debt to God, and thereby free us from the penalty of death. We know that his faithful followers can qualify for life eternal by believing in him and living as good Catholics. But aren't the Jews and others outside the Church damned?

A: Not if they have tried, in their ignorance of the Savior, to please God with all their might. Christ did not die to pay some debt on our behalf either to the devil or to God. He died to pour charity into our hearts. Those who learn to love God, not just to obey him mechanically, may be saved whether they are Christians or not.[11]

This ended the class, but not the discussion. Shouting and gesticulating, the students poured into the street, rehashing Abelard's main arguments and raising objections that had not occurred to them while under his spell. Well into the night, crowded around the tables of local taverns or packed into humble Left Bank lodgings, they would struggle to make sense of individual sin and Original Sin, the saving work of Christ, and the Jews' moral responsibility—*et non*—for killing the Savior. What excited them most deeply, however, was not their master's specific teachings, as controversial and interesting as they were, but something more difficult to describe: an atmosphere, a spirit, a state of mind. Years later, one student who had gained great fame as a political theorist and administrator—John of Salisbury—recalled the excitement of studying with Europe's master dialectician.[12] Enthralled by the power of ideas, stirred by the thrust and parry of debate, fascinated and a bit frightened by logical reasoning that challenged long-accepted truths, the students understood that they were participating in something new, important, and potentially dangerous.

ABELARD'S STUDENTS had not had time to gossip about Heloise, now a well-known abbess directing the affairs of a convent outside Paris, but everyone knew her story. In his mid-thirties, at the very height of his fame, their teacher had fallen in love with the niece of a canon of the Cathedral of Notre Dame—a young woman half his age, although almost as clever as he. "In looks she did not rank lowest," he later recalled, "while in the extent of her learning she stood supreme."[13] Courting danger almost as eagerly as he wooed Heloise, he had written her love poems that were quoted all over Paris, gotten her pregnant, insisted (against her better judgment) on marrying her, and then, to protect her from her family's wrath, packed her off to a convent. Years later, in a bitterly repentant letter, he would picture himself as a cruel seducer motivated by "the fires of lust,"[14] but his autobiography makes it clear that he was as innocent as she was in matters of the heart, and utterly swept away by his first great love.

> We were united, first under one roof, then in heart; and so with our lessons as a pretext we abandoned ourselves entirely to love. Her studies allowed us to withdraw in private, as love desired, and then with our books open before us, more words of love than of our reading passed between us, and more kissing than teaching. My hands strayed oftener to her bosom than to the pages; love drew our eyes to look on each other more than reading kept them on our texts. To avert suspicion I sometimes struck her, but these blows were prompted by love and tender feeling rather than anger and irritation, and were sweeter than any balm could be. In short, our desires left no stage of love-making untried, and if love could devise something new, we welcomed it. We entered on each joy the more eagerly for our previous inexperience, and were the less easily sated.[15]

Every student—indeed, virtually every reader in France—knew these lines, which Abelard had included in his aptly named memoir, "The History of My Calamities." Even those who could not read knew the terrible price that he had paid for that love affair. Peter had sent his wife to a convent at Argenteuil as a temporary measure, intending to rejoin her when things quieted down in Paris, but her uncle, believing that he had cast her off, dispatched a group of "friends and relatives" to avenge the insult to his family's honor. The love-stricken scholar became a victim of the contradictions of the age, for while the Church preached strongly against the custom of clan retaliation, aggrieved families continued to practice it with gusto. Abelard writes that his assailants "took cruel vengeance on me of such appalling barbarity as to shock the whole world; they cut off the parts of my body whereby I had committed the wrong of which they complained." News of the atrocity spread quickly, for the next morning, "the whole city gathered before my house, and the scene of horror and amazement, mingled with lamentations, cries, and groans which exasperated and distressed me is difficult, no, impossible, to describe."[16]

The wounded man's comrades captured one of his attackers along with the servant who had been bribed to admit them to his chamber. Motivated by the same spirit of revenge that had maimed their friend, they administered an "appropriate" punishment on the spot: they blinded the two wrongdoers, then castrated them. The incident is redolent of an earlier, darker era of tribal justice, when vengeance was a private matter and violent men swung between the poles of aggression and repentance. At Abelard's urging, Heloise remained in the convent and took her vows as a nun, thus embarking on a religious career that would lead her to become a beloved and greatly respected abbess. Peter was already a churchman of sorts, since one could not be an intellectual in twelfth-century France without taking the minor orders of the Church. Clerical scholars were permitted to marry and to live in the world, but the mutilated and chastened philosopher entered the monastery of Saint Denis and became a priest, a vocation that he took as seriously as Heloise did hers. Years later, Heloise wrote him a touching letter in which she confessed that she was still haunted by "longings and fantasies" caused by memories of their youthful passion.[17] His all-too-priestly response was to condemn the "wretched, obscene pleasures" in which they had once engaged, and to implore her to stop complaining, since their fates clearly represented the judgment of a just God.[18]

One might not guess that the society which spawned this primitive drama of revenge and renunciation was undergoing one of the most remarkable periods of change in its history—the great awakening that some call the "medieval renaissance." But the story itself provides abundant evidence of that transformation.

Peter Abelard was the eldest son of Berengar, a vassal of the Duke of Burgundy with a small estate in Brittany. Ordinarily, he would have inherited his father's military profession along with his estate, but a growing Catholic Church now offered ambitious, intelligent young men more opportunity for self-fulfillment, fame, and social advancement than did the minor nobility. Around the time of Peter's birth, Pope Gregory VII had astonished all Europe by asserting the Church's supremacy over the secular authorities. The pope made it clear that he would not hesitate to excommunicate any prince who refused to recognize the rights of the Church and declare that the ruler's subjects were freed of their obligation to obey him. This was no empty threat. Everyone knew how Gregory had deposed the German emperor, Henry IV, in order to force him to recognize the Church's exclusive right to appoint bishops, and how a repentant Henry had stood barefoot in the snow outside the pope's castle at Canossa until Gregory forgave him and gave him back his kingdom. Other kings would find more effective ways to resist the claim of papal supremacy, but Gregory's successors continued his efforts to strengthen Christian institutions by revitalizing the monasteries, reforming the clergy, and developing an educated class of lawyers and scholars to extend the Church's influence throughout society. In this light, it is not surprising that Berengar decided to have his sons taught to read and write, and that he did not object when his most gifted child, "carried away by a love of learning," renounced his rights of inheritance in order to join the ranks of the churchly intellectuals.[19]

How Heloise received her education is not known, but as a canon's niece she was also a member of a privileged group that was newly ambitious for learning. Despite the general oppression of women and their exclusion from public life, a few women of

high status, like the German abbess and mystic Hildegard of
Bingen, managed to gain an education and make their mark on
European culture.[20] More important, although the Church remained stridently antifeminist, cultural and moral values in the
new, more civilized Europe were being feminized. In these years,
the cult of the Virgin Mary attained its greatest influence among
the laity, Jesus was adored as "the bridegroom of the soul," and
compassion became one of the primary Christian virtues.[21] Even
the tale of carnal love publicly recorded in Peter Abelard's autobiography provides evidence of a cultural revolution. Abelard's
book was a new sort of document—not a generic morality play
but a story emphasizing the individual personalities of the lovers
and revealing the intimate details of their relationship. One historian calls it "the critical turning point in the twelfth-century rediscovery of personality." "The important point," he notes, "is
that Abelard wished to reveal himself to the world as a unique individual whose biography could not be confused with anyone
else's. It is not the universal and ideal that he wished to portray,
but the particular and individual."[22]

What underlying causes generated this profound shift in cultural values? The question is still unsettled, but we know that, beginning in the eleventh century, the material and social conditions
of life in Europe changed dramatically. A sharp warming trend
melted the frozen northern seas, raised water levels in central Europe, and provided more than a century of good weather for
farming. Improvements in agricultural techniques increased food
production and permitted a huge percentage increase in population. As the incessant waves of migrations and invasions that had
made European life so dangerous and disorderly slowed and then
stopped, the pace of economic expansion accelerated. People
cleared forests and drained fens to create new farmlands, then
went off on Crusade to find new lands and opportunities in the

East. New social networks (brotherhoods, guilds, professions, religious orders, corporations) sprang up everywhere, supplementing the old relationship of lord and peasant. Commercial activity revived; villages morphed into towns, and towns became cities.[23]

Some idea of what all this meant for culture can be gathered when one realizes that in this same "century of great progress,"[24] the troubadours invented European love poetry, a fervent movement of moral reform moved from the monasteries into city streets, and young people hungry for knowledge poured into the church schools that were soon to become Europe's first universities. Coursing through society were two powerful currents of thought and feeling: a surge of religious piety and a great yearning for knowledge. Today many people would consider these diametrical opposites: the more religious passion, the less scientific inquiry, and vice versa. But in medieval times (and on occasion since then), they seemed twin aspects of the same aspiration: to develop and exercise one's capacities as a human being, and by doing so, to breathe new life and meaning into stale rituals and traditional formulas. The new religious zeal expressed itself in passionate devotion to Jesus and Mary, spontaneous movements to purify the Church, and militant Crusades against non-Christians. Abelard's contemporaries were discovering what it felt like to love a humanized Christ and his altogether human Mother, to bond with fellow believers, and to let these emotionally charged beliefs influence their everyday behavior. At the same time, many were experiencing, almost as if intoxicated, the joys of logical reasoning.

A new demand for understanding—a demand to "know" the truths of religion in addition to believing them—drew students from all across the Latin world to cities like Paris, Bologna, and Oxford, where pioneer thinkers such as Abelard were creating a new fusion of philosophy and religion that they called theology. For centuries, most Christians had assumed that the great truths about God, humanity, and the Church could be discovered and defended in only two ways: by reading sacred books and by meditating or praying. Reason had its uses—for example, in interpreting ambiguous passages of the Bible—but even here, faithful believers were taught to accept the interpretations offered by the Fathers of the Church as authoritative. The human intellect, after all, was weak, unreliable, and hopelessly infected by passion: an emblem of man's "fallen" state. Why trust its quibbles and machinations, when the point was to develop the virtues necessary for salvation: faith and obedience? "Faith believes," said Bernard of Clairvaux in a famous attack on Abelard, "it does not dispute."[25] As the European awakening accelerated, however, and people's minds began to turn from an exclusive concern with the next world to an engagement with the world at hand, some of Christendom's best thinkers began to wonder whether human reason might not offer another path to religious truth. Like former invalids rediscovering the use of their atrophied limbs, they began to appreciate the power and the joys of reasoning. As *joie de vivre* revived in the West, so did *joie de penser*.

That joy of thinking animates one of the most provocative pieces of writing of the age, a book consisting of two essays written around 1100 by a brilliant Italian churchman named Anselmo. Saint Anselm, as he is now known, was the prior of the Norman monastery at Bec, and after that, archbishop of Canterbury. In his essays, called *Monologion* and *Proslogion*, he adopted "the role of someone who reasoning silently to himself investigates things he does not know." Anselm knew, of course, that God existed; this was not the question that concerned him. The question was whether this fact—God's existence—was knowable by faith alone, or "whether it might be possible to find a single argument that needed nothing but itself alone for proof, that would by itself be enough to show that God really exists."[26] His answer, astonishingly, was that there was such an argument—a "proof" that has provoked discussion among theologians and philosophers to this day.

We have an idea of an absolutely perfect being, Anselm argued, something "that is best and greatest and supreme among all existing things."[27] Since we can imagine fantastic things that do not exist, it might seem that the idea of an absolutely perfect being exists only in our minds. But things that exist outside our minds as well as inside them are greater and more perfect than things that we only think about. Therefore, to have the idea of an absolutely perfect being means that such a being must exist, since, if it did not, there would be a being more perfect than the one we have conceived.

The argument seems at first mere wordplay—a logical trick. This is exactly what the monk Gaunilo asserted in a slashing attack on Anselm's theory, which was published soon after the archbishop's essay first appeared. According to Gaunilo, we do not necessarily have an idea of an absolutely perfect being, and, even if we did, this would not prove that such a being exists outside the mind. We can imagine an island more beautiful than any existing island, but, obviously, this does not mean that the island actually exists. In fact, remarked the fearless monk, if someone tried to convince him that the perfect island must exist, "either I would think he was joking, or I would not know whom I ought to think more foolish; myself, if I grant him his conclusion, or him, if he thinks he has established the existence of that island with any degree of certainty."[28] The actions that Anselm took in response to this attack were easily as important as the content of his answer. He published Gaunilo's blunt criticism as an addendum to his essay, and appended a rejoinder of his own in which he defended his position against the monk. It did not matter that Gaunilo was a person of lower status and lesser reputation than he. What mattered was the quest for truth. Having established this precedent for principled debate among future theologians, Anselm answered his adversary point by point. We can conceive of a perfect being, he insisted, even if our understanding is incomplete. To deny this is like saying that "someone who cannot gaze directly upon the purest light of the sun does not see the light of day, which is nothing other than the light of the sun."[29] Moreover, the case of God is not like that of the hypothetical "lost island," since the only thing that must exist outside the mind as well as in it is "something than which nothing greater can be thought."[30]

Anselm's argument may well be defective. Thomas Aquinas thought so, as did many later philosophers. Yet the debate exposed one of the central problems of the new theology: how to talk about God in terms that were "reasonable"—that is, in terms that made sense when talking of beings other than God—when the Supreme Being was, by definition, unique. It also opened up a related issue that became something of an obsession among medieval thinkers, and that has continued to interest philosophers ever since: the relationship among words, mental concepts, and things that exist outside the mind. Moreover, Anselm's method of argument provided a model for disputation in the new schools now springing up all over Europe. It was not enough to make a reasonable argument. One must also recognize the opposing arguments, state them strongly, answer them point by point, and then use these answers to restate the original argument more fully and convincingly. Progress in thinking was to be made by confronting contradictions and overcoming them—a process that Aristotle had called "dialectic."

Anselm was a pioneer of the new theology, but few thinkers of Abelard's generation dared to reason in such a solitary way, dreaming up ideas on sensitive subjects out of their own imaginations. Churchmen were used to consulting authoritative texts like the Bible and the writings of the Fathers and "glossing" or interpreting them. The activity to which they applied the new tools of logical reasoning was therefore interpretation—a matter far less "academic" than it sounds, since changes in society had produced a desperate need for new interpretations. Consider Jesus' admonition to the young questioner who asked him "What good deed must I do, to have eternal life?" "If you would be perfect," Jesus said, "go, sell what you possess and give to the poor, and you will have treasure in heaven; and come, follow me."[31] So long as social relationships in Europe remained relatively stable, a text like this would not generate serious conflict. In early medieval times, Jesus' call could be interpreted as a simple admonition to leave one's farm and family and become a priest or a nun. But what did the passage mean in a world in which the Church itself had become a great property owner and monasteries controlled vast estates? What did it mean in the burgeoning cities now filling up with merchants, moneylenders, and the surplus population of the countryside? This particular problem of interpretation—the meaning of the apostolic virtues in a commercializing, urbanizing Europe—would wrack Christendom for centuries, producing heretical, anticlerical movements outside the Church and passionate reform movements within it.

What to do when, because of unexpected social changes, sacred texts seemed to conflict or to produce controversial results when applied to real-life situations? In such cases, simple appeals to the Gospels or the authority of the Church Fathers were quite useless. The great need was for rational methods of interpretation that could produce answers consistent with Christian traditions yet applicable to changing circumstances. Moreover, Christian scholars and thoughtful laypeople were hungry for ideas that would help them make sense of what they already believed. Their orthodoxy was not in question, but they were increasingly dissatisfied with the traditional parent's answer to the curious child: "It's so because I say it's so!" The motto that best defined the new spirit of inquiry was Saint Anselm's: "Faith in search of understanding." As Abelard put it, in describing why he wrote a controversial treatise on the Holy Trinity,

> I first applied myself to writing about the foundation of our faith with the aid of analogies provided by human reason, and I wrote a treatise of theology—on the divine unity and trinity—for our scholars, who were asking for human and philosophical reasons and clamoring more for what could be understood than for what could be said. They said in fact that the utterance of words was superfluous unless it were followed by understanding, and that it was ridiculous for anyone to preach to others what neither he nor those taught by him could accept into their understanding.[32]

Scholars interested in discovering these "human and philosophical reasons" for belief also began with authoritative texts, but these were very few and very old. The works that would soon trigger major battles among Christian theologians—Aristotle's physics and metaphysics, his ethical theories, and his work on the soul—were just now being translated into Latin and were not yet available to most European scholars. The only Aristotelian works in circulation were the few treatises on logical reasoning known as the *Organon,* originally translated into Latin and commented on by Boethius. For centuries these writings had been gathering dust in Catholic monasteries, but now, with great changes brewing in European society, they suddenly assumed new importance. In part, this is because their subject was not just "logic," in the sense of formal rules of reasoning, but thinking in general. Aristotle's *Categories, On Interpretation,* and the other books of the

Organon analyze what we know, the way we categorize things that can be thought about, and the relationship of words to reality, as well as the major types of reasoning, the uses and misuses of logic, and how to spot a fallacious argument. For ambitious thinkers like Abelard, reading them must have been a thrilling experience. In a very short time, these ancient translations became the basis for what scholars called the *logica modernorum*, "the fastest growing and most creative area of medieval philosophy."[33] A suggestive modern parallel is computer technology, which not only extends people's thinking power in a mechanical way but also stimulates the imagination, creates new communications networks, and broadens the field of inquiry.

The great question, of course, was what would happen if the field of inquiry were broadened to include questions long considered outside the appropriate ambit of reason. Anselm of Canterbury's work suggested that God himself was not exempt from rational analysis, and Abelard agreed. "Man ought to direct his reason to nothing more readily than to the God in whose image he was made," he said, "since it is through his reason that he is like unto God."[34] But it was clear that applying the new intellectual technology recklessly could produce problems. Consider the case of Berengar of Tours, whose special interest was the Eucharist, that crucial part of the Catholic mass in which the bread and wine offered to the congregation become the body and blood of Christ. Everyone agreed that after the priest speaks the words, "For this is my body," the body of Jesus Christ is actually present in the bread, so that worshipers consuming this sacrifice are spiritually blessed and prepared for immortality. But the inquisitive Berengar, while accepting the miracle without question, wanted to know how it "really" takes place. Does the body of Christ entirely replace the bread? Some authorities thought so, but Aristotle had asserted in *Categories* that every earthly substance (bread, for example) has characteristics or "accidents" like shape, taste, and color which cannot exist unless the substance itself also exists.[35] Since the bread used in the Eucharist retains its "accidents," Berengar argued, it cannot be transformed entirely into something else. A better explanation is that the divine substance is added to the bread or unites with it. Both the bread *and* the body are present in the Eucharist.

This is the sort of argument that many people today consider the height of foolishness—a typical scholastic attempt to explain the inexplicable. Either one believes in the miracle of the Eucharist or one does not, says the modern mind. It makes no sense to try to account for such things scientifically. But Abelard and his colleagues were determined to follow Boethius's prescription: If possible, reconcile faith with reason. In some cases, of course, reconciliation might be impossible. There were matters of faith that seemed clearly out of reason's reach, like the manner in which God begot a Son. But other divine activities seemed perfectly comprehensible, like the punishment of Israel for the sins described by the Prophets, or the orderly patterns of motion given by the Creator to the heavenly bodies. And in the middle range, there were phenomena partaking of the miraculous—like the Eucharist—that might be better understood by showing the extent to which they were consistent with natural processes or analogous to them. This sort of analysis would not "prove" the doctrine, of course, but it might make it more convincing to unbelievers, as well as more satisfying to intellectuals hungering for understanding.[36]

Abelard understood that Berengar's argument had been rejected by the Church. The prevailing view was that "transsubstantiation," not "con-substantiation," takes place in the Eucharist. But Abelard appreciated the French scholar's insistence that when the views of the authorities are in conflict, one must decide which view makes more sense by using the tools of reason developed by Aristotle. "[It] is clearly the property of a great heart to have recourse to dialectic in all things," Berengar had written, "because to have recourse to dialectic is to have recourse to reason; and he who refuses this recourse, since it is in reason that he is made in the image of God, abandons his glory, and cannot be renewed from day to day in the image of God."[37] In time, this daring sanctification of reason would become accepted Catholic doctrine, with the exception of the phrase "in all things." Some mysteries, insisted conservatives like the great Cistercian abbot Bernard of Clairvaux, were too delicate and holy to be profaned by the application of Aristotle's logic. As Abelard would soon discover, passionate rationalists who entered those sacred precincts did so at their peril.

When Peter Abelard began his studies in Paris as a young man, there was as yet no university in France, nor was there any established method of selecting professors. Teachers set up shop in church and cathedral schools, attracted students on the basis of their reputation and brilliance on the lecture platform, and charged them for the privilege of attending classes. If the students decided to study with another teacher, they bade their comrades farewell and departed. If the professor had a better opportunity to teach elsewhere, he said good-bye to his students—or convinced them to come along—and wandered along to his next post. The situation, like so many in twelfth-century Europe, was chaotic but stimulating. In an age not known for free markets in goods or commodities, there was for a short time something quite close to a free market in higher education.

Abelard had chosen to attend the cathedral school of Notre Dame, where young men from all over Europe came to study logic, rhetoric, and grammar, the "trivium" of courses required for more advanced study in law or theology. His teacher, William of Champeaux, was considered one of the best logicians in France. As the archdeacon of the cathedral and a renowned scholar, William was accustomed to a certain deference on the part of his students, but Peter challenged him almost at once, insisting with aggressive certitude and flashes of sarcastic wit that William's premises were fundamentally wrong, his reasoning defective, and his conclusions indefensible. Abelard's manner must have been insufferably arrogant. Nevertheless, this was a declaration of war that the distinguished professor could not ignore, for if his students came to believe that Peter was the superior analyst and teacher, they might abandon the older man and come to study with him.

William defended himself as best he could against Abelard's verbal assaults, but he was no match for the young Breton. Peter withdrew from the school and, followed by a number of William's students, began lecturing on his own in the nearby city of Melun. His fame spread quickly. Many more admirers came from afar to study with him, and the following year, like a general maneuvering his troops toward an occupied capital, he moved the school to a town closer to Paris. Then, for reasons that are not clear, he broke off his offensive and returned home to Brittany. Perhaps he was not ready, emotionally speaking, to follow up his successful rebellion by establishing himself as the archdeacon's successor. When he returned to Paris two years later, however, it was to bring his struggle with William to a triumphant conclusion.

What was the subject of this argument? The great questions then agitating teachers and students in Paris (as one might expect) were those of epistemology: the theory of knowledge. How, other than by reading sacred books and meditating or praying, do we learn about reality? What is the reality we learn about by using our reason this way? And what is the relationship between the language that we use to describe things and the things that language describes? William of Champeaux presented the traditional Christian answers, which were based on Plato's ideas, as developed by the Neoplatonists and by Saint Augustine. We learn by a divine illumination that permits us to grasp general concepts like Goodness and Justice, Man and Woman, and, for that matter, Apple and Pear. Learning these "universals" first is what permits us to recognize individual examples of each type or species: this act of goodness, that man, or that apple. Furthermore, William argued, when we apprehend the universals, we apprehend Reality. Individual men or apples are real, too, in the sense that they are more than dreams or apparitions. But individuals are imperfect copies or approximations lacking the permanence and perfection of the universals. If we contemplate these universals, really focus on them, we can sense that they are One—that they have a common source in the even more universal reality of God. For this reason, universal words like "Goodness," "Man," and "Apple" do not represent mere mental concepts. They stand for entities that exist "out there" as things really real. They are spiritual realities created by God when he brought the universe into existence.

By Abelard's time, a number of thinkers had begun to question this "top down" theory of learning, language, and reality. One of them was Roscelin de Compiègne, a radical theologian with whom Peter had probably studied as a teenager. To combat the Platonic notions that we grasp universals first and that they are the primary realities, Roscelin wheeled out Aristotle's logic, which asserted that the first things we learn, and the primary realities in our universe, are the individual things that we apprehend through our senses—not *the* Apple, but *this* apple, a particular substance with its individual properties ("accidents") of redness, juiciness, edibleness, being on the table, and so forth. First, *this* apple impresses itself on our minds. Then, when we have seen, touched, smelled, tasted, and thought about other objects like this one, we develop a concept and a word that expresses their likeness. According to Roscelin, the universal "Apple" is the result of a mental process that perceives similarities between other round, red, juicy objects and this one, and dissimilarities between this one and the ovoid, yellowish, different-tasting objects we eventually group under the heading "Pear." The universal exists, but only as a name. What is really "out there" is the individual.

Roscelin's "nominalism" was at the pole opposite William of Champeaux's "ultra-realism." When Abelard challenged William after his return to Paris, however, he offered a new solution to the problem of universals—one that would be accepted by European philosophers for the next two centuries. First, he demolished William's ultra-realism by showing that it was absurd to maintain that the individual members of a universal class—men, say—were essentially the same. Were Socrates and Cicero the same in essence because they were both men? Nonsense, Peter declared. "Animal" is a category even more universal than "Man," but this does not mean that Socrates is essentially the same as an ass! In the last analysis, Socrates is Socrates—an individual similar in some ways to Cicero, and similar in other ways to an ass. Compelled by such arguments to retreat, William publicly repudiated his previous view and now maintained that the individual members of a general class were not essentially the same, but that they were essentially similar. This did not help. Even nominalists accepted the similarity of individuals, but the idea of an "essential similarity" seemed meaningless. At this point, according to Abelard, William's students began to leave him in droves.

The competition between the two philosophers continued for a time. While William and Peter fought over who would occupy the professorial chair at the cathedral school of Notre Dame, their students came to blows in the street. But Abelard's victory on the terrain of ideas was generally recognized, especially after he also disposed of Roscelin and his nominalism. The problem of extreme nominalism was this: If only individuals are real—if general concepts are merely words—we have no way of showing systematically why Socrates is more like Cicero than the ass, or why Socrates and the ass are more alike than Socrates and the apple or Socrates and the sun. In fact, without meaningful universal concepts, philosophy itself becomes impossible. Abelard's solution (called "conceptualism" by some) untangled the knot. Roscelin was right about one thing: universal words represent mental concepts, not ultimate realities. But he was wrong to maintain that these concepts exist only in language. The similarities between individual members of a species or a class constitute a fact, not just a word or a totally subjective perception. Even though they are not the "really real" Ideas of the Platonists, they have a certain more-than-mental reality of their own.

What is fascinating about this solution is that Abelard arrived at it without knowing that Aristotle had come to precisely the same conclusion in a book not yet available to European scholars in Latin.[38] What Peter was really attempting to do was to shift the debate in the schools away from the question of what was "really real," in order to focus attention on the role played by individuals and universals in logic and in language. There, in his view, Aristotle's approach was clearly preferable to the Neoplatonism that had long dominated Christian thinking. First, through our senses we become conscious of concrete individual things. Then, through a process of abstraction we arrive at general classifications. In a way that traditionalists could not help considering subversive, Abelard launched a typically Aristotelian attack on the idea that universals could somehow exist even if they had no individuals to "attach" to. Christian tradition had long celebrated the general type and trivialized the individual. Abelard proposed to rectify this imbalance.

Now we begin to see why the thinkers of the medieval renaissance involved themselves so intensely in this debate. Earlier Christians had been taught to consider themselves members of a race: not just a biological but a moral species, so unified in spirit and in destiny that the sin of Adam and Eve, their original father and mother, could be attributed directly to each of them. The "really real" universal, Man, implied that people's individual differences were nonessential, unimportant, even an obstacle to their salvation—a principle rigorously enforced by the rules that governed the lives of the vast numbers of Christians ensconced in monasteries and convents. As one historian points out, even one's salvation or damnation was considered not so much an individual reward or punishment for good or bad behavior as a consequence of one's membership in the Christian community and God's unfathomable justice.[39] The traditional social system in Europe reinforced this trivialization of individuality, since a person's unique character counted for very little in comparison with his or her membership in a general class like the peasantry, the priesthood, or the nobility. Now, however, this ancient Platonic ice was beginning to melt. Most people might still be defined by their membership in large hereditary groups, but some were becoming mobile. Wandering scholars and troubadours, traders and Crusaders, itinerant preachers and country folk moving to the city—all were developing a new sense that, no matter what universal class they belonged to, their individuality mattered.

Another reason that the issue of universals generated such ferocious debate was its implications for theology: how people thought about God. In an age of increasing sophistication and growing interest in the natural universe, many scholars were aware that the Creator and Sustainer of everything could not be conceived of, except by simple people or poets, as a human being writ large. One theologian even maintained that to call God the "Creator" or a "Supreme Being" was to anthropomorphize him, since God is so much greater and more mysterious than any created being.[40] On the other hand, though, the members of this rapidly changing society craved more than ever a personal relationship with God, and Christianity had long flourished by satisfying this need. The Christian God was not only one person but three, and the people of the medieval renaissance were passionately interested in all three persons of the Trinity. God as the Creator might be unimaginably mysterious, but Christians of the twelfth century looked to the Father for justice, loved and grieved for the Son as if he had just been crucified, and invested their hopes in the Holy Spirit—the Comforter—a symbol of the great regeneration that had already begun.

To Christians, it went without saying that God was a Trinity. But how could inquiring people using the tools of reason make sense of this Three-in-Oneness? Were the three *hypostases,* as the Greeks called them, or *personae,* as the Latins said, separate individuals? If so, what did the universal word "God" represent? Roscelin, the extreme nominalist, dared to draw the logical conclusions of his own philosophy. He apparently maintained that the Father, the Son, and the Holy Spirit were individuals, and that "God" was a term expressing their unique likeness and integration. It is not certain exactly how Roscelin expressed himself—he would never have denied the oneness of God directly—but we do know that a Church council that convened to investigate his teachings convicted him of the heresy of "Tritheism," or of maintaining, in effect, that there were three Gods. Roscelin wisely admitted his error, apologized, and was later allowed to resume teaching.

But what if the One God were considered to be an individual? A philosopher taking the hard "realist" position that only the universal was truly real could easily fall into another heresy directly opposed to Tritheism. This was "Sabellianism," the doctrine that the Father, Son, and Holy Spirit were mere aspects or behaviors of God, rather than real persons mysteriously united in a single divine Reality. Not only that, since the greater universals were thought to contain and to exude the lesser universals, ultra-realists often skirted the edge of the heresy known as Pantheism: the idea that the universe is part of God rather than something separated from him by the act of Creation. Given the risks of discussing the Trinity in philosophical terms, one wonders why Abelard would have taken on the subject at all, especially when his intellectual enemies were waiting impatiently for an opportunity to pounce. Very likely, since he was a far greater theologian than Roscelin, he thought he could succeed where his old instructor had failed. Perhaps, since he was celebrated everywhere as the scholar who had solved the problem of universals, he could not resist the challenge of applying his solution to the problem of the Trinity. Or he may simply have underestimated the power of less-brilliant enemies to do him harm. In any case, around the year 1120, Abelard published a little essay on the Trinity that was to prove more damaging to him than all the knives of Heloise's avengers.

Abelard wrote his treatise on the Holy Trinity, he said, in response to requests from his students, who believed that "it was ridiculous for anyone to preach to others what neither he nor those taught by him could accept into their understanding."[41] In a sense, the doctrine of the Trinity was the ultimate test of the new theologians' ability to use logical reasoning to explain and justify difficult propositions of faith. At first glance, the doctrine seemed a slap in the face of reason. How could three real persons comprise a genuinely singular God? The Breton's answer was elegant and, to a critic inclined to give him the benefit of the doubt, not obviously heretical. If one approached the treatise in a hostile spirit, however, searching for possibly heretical statements, it offered enemies plenty of ammunition.[42]

Abelard began by affirming the idea that God must be a single, unified being. The real issue, he declared, was how to define the differences among the three persons of the Trinity. The Father, Son, and Holy Spirit cannot differ in substance or in number, for God is One. Nor can they differ in omnipotence, omniscience, eternity, creativity, or any other substantial attribute of God, since to assign these attributes to different members of the Trinity would be to rank them one above the other, as well as to split God's essential unity into parts. No, the primary differences among the divine persons that we can recognize are those noted earlier by Saint Augustine: the Father is unbegotten, the Son is begotten, and the Holy Spirit proceeds from both the Father and the Son. The three *are* separate persons, but not in the same sense that three men or women are separate. To try to grasp this unique combination of separateness and unity, Abelard argued, one must have recourse to analogies. For example, things can be separate in their roles or functions, and yet unified, as when we observe a royal seal made of copper in the form of a king's image. The copper's role is analogous to that of the Father, the image's resembles that of the Son, and the act of sealing is like that of the Holy Spirit. Or things can be separate in name and yet one in substance, as when we speak of the weapon, the sword, and the blade. In the case of the Trinity, the Bible associates the names Power with the Father, Wisdom with the Son, and Goodness with the Holy Spirit.

Clearly, these were only rough analogies—logical devices used to permit people to gain some rational appreciation of matters that were ultimately beyond human understanding. But Abelard's enemies would leap on them as evidence of his incurable heterodoxy. On the one hand, his insistence that the persons of the Trinity could not be thought of as truly separate exposed him to the charge of Sabellianism: reducing the Father, Son, and Holy Spirit to mere names or functions of God. On the other, his analogies, if taken too seriously, could be seen as evidence of Arianism: the heresy that ranks the Father above the Son and both above the Holy Spirit. What was really at stake here was the whole theological enterprise, which some traditionalists bitterly opposed on the ground that the most fundamental doctrines of Christianity could only be accepted on faith, not reason. When Peter's essay was published by his students, two former students of his, now the joint heads of the cathedral school at Rheims, denounced it as heretical and called for a Church council to investigate its teachings. Abelard considered the charges outrageous. He had no idea that, for him, what seemed an absurd accusation might be the beginning of the end.

IN 1121, A COUNCIL of bishops and scholars assembled in the city of Soissons to rule on the orthodoxy of Abelard's treatise on the Trinity. Characteristically, the embattled dialectician took the offensive, certain that he could prove the harmlessness of his teaching in open debate. Every morning he appeared in a large hall in the city to discuss and defend his ideas. There, one of his ex-students made the mistake of confronting him publicly. By the time Peter had finished with him, the poor fellow had taken such an intellectual beating that he seemed to be espousing an obvious heresy himself. Fearing a repetition of this scene at the council, but unwilling to permit the philosopher to return in triumph to Paris, the council members hesitated, debated, decided to defer a decision, then rescinded that decision, and finally condemned the treatise without a hearing on the grounds that Abelard had not received the permission required to publish it. Despite the impropriety of this procedure, Peter was compelled to throw the book into the flames with his own hands.

Abelard left the Council of Soissons astonished and humiliated. In the familiar surroundings of the classroom, or in earnest debate with colleagues at the cathedral school, he had never felt endangered. He knew he had enemies, of course, some of them quite powerful, but their open animosity had never infringed upon his sense that, at least since *"l'affaire* Heloise," nothing could ever hurt him again. Now, however, he was damaged in a knight's most sensitive spot: his reputation. Returning to his former teaching position was impossible. Peter would spend the next ten years at a series of inhospitable monasteries far from his beloved Paris, an exile in his own country.

Even so, his legend grew. Escaping from one particularly ghastly monastery to which he had been assigned, he settled on a lonely spot of land in the country given to him by the local bishop and built a small oratory there that he dedicated to the Holy Spirit—the Paraclete. In a matter of weeks, students learned of his whereabouts and "began to gather there from all parts, hurrying from cities and towns to inhabit the wilderness, leaving large mansions to build themselves little huts, eating wild herbs and coarse bread instead of delicate food, spreading reeds and straw in place of soft beds and using banks of turf for tables."[43] If Abelard could not return to his students, the students would come to him. A year or two later the school was closed, but he managed to turn the property over to Heloise, who was soon named Mother Superior of a convent built on the site of his old oratory. By the early 1130s, he was back in Paris, corresponding frequently with Heloise and teaching at the monastery on Mont-Sainte-Genevieve. Since the contents of his work on the Trinity had not been condemned, he felt free to expand and publish it, with a lengthy discussion of other doctrines, in his *Christian Theology*. He also wrote his major work on ethics, *Scito Teipsum* (*Know Thyself*); his *Dialogue Between a Philosopher, a Jew, and a*

Christian; and a commentary on the letters of Saint Paul. But the sense of impending disaster that had darkened his life since Soissons never left him. He was more famous than ever, but fame would not immunize him from attack when his enemies decided to strike again.

One wonders what Abelard's life would have been like if he had not been such a charismatic teacher, or if he had cultivated the skills of diplomacy rather than making enemies of those he had bested in debate. Diplomacy, however, was never his strong suit. He seemed driven to state his views in ways that made passionate opposition inevitable . . . and then to portray his opponents as dolts and windbags. As one critical admirer remarks, "There is was not a single one of his teachers with whom he had not quarreled, and whom he did not ridicule with mockery as spiteful as it was epigrammatically witty."[44] The list of these enemies was long, but it posed no immediate threat until his writings came to the attention of another popular teacher, William of Saint-Thierry. Convinced that his rival's views were deeply subversive of traditional Christianity, William fired off salvos of letters to his good friend Bernard of Clairvaux, asking him to step in on the side of orthodoxy against the arrogant Breton.

This was by far the worst thing that could have befallen Abelard. It was one thing to offend leading logicians and theologians. Even the bishops at Soissons could be seen as nasty but ineffectual opponents. But Bernard was one of the most powerful figures in Christendom—some said, even more influential than his good friend Pope Innocent II. A famous writer on mystical themes and leader of the Cistercian order, he combined a passion for Church reform and social purification with a talent for rough-and-tumble politics. Upon receiving William of Saint-Thierry's letters, Bernard read the accompanying documents carefully, studied Abelard's writings, and made up his own mind. In the winter of 1139–1140, he wrote a series of letters denouncing Abelard as a heretic, bound them into a treatise called *Against the Errors of Abelard,* and sent the document to the pope with a request that Peter be investigated and disciplined by the Church.

In some ways, Bernard of Clairvaux could be considered a bitter-end traditionalist. The idea of exposing sacred mysteries like the Holy Trinity to glib analysis and classroom discussion seemed to him nothing less than a form of impiety—a violation as gross and distasteful as desecrating a church. Abelard "has defiled the church," Bernard wrote to a Roman cardinal, "he has infected with his own blight the minds of simple people. He tries to explore with his reason what the devout mind grasps at once with a vigorous faith. Faith believes, it does not dispute. But this man, apparently holding God suspect, will not believe anything until he has first examined it with his reason."[45] Another letter accused Peter of manipulating the minds of his students:

> He shifts the boundary stones set by our forefathers by bringing under discussion the sublimest questions of Revelation. To his totally unseasoned students, mere beginners in theology, who have scarcely outgrown dialectics and are barely qualified to grasp the elementary truths of religion—to such he exposes the mystery of the Trinity, the inner sanctuary and the royal tabernacle. He presumes to imagine that he can entirely comprehend God by the use of his reason.[46]

A harsh denunciation, to be sure. Nevertheless, Bernard was no unthinking fundamentalist. Toward Abelard he adopted the stance of the defender of tradition against innovation. But the abbot was, in some ways, more radical than his academic adversary, since he was part of the Gregorian movement that aimed at purifying the clergy, renewing and unifying Christian society, and asserting the Church's power to discipline disobedient princes.

As the chief leader of the Cistercian monks, he had launched a devastating attack against the older monasteries, which he believed had become far too comfortable and routine. As a preacher, he was the bane of heretics like the Catharists of southern France. He would shortly preach the Second Crusade against the Muslim unbelievers in the East. But he was also famous throughout Europe for advocating a gospel of love featuring compassion for the crucified Jesus and adoration of his sinless Mother. Moreover, as Abelard was now to learn, the abbot was a formidable rhetorician.

"His books have wings," Bernard wrote to Innocent II, complaining of the philosopher's broad and pernicious influence. "His writings have passed from country to country, and from one kingdom to another. A new gospel is being forged for peoples and for nations, a new faith is being propounded, and a new foundation is being laid besides that which has been laid."[47] One can easily understand why Bernard would find Abelard's teachings both alarming and distasteful. For him, the foundation of faith was religious experience, not intellectual analysis; love, not logic, was his watchword. Deeply suspicious of the Breton master's cold intellectualism and repelled by his flamboyant style, Bernard exaggerated his heterodoxy at every turn. But his own position, "Faith believes, it does not dispute," was a brilliant piece of rhetorical obfuscation. The Fathers of the Church were believers *and* disputants, as was the revered Anselm of Canterbury, whose motto, "Faith in search of understanding," might have been Abelard's as well. Clearly, Master Peter was no mystic, and there is no doubt that he dared to analyze doctrines whose discussion had been considered taboo. But he never dreamed of propounding a new faith, nor did he imagine for a moment that he could "entirely comprehend God by the use of his reason."

In 1139 or 1140, Bernard came to Paris to speak publicly against Abelard's theology at the cathedral school of Notre Dame.

He may also have seen Abelard at this time and attempted to persuade him to repudiate some of his teachings, but the evidence of this meeting is skimpy and unreliable.[48] In any case, Peter recognized that his enemies were mobilizing actively against him and decided to beat them to the punch. He learned that a large gathering of churchmen and high officials had been scheduled for June 3, 1140, in the cathedral city of Sens. King Louis VII would attend in order to view the cathedral's relics, and a throng of bishops and nobles was expected as well. This would be a perfect opportunity for Abelard to do what he did best: take the public stage as a lecturer and disputant.

Through his students, Peter asked Archbishop Henry of Sens to arrange a public disputation between Bernard and himself before the assembled notables. The archbishop was a friend of Bernard's, but, lured by the idea of sponsoring such a historic spectacle, he seems to have accepted the proposal without first conferring with the abbot. Abelard immediately wrote letters to his students throughout Europe asking them to come to Sens in June to support him. Bernard, on the other hand, was dismayed by the thought of doing battle publicly with Europe's champion dialectician. Evidently, he first determined not to accept the archbishop's invitation, but finally he consented to come. Whether this was because he was "burning with the fire of the Holy Spirit," as one writer suggests,[49] or because he had resolved on another less creditable stratagem, Bernard arrived at Sens several days before the scheduled disputation.

Once ensconced in the archbishop's quarters, Bernard prevailed upon him to call a secret meeting of the bishops on the night of June 2. There, in Abelard's absence, he read out a list of nineteen charges against the philosopher based principally on his *Christian Theology*, discussed them, and almost certainly gained the bishops' promises to support Abelard's condemnation. (Bernard was to attempt the same tactic seven years later at a heresy trial in Rheims, but this time the cardinals refused to participate in the unauthorized meeting on the grounds that his treatment of Abelard at Sens had been unfair.[50]) In any case, Abelard arrived the next morning for the disputation, only to find that the format was that of a trial, and that he was expected to play the role of the defendant. Bernard read the list of alleged heretical propositions, and, according to the custom of heresy trials, demanded that Abelard either defend them, renounce them, or deny that they were his.

Peter was silent for a long time. The bishops and assembled notables waited impatiently for his response, but he seemed sunk in thought. Just when the tension in the room was at its height, he spoke a few sentences. He declined to participate in the proceedings and appealed directly to the pope to decide the issues presented. Then he walked out of the hall, leaving a crowd of stunned officials and students in his wake.

Abelard never explained why he did not accept Bernard's invitation to defend his views at Sens. It was the most distinguished audience he had ever played to, and he was a born performer. Clearly, if Bernard had dared engage him in debate, he could easily have defended himself against the less experienced dialectician. Even so, one can imagine Peter's heart sinking as he listened to the reading of the charges and watched the impassive faces of the assembled bishops. Very likely he realized that the deck had been stacked against him—that Bernard would probably not dispute with him in public, and that even if he did, his performance would count for naught. Possibly he felt his energy desert him, since, at the age of sixty-two, his health was already failing. Or perhaps he had simply had enough of the show. If he was, indeed, a heretic, a greater power than the Council of Sens would judge him. And if he was not, students would still be reading his books long after he, Bernard, and Heloise were laid to rest.

In any event, Peter's exit left the council in an uproar. The bishops adjourned for lunch, and, after returning, condemned the nineteen allegedly heretical propositions. According to a monk who was present at the council—a partisan of Abelard—some of the judges were so drunk with lunchtime wine that when they attempted to pronounce the word "Damnamus" (We condemn), they could succeed only in muttering "Namus" (We swim). Bernard immediately wrote to Innocent II reporting the results of the council and asking him to confirm its judgment. Abelard left for Rome to make his appeal in person, but stopped to rest at the abbey of Cluny, whose abbot, Peter the Venerable, was an old antagonist of Bernard's. A few weeks later, at Cluny, Abelard received the pope's decision in his case. Innocent II condemned him as a heretic, excommunicated his followers, ordered his books to be burned in Saint Peter's Square, and commanded him to retire to a monastery, there to be perpetually silent.

This harshness proved unnecessary. Abelard's health was broken (he probably had Parkinson's disease), and he had no further taste for theological battles. Peter the Venerable wrote to Innocent II to report that he and another abbot had mediated between Abelard and Bernard, that the two men had formally reconciled, and that Abelard desired to remain at Cluny as a monk. The pope suspended Abelard's sentence, and the philosopher lived out the remaining eighteen months of his life as a simple Cluniac monk. At some point before his death, he sent Heloise a moving Confession of Faith containing a phrase that has often been cited in defense of his orthodox intentions: "I do not wish to be a philosopher if it means conflicting with Paul, nor to be an Aristotle if it cuts me off from Christ."[51] When Abelard died, Heloise asked for and received his body, which was buried at the Convent of the Paraclete. Twenty-one years later, she died and was buried beside him. Centuries later, after a series of moves, the lovers' bones came to rest at Père-Lachaise Cemetery in Paris, where one may visit them today.

Did Abelard and Bernard reconcile before the Breton's death? It is possible, considering that the two opponents had more in common than either man recognized. Each in his own way sought to infuse habitual beliefs and formalized rituals with new meaning. Abelard's mission was to make sense of religious doctrines that, to many of his students, had begun to seem like empty words and phrases. The same impulse, to revivify a Christianity in danger of becoming a collection of routinized formulas and gestures, drove Bernard to advocate a revivalist gospel of active love, committed action, and spiritual union with Christ. Having offended the most powerful politician in Christendom, the haughty and tactless Abelard paid the price. But the impulse that motivated his work—the craving to understand—would turn out to be as irrepressible as the craving for authentic religious experience. In the next generation, an Aristotelian movement far larger and more radical than Abelard's would challenge the authorities in the universities, while a surge of popular evangelism made Bernard's brand of piety seem conservative and tame. How the Church responded to these twin challenges would largely determine the future of science and religion in the West.

CHAPTER FOUR

"He Who Strikes You Dead Will Earn a Blessing"

ARISTOTLE AMONG THE HERETICS

WHEN BERNARD of Clairvaux returned home in triumph from the Council of Sens, he might have congratulated himself on defeating Europe's greatest debater without a fight. Bernard's partisans put out the story that Abelard had failed to speak at the council because the abbot's just accusations had convinced him that he must be in the wrong—a tale that made its way afterward into a number of Catholic histories.[1] It is true that little was heard from the philosophers of the schools after Abelard's condemnation, but there were reasons for this which were more significant than Bernard's victory. For most of the twelfth century, notes one historian, "the philosophers of Christian Europe were too busy reading Aristotle and the other Greek writers to engage in critical, original, and systematic speculation."[2] Beginning in the 1150s, Latin editions of the rediscovered writings began to flood the libraries of Europe's scholars. By medieval standards, the output of the translation centers in Spain, Provence, and Italy was enormous, numbering in the thousands of manuscripts. These books appeared in waves, beginning in mid-century with the works of the "new logic," and continuing decade after decade with Aristotle's metaphysical and scientific books, the treatises on psychology and ethics, and, finally, the essays on politics and aesthetics, each accompanied by relevant Arab commentaries. It was not until the turn of the century that these materials would be digested and sufficiently understood to become the basis for a new challenge to Christian orthodoxy.

The schools were quiet—at least for now. But if the abbot of Clairvaux was feeling victorious after Sens, he had an unpleasant surprise coming. While he had been worrying about the heretical writings of a few Parisian intellectuals, a far more immediate danger to the Church's authority was gathering strength in the streets. A vast movement of popular evangelism hostile to the "corrupt" Catholic clergy had begun to make its presence felt throughout Europe. As yet, the pietistic movement lacked intellectual leadership, but if the dissidents ever found influential spokesmen among the scholars or supporters within the ranks of the nobility, the threat of a schism would become real. The thought was enough to give Bernard nightmares, and to send him on a mission to stamp out the flames of religious extremism while there was still time to do so.

Oddly enough, Bernard himself was one of those indirectly responsible for the new movement's existence. In Church politics, he was a Gregorian—one who agreed with the late pope, Gregory VII, on the urgent need to reform the Catholic clergy, a fast-growing agglomeration of priests, monks, nuns, church officials, teachers, and other employees that, in urban areas, amounted to some 10 percent of the population.[3] The root of the problem, as the reformers saw it, was that the clergy had developed too intimate a relationship with the secular world. Intimate, indeed, considering that in those days, "bishops commonly cohabited with women, fathered children by them, and looked after the interests of their 'nephews.' The cathedral clergy's children were a significant segment of urban populations. The parish priests were generally married and heads of households."[4] Clerical marriage or concubinage was one worldly practice condemned by the Gregorians. Others included the buying and selling of Church offices, the accumulation of needless wealth by churches and monasteries, failure to attend to the needs of the poor, and giving free rein to oppressive secular authorities. Men like Bernard believed that they could eliminate these evils by purifying and professionalizing the clergy and imbuing the Church's servants with a passion for selfless service. The problem they had not been able to solve was how to accomplish these goals in a society that defined every group's identity, status, and power on the basis of its relationship to landed property.

Gregorians such as Bernard attempted to keep the reform impulse alive, but fifty years after the great pope's death, the movement's limitations had become apparent. Some progress had been made in reorganizing the clergy and inspiring some of its members with a renewed sense of spiritual mission. But the Church overall was more than ever part of the feudal "establishment," as wedded to lands, possessions, and power as any feudal baron or earl. Few influential clerics were willing to give up their property and privileges, nor, despite the popes' complaints, did secular princes readily defer to the princes of the Church. On the contrary, powerful monarchs such as those of France and England increasingly set the standards to which bishops willingly or unwillingly conformed. Notwithstanding the efforts of ascetic reformers, the general level of morality and religious zeal among the clergy fell far short of earlier expectations. Just as the fires of "top-down" reform were burning low, however (and, to some extent, because of this), a great wave of religious fervor swept the population at large, particularly those living in Europe's burgeoning towns and cities.

In retrospect, at least, this is not surprising. The dramatic changes transforming the West—the explosion in population, the growth of cities, the revival of trade, and the circulation of new ideas—were exciting, but profoundly disturbing. Europe as a whole resembled a monk who emerges from his cell after years of seclusion, wandering confusedly in a profane world. A host of new questions demanded answers. How could the Church's otherworldly ideals be adapted to life in an increasingly inquisitive, individualistic, pleasure-seeking society? Who would care for believers tempted or confused by new possibilities for good and evil? Who could provide reliable models of good moral conduct? For masses of ordinary Christians, the last place to discover answers to such questions was among the "secular clergy" (bishops and parish priests not in monastic orders). The Church's agents had become as compromised by worldly entanglements as the laity—perhaps more so, given their privileged status. The result among ordinary believers was intense frustration, driven as much by self-criticism as by scorn for the unholy priesthood. Leaders like Bernard and Pope Innocent II sensed the potential of these feelings to produce aggressive anticlerical action, and tried to direct religious energies outward, against the Muslim occupiers of the Holy Land and growing numbers of heretics closer to home. But the impulse to purify the Church from within could not be contained. As such impulses will, it summoned up a host of would-be satisfiers. Seemingly out of nowhere, wandering preachers appeared in the streets of Europe's thriving towns and cities, calling both clergy and laypeople to account for their sins, and announcing the advent of a new era of spiritual renewal.

Henry the Monk was one such wanderer. At the same time that Abelard was gaining notoriety in Paris, Henry appeared at the gates of Le Mans "carrying a cross on an iron-tipped staff, bearded, barefoot, and with poor clothing."[5] In almost no time, extraordinary things began to occur in that city. Henry transfixed the townspeople with his denunciations of corrupt, property-hungry bishops and priests. He preached against luxury, linked simplicity with salvation, and urged his listeners to make bonfires of their fancy clothes and ornaments. Most passionately, he condemned the new, onerous rules that forbade marriages between distant cousins and that made marriage a sacrament of the Church, to be controlled (and taxed) by the priesthood. Love, he said— "the consent of the persons alone"—sanctified marriage.[6] And Christian love could save even the unchaste from hellfire and damnation. On one memorable Sunday, Henry called the prostitutes of Le Mans to the town square, where, in accordance with his instruction, they stripped off their fancy clothes and cut their hair. Then he had them cast these symbols of their former lives into the fire. They put on new clothes, purchased for them by generous townspeople, and respectable young men (recruited in advance) stepped forward to marry them.

Acting as an itinerant evangelist, Henry simply bypassed the local clergy. Even so, he left Le Mans without being arrested or charged with any offense. In part this was because it was not heretical to call for priestly celibacy and poverty, a return to simplicity, the rehabilitation of prostitutes, or marriages based on love. Very likely it was also because his stay in the city was of limited duration, and probably of limited effect. Most important, Church officials did not yet recognize this sort of evangelism as a threat to Christian orthodoxy and to their own role in society. This became clearer to them later, when Henry and some of his fellow preachers began challenging the clergy's sacramental role more directly.

If priestly rituals like marriage were empty without the consent of the parties, some evangelists asked, how could one defend other rituals that seemed entirely formal, like infant baptism? There is no evidence that Henry the Monk ever met Abelard or even knew of him, but he shared the conviction that a willing intention—what Abelard called "consent"—was necessary to give acts ethical meaning. If this were so, could sprinkling holy water on a squalling infant have the saving effect claimed for it by the traditionalists? And what was one to think about the Eucharist—the heart of the Catholic mass? Could the miraculous transubstantiation of the bread and wine be the result of a few "magic words" spoken by an indifferent or corrupt priest? In ancient times, a North African bishop named Donatus had thrown the Church into an uproar by denying that sinful or indifferent clergymen could validly administer the sacraments of the Church. Ever since Saint Augustine's time, the official answer to this heresy had been to affirm that the priest's office was holy even if its current tenant was not. But the tendency to question the necessity and justice of the priestly role was particularly tenacious in a society in which many laymen, as well as renegade monks like Henry, seemed to be living more Christian lives than the average clergyman.

In part, this questioning grew out of a craving for personal and institutional purity, which sent crowds flocking to hear the unauthorized sermons preached in village squares by traveling holy men. But it was also a result of the same passion to understand that motivated the careers of theologians such as Abelard and his scholastic successors. Just as intellectuals wanted to understand religious doctrines, believing laypeople wanted to make sense of the sacraments. (Abelard himself, although no anticlericalist, had denied that priests could absolve sinners merely by reciting a ritual formula.[7]) The thirst that needed quenching was a thirst not merely for purity but for meaning. Bernard himself eventually preached against Henry the Monk in the city of Toulouse, and the evangelist's career apparently ended there, but the movement that had spawned him did not abate. The great question was whether the techniques of coercion that had silenced Abelard and Henry would be effective to control the new forces of self-expression and dissent gaining strength throughout Europe.

Clearly, if these flames were to spread, the Church could not simply follow Bernard's lead and hope to maintain its position as the supreme spiritual authority and political arbiter in the Christian West. The Gregorian movement had now reached a point that will be familiar to modern readers—the point that a reform movement grown stale begins to spawn genuinely revolutionary alternatives. Itinerant evangelists like Henry the Monk provided a foretaste of a mass movement that would soon mobilize tens of thousands of laypeople to follow brilliant organizers such as the Lyons businessman Peter Waldes and the Italian spiritual genius Francis of Assisi. Intellectual innovators like Peter Abelard would prove tame, indeed, compared with a new breed of thinkers whose shockingly radical ideas were now beginning to circulate from southern France to the Rhineland. Most dangerous of all, a growing number of secular leaders who deeply resented Rome's political power might form a common front with the dissenting evangelists and intellectuals. To deal with some of these threats, repression—indeed, a repression far more violent than the silencing of a few heretics—might be considered necessary. But awakened people striving to satisfy basic human needs are not easily repressed. If the Church wished to maintain its internal unity and its hegemony in Europe, it would have to discover leaders capable of absorbing and utilizing the forces of dissent, not just smashing them. And this would mean transforming Catholic institutions from within, not merely defending them against external attack.

Rome awaited such a far-sighted leader. Meanwhile one case in particular came dangerously close to realizing Bernard's nightmare—a fusion of popular evangelical protest with intellectual leadership and secular support. One of Bernard's letters attacking Peter Abelard contains a curious sentence that seems to be written in code. "The French bee," says the abbot darkly, "has been buzzing to the bee from Italy."[8] There is no mystery about the identity of the "French bee"; Abelard's name is sometimes rendered in English as Abeillard because its first few syllables sound like *abeille*, the French word for bee. But who is the "Italian bee," and why does Bernard mention him?

The answer is that the mysterious Italian is not a "bee" but a "B." Arnold of Brescia was as controversial a figure as Abelard, and in many ways far more dangerous to the established order. He came from his native Lombardy to study with Abelard in Paris when the great dialectician was in mid-career. Not much is known about the two men's relationship after Arnold returned home, but they must have maintained some sort of contact, for when Peter came to Sens to face Bernard and the council of bishops, his former student was at his side. The same papal decree that condemned Abelard to silence and perpetual confinement in a monastery dispatched Arnold to a different monastery under the same harsh terms. But while the defeat at Sens effectively ended the ill philosopher's life, Arnold had another fifteen years in which to advocate his own sharp-edged version of the truth.

The two allies were cut from different cloth. While Abelard was a theoretician who came late (and involuntarily) to the regular priesthood, Arnold became the prior of a monastic community immediately after completing his studies in Paris. *The Catholic Encyclopedia,* seldom complimentary to heretics, describes him as fitted for his office "by the austerity of his life, his detachment from earthly things, his love of religious discipline, the clearness of his intellect, and an originality and charm of expression that he brought to the service of a lofty ideal."⁹ That ideal, and the manner of achieving it, also distinguished him from Abelard, for while Peter was a leader in the intellectual sense, but without any practical organizing ability or political ambitions, Arnold was, incurably, a man of action. Never was he happier—or more dangerous to those in authority—than when he was at the head of a popular movement, infusing masses of people with his own zeal to purify the Church by ridding it of wealth and earthly power.

Unlike the itinerant evangelists who moralized about the evils of property, Arnold used his scholarly training to develop a sharp critique of the Church's entanglement with society. According to him, the Gregorian reforms had been hamstrung by the prevailing definition of ecclesiastical office as a form of property (or "benefice"), and the insistence by popes and bishops on playing the role of great feudal landlords. Since land was held in feudal times in exchange for services, including farm labor and military service, this inevitably involved the Church's rulers in exploitation of the lower classes and in warfare. As a result, those who ought to have taken the lead in spiritual renewal and the care of the poor (the monastic orders, for example) were paralyzed by their all-consuming dedication to maintaining and increasing their wealth. All these contradictions, Arnold boldly declared, were a product of the Gregorian popes' misguided efforts to establish their supremacy over Europe's secular rulers. In their efforts to bring the nobility to heel, the princes of the Church had succeeded only in making themselves princes of the earth. Even the Crusades, he declared, had become little more than land-grabbing raids that made a few feudal lords and a great many Venetian and Pisan traders rich.

Arnold did not hesitate to draw logical conclusions from these premises, and then to act on them. "Clerics who own property, bishops who hold regalia [land granted by the king], and monks who have possessions cannot possibly be saved. All these things belong to the prince, who cannot dispose of them except in favor of laymen."[10] In short, the Church should surrender its power and property to secular rulers, who were to distribute these lands and possessions to laymen. Furthermore, the clergy should not involve themselves in warfare and violence, as the knightly ruling class did. "It is not permitted to [priests] to bear the sword or the cup, but to preach, to affirm their preaching by good works, and not to wage war and cause strife in the world."[11] The militant abbot found an enthusiastic audience for these ideas in his native city of Brescia, a town nominally governed by elected consuls but actually under the thumb of the local bishop, who was also the region's largest feudal landowner. While the bishop was out of town, Arnold persuaded the townspeople to rise against him. Then he convinced the local clergy to surrender their property to the Commune of Brescia, and, says John of Salisbury, "so swayed the minds of the citizens that they would scarcely open their gates to the bishop upon his return."[12]

This uprising was no joke. Northern Italy was filled with towns whose citizens were anxious to assert their "liberties" against feudal landowners. With the city threatened by armed conflict between the bishop's forces and the commune, Arnold appealed to Innocent II, but the pope was profoundly unenthusiastic about defending insurrections of the laity against officers of the Church. Not surprisingly, Arnold found himself condemned and deposed for insubordination at the Lateran Council of 1139. Forbidden to preach publicly or to return to Brescia, he came to Sens the following year to support Abelard against Bernard and the assembled bishops. When his old teacher went into retirement at the Abbey of Cluny, Arnold entered the monastery of Saint Hilary on Mont-Sainte-Genevieve—the same place in which Abelard had formerly taught—and gave a course of lectures there on moral theology.

This Paris sojourn did not last long. Arnold could not resist the opportunity to denounce his high-ranking enemies as avaricious, sexually corrupt militarists who sought to "build the Church of God in blood." Not even the untouchable Bernard escaped the lash of his tongue. Arnold labeled Abelard's persecutor "a seeker after vainglory, envious of all who won distinction in learning and religion unless they were his own disciples."[13] Bernard responded by denouncing his critic to King Louis VII of France as "the incorrigible schismatic, the sower of discord, the disturber of the peace, the destroyer of unity,"[14] and urging his expulsion from France. The request was quickly granted. Arnold made his way to Switzerland, but Bernard hounded him out of that refuge as well, and in 1143 Arnold went to Bohemia, where he was befriended by the papal legate to that kingdom. Despite warning letters from Bernard, the legate persuaded Arnold to submit to Pope Innocent's successor, Eugenius III. Arnold met the new pope in Viterbo, Italy, where he promised to obey him and do penance for his past offenses. Eugenius then made a terrible mistake (from the point of view of the papacy). He sent the Brescian firebrand on a pilgrimage to Rome.

Rome in 1146 was Brescia writ large—a whirlpool of revolutionary ideas and sentiments stirred by the new piety, the local citizens' hatred of their papal overlords, and old dreams of restoring the power of the Roman senate. No doubt, Arnold meant to be obedient. But the Catholic hierarchy was as corrupt as any radical could wish; the people were awaiting a leader with his ideas and temperament; and in almost no time, he was helping to organize a popular rebellion against the pope. He branded the College of

Cardinals "a place of business and a den of thieves." Pope Eugenius was "a man of blood who maintained his authority by fire
and sword, a tormentor of churches and oppressor of the innocent, who did nothing in the world save gratify his own lusts and
empty other men's coffers to fill his own."[15] No one could possibly owe obedience to a prelate who, among his other vices, had
deprived Rome, "the fountain of liberty," of her independence.
In 1146, under Arnold's leadership, the Roman citizenry expelled
Eugenius from the city. For the next three years, Rome was a democracy ruled by an elected senate, while Arnold convinced or
compelled the clergy to abandon their possessions and adopt an
apostolic way of life.[16]

Eugenius III excommunicated the rebellious Lombard in
1148, an act that Arnold declared of no effect, since the pope was
"no longer the real *Apostolicus.*"[17] One year later, Eugenius returned to Rome at the head of an army, but the armed commune
expelled him again within a few months. At this point, however,
power began to shift against Arnold and his lower-class allies. In
order to defend the city against the pope, he had solicited the aid
of Conrad III, the German emperor. Germany's "Holy Roman
Emperors" had long controlled much of northern Italy and cov-
eted the rest of the country, but Conrad was no more interested
than Eugenius in supporting a rebellion against the established
feudal order. In 1152, Arnold wrote to Conrad's newly elected
successor, Frederick Barbarossa, asking him to accept his crown
from the Roman people rather than the pope, and offering him
control of the city.[18] Better an outside secular ruler, he thought,
than a corrupt pope. Like his predecessor—and for the same reason—the emperor demurred. Meanwhile, Arnold's movement
was splitting along class lines. While the poor and many of the in-
ferior clergy continued to support him, wealthier citizens, most of
the nobility, and priests resentful of their new poverty turned

against him. When Arnold's opponents won the senatorial elections, the rebel leader discovered that he was no longer safe in his adopted city.

Imprisoned for a short time by a hostile Roman cardinal, Arnold was freed by a sympathetic nobleman who offered him refuge on his estate in the countryside. But he was now a man in flight, and his time was running out. The election of Adrian IV as pope in 1154 sealed his fate. When the new pontiff crowned Frederick Barbarossa emperor, Frederick promised to compel Arnold's protector to hand him over to imperial soldiers. The rebel was hunted down and captured in 1155, bound hand and foot, and delivered to the Roman Curia—the same Church officials that he had savaged verbally and dispossessed eight years earlier. Accounts differ as to exactly what happened to him at that point. The Curia tried him but the charges remain obscure, since, while obviously insubordinate, he had not preached heresy or violated canon law. Some say that Pope Adrian himself ordered him to be hanged after the trial. Others maintain that the Roman officials he had treated harshly during the period of the commune kidnapped him from the pope's prison and executed him. The penultimate scenes of this drama remain obscure, but many witnessed its finale. Arnold made his last public appearance on the city gallows. We are told that he died bravely after praying for his salvation, and that his body was cremated and the ashes thrown in the Tiber River. A chronicler of the time explains why. This was done, he says, "for fear, lest the people might collect them and honor them as the ashes of a martyr."[19]

THE CHURCH HAD REASON to fear Arnold of Brescia's ghost. In Lombardy and then in Rome, the volatile abbot had managed to combine three elements that, cleverly mixed, were capable of igniting a violent explosion: anticlerical anger, evangelical zeal, and secular political ambition. Add a fourth ingredient not present in Arnold's case—a credible challenge to orthodox theology—and one would have the recipe for a revolutionary movement like that led a few centuries later by Martin Luther. Perhaps because this danger was not yet manifest, the official responses to dissent during most of the twelfth century were relatively moderate. It was the popes, after all, who had launched the campaign to reform the clergy and who still supported the movement of popular piety, except where it went to excess. As a result, unorthodox teachers such as Peter Abelard and overzealous evangelists like Henry the Monk were criticized and silenced, but not burned. Rebellious activists were sometimes executed, but even the "Italian bee" would probably have survived had he not moved from preaching ecclesiastical reform to fomenting civic revolt. So long as dissenters did not controvert the Church's sacred doctrines or challenge its organized power directly, the hierarchy could afford to be magnanimous.

This relaxed state of affairs would not last much longer. The European awakening was gaining momentum. The boundaries of Christendom were expanding, bringing Christian travelers, soldiers, traders, and scholars into contact with other cultures and opening Europe's doors to an influx of new ideas. One result, horrifying to Catholic leaders, was the formation of a large, belligerently anti-Catholic sect with its base in southern France. In the Midi, northern Italy, and the Rhineland, a dualistic doctrine imported from the Byzantine Empire inspired tens of thousands of believers who called themselves Cathari—the Pure Ones—to organize what was, in effect, a counter-Church. The high moral standards and dedication to service of their leaders (the *Perfecti*) gave them enormous popular appeal. They converted some members of the local nobility and even managed to win the tacit approval of certain Catholic bishops and priests. Moreover, a number of the *Perfecti* were intellectuals who devoured the newly translated works of Aristotle. Confronted by Catholic polemicists seeking to win their followers to the true faith of Rome, they would prove to be formidable opponents in debate.

That the Cathar threat was not immediately recognized was probably due to the movement's superficial similarity to other evangelical groups, some of them quite large, that practiced voluntary poverty and service to the poor, revered selfless leaders, lived communally, translated the Bible into vernacular tongues, and preached without authorization to all who would listen. Most of these advocates of the "new piety" were interested in reforming the practices of the Catholic Church, not in challenging its basic doctrines. Yet there was something more about these new dissenters that alarmed observers such as Eversin of Steinfeld, a Cistercian monk who encountered them in 1144 and wrote about them to his superior, Bernard of Clairvaux. Eversin's report focused on a group of protestors captured near Cologne who had "defended their heresy with quotations from Christ and the apostles." "When they saw that they were making no headway," the monk wrote,

> they asked for a day to be fixed on which they might bring forward men from among their followers who were expert in their faith. They promised that if they saw their masters refuted in argument they would be willing to rejoin the church, though otherwise they would rather die than abandon their views. After this they were urged for three days to come to their senses, and refused, and then were seized by the people, who were moved by great enthusiasm, (though we were against it), put to the stake, and burnt. The amazing thing was that they entered and endured the torment of the flames not merely courageously but joyfully. I wish I were with you, holy father, to hear you explain how such great fortitude comes to these tools of the devil in their heresy as is seldom found among the truly religious in the faith of Christ.[20]

This demand for a public disputation, as well as the believers' thirst for martyrdom, represented something new. According to Eversin, the members of the group held to a number of peculiar beliefs and customs. They refused to consume milk, meat, or any other products of procreation, and they condemned marriage, which they considered fornication. They consecrated their food and drink as the body and blood of Christ by saying the Lord's Prayer, and baptized by the simple laying on of hands (a ritual known as the *consolamentum,* which was also used to give the dying last rites). They divided themselves into groups of ordinary believers and a spiritual elite whose members they called Perfect Ones (*Perfecti*)—men and women who were said to live lives of remarkable virtue. Determinedly nonviolent, they considered all wars unjust and opposed capital punishment. And, most shockingly, they denied the authority of the Catholic Church and the efficacy of the sacraments, except for the *consolamentum.*[21]

This report and others dismayed Bernard, who had encountered members of the same sect on a preaching mission to Languedoc in southwestern France, where they seemed to be especially popular. Further investigation made it clear that the new organization was not merely an eccentric Catholic protest group but a non-Catholic religion. At first, there had been some confusion about this. The Cathars were clearly "dualists" who counterposed the holiness and beauty of the spirit to the venality and temptations of the material world—but many good Catholics also preferred spiritual gifts to material goods, celibacy to marriage, and charismatic worship to the rites of the organized Church. The Cathars took one giant step further, however. According to their leaders, there had been two Creations, not just one. At the same time that the good God created the universe of the spirit, an evil God co-eternal and co-equal in power with him created a parallel material universe. No mere fallen angel, the

God Satan raided heaven to capture and imprison the angels in the human bodies that he had fashioned for that purpose.[22] Thus were human souls imprisoned in inhospitable, mortal flesh. And thus began the war between Good and Evil, which continues to this day—an unending struggle whose major battles have been the fall of Man (a victory for Satan) and the life and resurrection of Christ (a victory for God).

Cathar ethics followed inexorably from this major premise. God sent Jesus to show us the way to triumph over the body and to escape the vicious chain of sexual reproduction. Each person should therefore seek, like Christ, to purify himself by loving his neighbor and overthrowing the tyranny of the flesh. For the Perfect Ones, this meant renouncing marriage, living nonviolently, and devoting their lives entirely to the welfare of others. For ordinary believers the demands of the faith were not so stringent, but included renunciation of the Roman Church and its "superstitious" rites, as well as commitment to a life of communal responsibility, vegetarianism, and virtue.

What interested the Cathars' critics most were the more extreme manifestations of their antimaterialist beliefs. Some zealots viewed childbirth with horror—another soul condemned to imprisonment in a corrupt body—and, although the evidence is skimpy, others may have ended their lives in old age or when seriously ill by fasting to death: a form of ritual suicide known as the *endura*.[23] The inclination to define body and soul as separate and conflicting entities led some Cathars to believe in the transmigration of souls, with each soul's progress in self-purification rewarded by its rebirth in a more worthy body, and the souls of the Perfect Ones returning to God. At the other extreme, reports abounded of loose sexual practices by members of the church, whose disapproval of marriage and childbirth was said to free them for nonreproductive sex. But these were the same sort of rumors spread by the Romans about the original Christians, and about as well founded. There is little evidence that Cathar beliefs produced behavior radically different from that of pious Catholics, or that the faith's dissident status rendered its members rebels against common notions of morality and decency.[24]

The contrary was the case. The generally high moral standards observed by faithful Cathars stood in stark contrast to the violence, cruelty, and corruption endemic to a rapidly changing society. In Languedoc, and to a lesser extent in Provence and northern Italy, the new church commanded strong support among all social classes—so much so that Catharism quickly became the unofficial religion of the south. The poor believed (with some justification) that the Perfect Ones were clearly superior in personal holiness and pastoral skill to the Catholic clergy. The urban middle classes—doctors, lawyers, artisans, and merchants—responded to the faith's purity and simplicity, and acted as its unofficial missionaries when they traveled to other regions. Women were particularly active in the church, and played a role as *Perfecti* equal to that of men. And the nobles saw Catharism as an expression of the regional autonomy that they wished to defend against the ambitions of "foreign" popes and princes. Count Raymond VI of Toulouse, hero of the troubadours and one of the greatest princes in Christendom, had no great desire to suppress the heretics, whose ranks included many of his noble friends and relatives. Nor did the Catholic bishops of Carcassonne, Béziers, Albi, and other cities of Languedoc, many of whom had learned to tolerate their Cathar competitors even while disputing against them.

Especially considering the wealth and brilliant culture of the Midi, this regional solidarity could be turned into a weakness if the Catholic authorities in Rome decided to invite land-hungry knights and princes from the north to help punish the southern heretics. This gruesome possibility became increasingly likely as the extent of Cathar alienation from the Catholic Church became clear. Although Rome dispatched several teams of Cistercian missionaries to preach in the "infected" regions, the results of these campaigns were negligible. Not only did the visiting evangelists, with their fine linen and well-appointed retinues, show up badly in comparison with the local "Good Men" (as the Cathar activists were called), but they were not prepared for the disputations to which learned heretics challenged them at every opportunity. Modeled after the disputations at the universities, these debating contests were held at cathedrals, in town squares, or at other places open to the public. Quite often the disputants argued before a jury composed half of Catholics and half of Cathars, with the aim of seeing which side could convert one or more hostile members of the jury, and so be awarded the palm. At one famous disputation held at Carcassonne in 1204, the pope's legate, Peter of Castelnau, argued the Catholic case against the Cathar bishop of the city, Bernard de Simorre, before a jury of thirteen Catholics and thirteen Cathars, with King Peter II of Aragon looking on. Despite the Catholic king's presence, the contest was a draw. In general, the Catholics made no more converts at these events than did their Cathar adversaries.[25]

Persuasion proving ineffective, the authorities turned increasingly to threats of force. The Third Lateran Council of 1179 not only condemned the Cathar heresy but also added that "The whole body of the faithful must fight this pestilence vigorously, and even at need take up arms to combat it. The goods of such persons shall be forfeit, and all princes shall have the right to enslave them." The council promised that anyone fighting against the heretics would earn two years' remission of penance and be in a position to be awarded their forfeited property, "exactly like a Crusader."[26] For the time being, this appeal went unanswered.

Rome did not yet have a leader able and willing to organize a genuine Crusade against a well-entrenched internal enemy, nor had Church leaders given up hope that the movement might exhaust itself in internal disputes and burn itself out, as other charismatic groups had done. Moreover, while unrepentant Cathars were burned at the stake in Champagne, Flanders, London, and Cologne, the strength of the movement in the south made it clear that a holocaust of bodies would be necessary if the ultimate penalty were demanded of that region's heretics.

For the time being, therefore, the disputations continued, raising issues of philosophy and theology that would be debated long after the Cathar movement ceased to exist. The new sect's representatives might not have participated so vigorously if they had known what the penalty would be for defending themselves so ably against their Catholic adversaries. Perhaps the Cathars felt invulnerable in their southern strongholds, or they may simply have been willing to run the risk of martyrdom for their faith, but they did more than hold their own in debate. Calling to their aid the methods and concepts of Aristotle's rediscovered philosophy, they threw the Catholics on the defensive and unwittingly sealed their fate.

CATHAR BELIEFS, it turned out, were not merely unorthodox and peculiar; they were systematic and, to people hungry for rational explanations, highly persuasive. Their reputation for virtue had won the heretics many unlearned followers, but it was their ability to support their doctrines with convincing arguments that brought educated Christians into their camp, and that made them a real danger to the intellectual hegemony of the Catholic Church. The dissenters were known to be avid readers—paintings of them frequently show them carrying books—and they used what they read effectively. Like their Catholic adversaries, they cited biblical texts that apparently supported their views, especially the numerous passages in the New Testament emphasizing the corruption of the material world and its churches. What most startled and troubled their opponents, however, was their ability to marshal support for their case by using methods and concepts derived from highly respected secular authorities—in particular, Aristotle and his commentators.

Their principal subject (amounting almost to an obsession) was the problem of Evil. How could a good God have created a universe as beset as ours is by death, decay, and moral failure? How could an all-powerful, just, and loving Creator allow plagues, natural disasters, and sinful impulses to exist? The question was of concern to many thinking Christians, but prior to the Cathar challenge few were inclined to see God's toleration of these worldly ills as a problem creating a serious doctrinal crisis. Most believers tended to accept the explanations originally offered by Saint Augustine, who declared that evil is not a thing created by God, indeed, not a thing at all but an insufficiency or "privation" of being.[27] Sin, or rebellion against God, said Augustine, is the product of our own free choice, not of the divine will. And—the clincher—God's inscrutable plan, if we could but understand it, would demonstrate that apparently evil events actually serve some higher purpose.[28]

The Cathar response to all this was apparently devastating, especially when delivered in public disputations by *Perfecti* who had studied Aristotelian logic in church schools or at universities. None of Augustine's explanations made sense, they argued, since the contradiction between a good and omnipotent God and a universe tainted by evil is real and cannot be made to vanish by theological sleight of hand. Evil is not an illusion, they insisted; it is a reality just as substantial as the material world which embodies it. Augustine himself identified sin not just with an absence of being but with concupiscence: the misuse of man's perverted will. But how could a good and omnipotent God have produced such a defective product? And how, in justice, can he damn his own sinful creatures (the vast majority of humans, according to Augustine) to eternal hellfire? Furthermore, said the Cathars, the attribution of evil impulses and events to some inscrutable plan of God's is no more than an appeal to ignorance. If God's plan is unknowable, how do we know that it aims at our good? Indeed, how can we know anything about it at all? The conclusion that he must have our welfare at heart even as he permits us to suffer simply ratifies the original assumption of a good and omnipotent deity. But is this assumption warranted by the empirical evidence? Or is there a more satisfactory explanation?

As exotic or "Eastern" as some Cathar beliefs and practices might seem,[29] these questions were very much in tune with the same rationalist spirit—the desire to make sense of things—that was then transforming Catholic theology, as well as stimulating Europe's fast-growing interests in natural science and higher education. To the charge that their creation story was a wild-eyed fantasy, the Cathars responded by analyzing the Old Testament story of Job, the "blameless and upright man" who loses everything on a whim of Jehovah's.[30] Clearly, said the Cathars, this unpleasant story, in which God taunts and bullies Job until he accepts the paradox of a good God who makes people suffer, does not constitute an answer to the question of the problem of evil, but a refusal to answer it. Worse yet, Jehovah's repeated proclamations of God's limitless power implicitly concede that he either causes evil deliberately (as in Job's case) or permits it to exist (as in the case of the fallen angels or Adam and Eve). The orthodox conclusion, then, is that humans using reason alone cannot make sense of the events and impulses they call evil. Here reason must yield to revelation, and logic to faith. Christians must simply accept the idea that since God is good and all-powerful, his infinite power and knowledge will be accompanied, in due course, by infinite justice and mercy.

To this the Cathars replied that there was one explanation of the phenomena that could be arrived at by using one's reason: God cannot be simultaneously good and omnipotent. If he created evil or permits it to exist, he cannot be good. But if he is good, he cannot be omnipotent, for if he were, he would not have saddled us with sin and suffering. The existence of good and evil implies the existence of two creative principles, or Gods, neither of them omnipotent. The God portrayed in the Book of Job and elsewhere in the Old Testament, a tyrannical brute infatuated with his own power, is the creator of the material universe, the source of all evil. The God of the New Testament, the source of mercy and love, is the creator of the spiritual realm, which includes his Son, the angels, and the souls of human beings. This ethical dualism not only makes sense, said the Cathars, it is a necessary conclusion, if we are to follow the principles of scientific reasoning laid down by Aristotle.

The only Cathar text that survives intact, a treatise called *On the Two Principles,* contains the following intriguing passage:

> But this [evil existing without a cause] would seem to be impossible, that is, that anything can begin without a cause, as it is written: "For whatever happens, it is impossible for it not to have a cause." And again: "Everything that goes from potency to effect needs a cause by which it is drawn to the effect." And even that which was, according to them [the Catholics] its cause, that is, good, needs it less than that which was not, that is, evil, as it is certainly written: "It is necessary for something to be before it can act."[31]

The argument is pure Aristotle. The phrases quoted are probably from an abstract or commentary on *Physics* or *Metaphysics,* books in which the Philosopher insists that to know something is to understand its causes, that there are no uncaused things or events in the universe, and that all potential things or events become actual because of the influence of some cause or goal.[32] The final sentence of the passage refers to the Aristotelian principle that any new activity in the universe must have a new cause, since things will otherwise go on as they had gone on before. The Cathar argument asserts that even if evil is not eternal (as they believed it was), it must have a cause, since otherwise whatever was producing good would have gone on producing only good forever. Similarly, although Catholic disputants might argue that evil is the result of free choice, the question, "What causes angels or men to choose evil?" must still be answered. The notion of an uncaused or self-caused event is an absurdity, since, as Aristotle says, everything that happens in the natural world has a cause. And since the Philosopher has demonstrated that the cause of something so general and fundamental as good must be a First Cause—a God—it stands to reason that the cause of evil must be a God as well.

The implications of this argument were troubling to many Catholics, not because they accepted the Cathars' conclusions but because the heretics were able to make such effective use of the new learning. The idea of a dual Creation was not only a blatant heresy, it was also a notion that Aristotle, with his belief in the unity of nature, would not have countenanced for a moment. Yet the rationalist method that the Cathars were applying was one that many Catholic theologians had also embraced. They, too, believed that religious doctrines ought to make sense in the way that Aristotle's theories made sense. That is, they ought to be comprehensible; they ought to explain (or at least be consistent with) observed phenomena; and they ought to be justifiable by the same sort of logical arguments that were used to prove other sorts of propositions. Some exceptions to this approach were recognized by Christian scholars. Issues having to do with divine things like the Virgin Birth, the three-in-oneness of the Holy Trinity, and the geography of heaven were generally considered to be outside the scope of logical reasoning. But was the problem of evil the same sort of trans-rational issue? Weren't the very evils whose origin was being debated by Catholics and Cathars normal features of the natural world? What sense did it make, then, for orthodox believers to declare that they were too mysterious for human beings to comprehend?

From the time that Aristotle's "lost" works and other works of Greek science were first introduced in Europe, the standard Catholic response to the new learning had been to accept its findings by placing them in the larger context of generally accepted religious truths—an operation that involved separating the sensuous here and now of the natural universe from the ineffable realm of the divine. Both Galen's medical science and Aristotle's biology, for example, strongly suggested that dead bodies remain dead. Believing Christians might respond that this was certainly true in the world of nature, but that it was also true that God could on rare occasions raise the dead—as Jesus had raised Lazarus—and that he would resurrect the saints bodily at the end of time, as promised by the Gospels. The apparent conflict between science and religion could be resolved by admitting the possibility of miracles as occasional exceptions to the regularities of nature, and the existence of a Divine Kingdom in which the laws of nature were abrogated. In this way, one could accept the undoubted truths of "natural philosophy" while remaining a faithful Christian. Another way to put this was that ordinarily God chooses to exercise his limitless power by allowing nature to operate autonomously, according to the principles described by Aristotle. But since God is omnipotent, he can—and sometimes does—do anything he wants to do.

The solution was neat, and in many cases quite serviceable. But what the disputations with the Cathars demonstrated was that certain vital issues resisted easy classification as either earthly or divine, as fit for scientific determination or beyond human comprehension. In some areas of inquiry, the task of separating the natural from the supernatural was far more difficult, and serious conflicts could therefore occur. The problem of evil was located squarely in this disputed territory, along with certain other issues, for example, the eternity of the world, the invariability of natural laws, and the nature of the soul. Dealing with such issues in a way satisfactory to educated Christians would require considerably more philosophical sophistication than the current crop of Catholic preachers could muster.

This was the second lesson of the Cathar disputations. If Catholics wished to defeat heretics skilled in using Aristotle's arguments in debate, they had better use preachers skilled in Aristotelian dialectics—specialists in disputation able to beat the Cathars at their own game. In 1205, one such specialist, a thirty-five-year old Spanish theologian named Domingo de Guzmán, a graduate of the University of Palencia, accompanied his bishop to a meeting of the papal legates in Montpellier. The fiery young man had hoped to preach to the Saracens, but a pope almost as young as he—Innocent III—had ordered him into forensic battle against the Cathars. His first act was to advise the legates that preachers against the heretics must immediately abandon their horse-drawn coaches, dismiss their cooks and valets, discard their fine clothes, and adopt the austere lifestyle of their opponents. Shortly thereafter, he would petition the pope for permission to found a new order of preachers in order to carry the struggle against Catharism across Europe. Young Dominic—to give him his Latin name—would eventually get his wish. But before the Dominican Order could be formally established, Inno-

cent III had preached a crusade against the Cathars, and all Languedoc was in flames.

Rarely do leaders make a great difference in history, but Lotar
of Segni was born to lead. The young Roman aristocrat received
the best education possible in late-twelfth-century Europe, earn-
ing a degree in theology from the University of Paris and in
law from the University of Bologna. At the age of twenty-one,
prodigiously early by medieval standards, he completed his studies and returned to Rome to take up a series of progressively
more important posts in the Church hierarchy. When Pope Celestine III died in 1198, Lotar was elected pope by a virtually
unanimous College of Cardinals, taking the name Innocent III.
Celestine III had handpicked another man to be his successor, but
no matter; Lotar was recognized as one of the most brilliant legal
minds of his time—a superb administrator, shrewd politician, patient diplomat, and passionate defender of the papacy's leading
role in European affairs. Moreover, he was a devoted admirer of
the great reformer, Gregory VII, and was determined to continue
his work. When he assumed the throne of Saint Peter, Innocent
III was only thirty-seven years old.

Three great challenges confronted the new pope and his administration: the persistence of Catharism in southern France
and Italy, the spread of evangelical protest movements throughout the West, and the "invasion" of Europe's new universities by
Aristotelian ideas. By almost any standard save that of human-
itarianism, his reign was a triumph. Innocent's overall political
perspective was what might be called far-sighted conservatism. To
advance the long-range interests of the Church, he was prepared
to make changes that more myopic traditionalists considered unacceptably radical. His preferred method of approaching problems (no doubt, a residue of his legal training) was line-drawing.
On one side of the line he placed those who directly challenged

the spiritual and organizational hegemony of the Church, or who were unrepentant heretics. Their fate was to be physically exterminated. On the other side were those whom the Church might use to its benefit, even though their ideas and attitudes seemed dubious or troublesome. Their fate, if they accepted it, was to be incorporated into the Catholic hierarchy under appropriate rules and regulations. This method, which did much to determine the future of Catholic organization and thinking for the next three centuries, dictated the destruction of the Cathars, the cooptation of the evangelical movement, and an ambivalent attempt to regulate the reception of Aristotle by the universities.

The pope's response to the persistence of Catharism seemed at first quite measured, considering how much he loathed heresy. On the theory that abuses of power by the Catholic clergy were stimulating the revolt, he sent his legates into Languedoc with orders to suspend a number of corrupt bishops from office and dispatched Domingo de Guzmán on a preaching and disputation tour throughout the region. He also accepted the declaration of repentance offered by Count Raymond VI of Toulouse, who had been excommunicated for tolerating heresy, and readmitted him to communion. But Innocent had no intention of permitting the Cathars to continue to organize a counter-Church in southern Europe. Furious at Count Raymond's continuing failure to act against the heretics, he privately informed the count's cousin, the king of France, of his duty as a Christian prince:

> It is your responsibility to harry the Count of Toulouse out of those lands which at present he occupies; to remove this territory from the control of sectarian heretics; and to place it in the hands of true Catholics who will be enabled, under your beneficent rule, to serve Our Lord in all faithfulness.[33]

Meanwhile, the pope instructed Peter of Castelnau, his chief representative in the Midi, to move against Raymond in his own territory. Castelnau induced a number of local barons, technically Raymond's vassals, to form a league dedicated to capturing and eliminating Cathar heretics. When invited to join the new organization, Raymond (quite predictably) refused to participate, and Castelnau retaliated by excommunicating him, thus freeing his subjects legally from their oaths of allegiance. He also put the county of Toulouse under interdict, which meant that until Raymond made his peace with the Church, Catholics of the region could no longer attend mass or take Holy Communion. The legate made no secret of his intentions. "He who dispossesses you will be accounted virtuous," he announced to Raymond, "he who strikes you dead will earn a blessing."[34] To shore up his threatened authority, the count was compelled to apologize, humble himself before Castelnau, and make numerous solemn promises to follow the pope's orders and join the campaign against the heretics. The ceremony of submission at the church of Saint-Gilles was apparently humiliating not just to Raymond but to his officers. The following morning, just as Castelnau and his colleagues were leaving the city, one of Raymond's men accosted them and ran the papal legate through with his sword.

Innocent III had not planned the assassination, of course, but it was the act of war he had been waiting for. Now he could summon all Christian kings and princes to join him in ridding the region of its excommunicated prince and in "exterminating" (his word) the Cathars, who were "worse than the very Saracens." The call to Crusade went out in the spring of 1208, promising the barons of Europe all the benefits of the Crusades against the Saracens, including a moratorium on their debts, remission of sins, and a right to claim properties forfeited by the heathen enemy. By July 1209, the largest army ever seen in southern Europe, composed of great lords like Simon de Montfort, vassal knights by the thousands, large mercenary bands, and hordes of pilgrims, was advancing down the Rhone valley. Its first target, the city of Béziers, was stormed almost immediately after being besieged, with horrifying results. Catholics and Cathars alike had abandoned their homes and taken refuge in the churches, but church doors could not keep the invaders at bay. "All inside were slaughtered wholesale," writes one historian, "women, invalids, babies, and priests, the latter clasping the Chalice or holding aloft a crucifix." One story, perhaps apocryphal, recounts that when the papal representative Arnald-Amalric was informed before the attack that the city contained many good Catholics as well as heretics, he replied, "Kill them all; God will recognize his own." The legate may not have uttered those words, but he most certainly did write Innocent shortly afterward, declaring proudly that "nearly twenty thousand of the citizens were put to death, regardless of age and sex."[35]

Carcassonne fell next. Most of its citizens saved their lives by surrendering and abandoning their homes and possessions to the Crusaders, but resistance to the "foreign" invasion flared up everywhere, and the campaign became a long war of attrition. In the end, of course, the depopulated and war-ravaged south had to give way. His army and resources exhausted, Raymond VII signed a peace treaty in 1229 that effectively ceded Languedoc to France. That same year, a great Church council in Toulouse established a new university in that city under papal control and gave the newly founded Inquisition vast powers to root out and destroy heretics. Not only were all women over the age of twelve and all men over fourteen required to swear an oath against heresy, they were forbidden to own either the Old Testament or the New Testament, lest they be led astray by erroneous interpretations. Pope Innocent's successors (he had died in 1216) brought the Inquisition's investigators and prosecutors into Italy, northern France, and Germany, where the chief Inquisitor, Konrad von Marburg, caused a memorable reign of terror before being assassinated in 1233. This was not the end of the Cathar resistance. Rebellions in France and Italy flared up from time to time until 1244, when the last rebel stronghold in Languedoc, the castle of Montségur, was captured and all its inhabitants massacred. Even then, groups of Cathars continued to meet and even to make converts. The religion persisted for another century in Western Europe (the last Cathar was burned in Italy in 1330), and somewhat longer in the Balkan regions where it had first begun.

Western Europe after the suppression of the Cathars was not the same society that it had been when Innocent III first assumed the papacy. An era of toleration and openness to new ideas had ended, and a new period of "strict normalization" and repression had begun.[36] Symbolic of the change was the Fourth Lateran Council convened by the pope in 1215, which not only condemned every major Cathar belief but required Jews and other non-Catholics to wear special clothing (in most places, a yellow badge) in order to warn good Christians against fraternizing too closely with them. The question was what all this might mean for Catholic dissenters who engaged in unauthorized evangelism and for the Aristotelian scholars now beginning to teach in the new universities. Was Latin Christianity about to take the turn taken by the Islamic world, when it isolated and marginalized its secular philosophers? Would Aristotle's books be thrown on the bonfires now consuming the Cathar tracts? For some time—indeed, for much of the thirteenth century—the answer would remain in doubt.

INTERESTINGLY, the principal source of resistance to expanding the anti-Cathar mobilization to include other potentially "subversive" movements was Innocent III himself. For all his ferocity where outright heretics and religious competitors were concerned, the pope remained a Gregorian, deeply devoted to radical reform of the clergy. His most remarkable achievement was to incorporate into the body of the Church many of the mass-based evangelical organizations that had terrified older conservatives like Bernard. Ignoring previous anathemas against them, Innocent negotiated compromise agreements that recognized certain groups as agents of the Church and sanctioned their activities, on condition that they reorganize their religious houses, moderate some excessive practices, and avoid preaching on theological matters. The last condition proved crucial, since what it permitted—popular preaching in the towns and cities by self-appointed evangelists— was a practice that was spreading throughout the West despite the assault on Catharism, and that was probably unstoppable.[37]

Innocent's greatest triumph was the incorporation of the group led by Francis of Assisi, a businessman's son, as the Order of Friars Minor. The move was a risky one, not only because of Francis's charisma, his selfless stubbornness, and the breathtaking growth of his movement, but also because of his unusually strong aversion to property. Most evangelists lived humble lives, but worked for a living. Francis insisted that his followers live as beggars and avoid owning even the buildings that housed them. How could an evangelist trying to found a large organization devoted to prayer and service even think of doing so without owning and controlling land? Was Francis, in effect, an Arnold of Brescia— one who would eventually call for pauperization of the Church and the transfer of its worldly goods and power to the secular authorities? Innocent's genius was to recognize that the saintly man from Assisi had no interest in challenging the political and doctrinal hegemony of the Church. In fact, since the impulses that motivated him—the urge to live apostolically, to serve the poor, to experience God's presence, and to preach his Word—were shared by significant numbers of zealous Catholics throughout Europe, the answer was to incorporate his followers in the body of the Church, where they might become a spiritually revitalizing and, in the long run, politically stabilizing force.

A story that circulated later told how, before meeting Francis for the first time, the pope had dreamed that the Basilica of Saint Peter's was threatening to collapse, but that one man was supporting the entire structure on his shoulders. Innocent was said to have recognized Francis as the hero of his dream. There can be no doubt that by incorporating the charismatic evangelist and his followers into the organizational life of the Church, the pope strengthened that vulnerable structure, as well as enhancing his own authority. But the line that so cleverly separated unrepentant heretics from manageable reformers did not answer the questions posed by the new learning that was now fascinating students in Europe's burgeoning universities. How should the university curricula be regulated? What sort of distinction, if any, needed to be made between groups of loyal or suspect intellectuals? What should the Church's attitude be toward the philosophy of Aristotle?

During Innocent's episcopate, the long period of scholastic silence that accompanied the "digestion" of Aristotle's writings came to a close. Now everyone wanted to talk about the Philosopher's works, especially those known as the "nature books": *Physics, Metaphysics, On the Soul, On Generation and Corruption,* and the treatises on natural science. This reception was part of a great revival of literary interest among educated Westerners, who were now reading chivalric stories, love poetry, warrior epics, astrological treatises, and the lives of saints in vernacular tongues as well as in Latin.[38] Even with this competition, however, no literature commanded a larger or more enthusiastic audience than Aristotle's works of *scientia*—worldly knowledge—which were devoured, along with his logical books, by the thousands of students now crowding into European universities.

The universities were also a new development. Originally created to serve the interests of the religious and secular authorities, these colorful, volatile, independence-minded communities were always threatening to overstep their authorized boundaries.[39] Their main purpose was to train privileged young men (and a few women) to be religious leaders, public servants, teachers, lawyers, and physicians, and—a particular interest of Rome's—to produce intellectual warriors capable of doing battle against religious competitors and heretics. Like the craft guilds being formed at the same time, they were legal corporations empowered to admit or reject members, define standards of workmanship, regulate internal promotions, and determine their own codes of conduct. Ultimately responsible to church or state officials, they exercised a high degree of day-to-day self-governance, with considerable power in the hands of the faculty and students. This structure created an intellectual and political space in which new ideas and research techniques could be generated and refined. Medieval universities enjoyed "far more academic freedom than similar institutions in Byzantium and Islam" as well as a strong sense of collective identity.[40] Almost inevitably, the same freedom bred unauthorized thinking and unruly behavior. "Town-gown" battles between local residents and students were frequent and violent, and insubordination by masters and students was congenital. Teachers and students in many universities formed a common front, and attempts to discipline or "correct" them were often met by passive resistance, shutdowns of classes, or breakaway movements that created new universities.

The authorities had reason to worry about the impressionable youths entrusted to the universities' care. Students matriculated at an early age—often as young as thirteen or fourteen. Hailing from diverse regions of Europe, they used Latin as their common language, but lived together in "nations" based on their communities of origin or in colleges designed to supervise the younger students. At Paris, where the recognized "nations" were French, Norman, Picard (Belgian), and English-German, quarrels between ethnic groups were frequent and often spilled over into the streets. The basic education there, as in other universities, took place in the faculty of arts, whose masters offered courses in grammar, rhetoric, logic, geometry, arithmetic, astronomy, and music—and, increasingly, in Aristotelian "natural philosophy." The cornerstones of educational method were the lecture and the *disputatio*—a formal debate that demonstrated the student's command of the materials and ability to argue all sides of a disputed issue. Students who obtained bachelor's degrees were immediately qualified to teach the liberal arts. Others went on to pursue master's and doctoral degrees in law, medicine, or the "Queen of Sciences," theology. The process was lengthy by modern standards; it took at least sixteen years, and often longer, to obtain a doctorate in theology. But graduates of the great schools were virtually assured employment by the burgeoning bureaucracies of the Church, state, and university.

The University of Paris, chartered in 1200, was immediately recognized as Europe's premier center for the study of theology. Bologna, founded some sixty years earlier, was best known for its law school, which had virtually created the profession of canon lawyer. Salerno and Montpellier were generally considered to have the best medical faculties, and Oxford soon achieved a reputation for expertise in natural science. Within the century, Europe would boast some one hundred universities, each cultivating a reputation in some specialized field of advanced studies. But at many of them—and certainly at Paris—the most exciting and troublesome community was the liberal arts faculty, filled with eager novice students and taught by young masters so numerous that they soon "came to constitute a university on their own."[41]

The masters were graduate students as well as teachers, but many came to prefer teaching in the exciting atmosphere of the arts faculty to pursuing their own doctoral degrees. At Paris, where philosophy was king, "the masters of arts were the permanent element of intellectual unrest and the driving force of intellectual revolutions."[42]

The arts faculties were therefore the first to feel the impact of the Aristotelian revolution. As the Philosopher's works became available in Latin, the masters modified the curriculum to include them, and the faculties of arts at leading universities soon became, in effect, schools of Aristotelian philosophy. Integrating Aristotle's logical books into the curriculum caused only minor controversies, but conflict blossomed with the appearance of his "nature books." The University of Paris was barely ten years old when a council of bishops presided over by the archbishop of Sens, Peter of Corbeil, decreed that "neither Aristotle's books of natural philosophy nor commentaries [on them] are to be read publicly or privately in Paris, and this under penalty of excommunication."[43]

This was an ominous and startling development. Although the university was a Church-run institution, it was unusual to forbid the study of any books there, much less books written in antiquity by the legendary Philosopher. Nonetheless, five years later, the ban was extended and broadened by the papal legate, Cardinal Robert of Courcon, a former University of Paris professor and boyhood friend of Innocent III. (Innocent had studied theology at Paris himself before the university was chartered.) Courcon drew up new university statutes that expressly permitted the reading of Aristotle's logical books in the faculty of arts, but that proscribed his "books of metaphysics and natural philosophy and summaries of these."[44] In addition, the liberal arts students were obliged to swear an oath stating that they would not read or discuss the works of three recent writers: David of Dinant, Amalric the Heretic, and Maurice of Spain.

The linking of the ban on Aristotelian science with these three names was not fortuitous. Historians have long debated what David of Dinant and Amalric of Bene (Amalric the Heretic's real name) actually believed and wrote, since, as was customary in such cases, the heretical books were burned even if their authors were not, and public discussion of their contents was taboo. We know something of David's writings, because the great Dominican scholar Albert the Great quoted from them in order to refute them, and some fragments of his work escaped the fire.[45] Amalric's beliefs are more obscure, but in the case of his followers, it seems that more than writing was involved. The "Amalricians" apparently acted—quite scandalously—on the basis of their heretical beliefs, as a result of which "a batch of persons infected with the heresy—priests and clerks from the schools, as well as a goldsmith from the neighbouring Grand-Pont—were handed over to the secular arm, some for the stake, others for perpetual imprisonment."[46] Their leader's corpse (he had died earlier of natural causes) was disinterred from holy ground and then burned.[47] The identity of "Maurice of Spain" presents an additional mystery. It seems clear, in any case, that the three men named by Cardinal Courcon were scholars whose beliefs were identified with Aristotle's metaphysics and natural science, and whose condemnation was intended to warn others not to follow their example.

Both David and Amalric taught at Corbeil, just south of Paris, where Abelard had also lectured for a time. It appears that the two scholars had become, in a sense, reverse Cathars, for while the Cathars insisted that the material universe, being evil, must have its source in an evil God, the Paris masters taught that the material universe was good, and that it *was* God.[48] David of

Dinant had clearly studied Aristotle's *Physics* and *Metaphysics* and his psychological treatise, *On the Soul*. What most impressed him about the universe described by the Philosopher was its unity and exclusivity. Everything in the natural universe is composed of matter and form—primary, inchoate material given an intelligible shape and purpose. Even the soul is compound, since it is the animating principle of the body. All the parts of this great whole are interrelated. And God, described by Aristotle as pure form, as well as the Unmoved Mover responsible for all change in the universe, exists in the closest possible relationship to his creation. As a logician, David argued that the differences between matter, soul, and God could not be described unless the three categories shared some common underlying feature, nor could the soul understand God and matter unless they had something fundamental in common. The conclusion that he reached—his own fusion of Aristotelian and Christian doctrine—was that existence itself was the common feature. God, who is pure Being, created the universe out of himself. Its form, or spirit, is his Spirit, and even its matter partakes of his Being. In the last analysis, David concluded, God, matter, and the soul are One.

Other theologians immediately recognized this doctrine as pantheism. Whether Jewish, Muslim, or Christian, most orthodox monotheists insisted on maintaining a sharp distinction between the Creator and his creatures. The world was created by God and man was made in his image, but this creation was not God himself nor was it made of "god-stuff." The distinction was especially important for Christians, who believed that the natural world was a fallen world, separated from the Kingdom of Heaven by sin and mortality. If the world was God, what would become of man's immortality and the hope of heaven? If humans were God, why would they need salvation or the forgiveness of sins? And, if they were sinless, what would prevent them from behaving in any way that they pleased? The scholarly David of Dinant was not interested in these issues, or, if he was, he left no evidence of it. But Amalric of Bene apparently took up these challenges with zest. We are told that he asserted that, although the material universe was immortal, just as Aristotle had said, its human inhabitants were not. From the point of view of Aristotelian science, their bodily resurrection was out of the question, and the survival of the soul after the death of the body was doubtful. According to Amalric, however, the men and women of earth did not require salvation in the afterlife. Since their souls (at least those of his disciples) participated in God's Spirit while alive, they were incapable of sinning, no matter what thoughts or actions they undertook.[49]

How far Amalric and his followers put their doctrine into practice is still not clear, but the idea that the souls of some contemporary Christians might embody the Holy Spirit was in the air at the time. A few years earlier, the utopian priest, Joachim of Fiore, had announced that the age of the Father (the Old Testament) had ended, the age of the Son (the New Testament) was nearing its close, and the age of the Spirit (when people would be saved by God's grace alone) would begin in a century or so.[50] Apparently the Amalricians believed that the inauguration of the Third Age was imminent or that it had already begun—not very good news for the Roman Catholic Church, since that eventuality would make organized religion unnecessary.[51] Amalric may have been emboldened to speculate this freely by his social position. He is said to have been the tutor of Philip Augustus, heir to the French throne, whom some Amalricians identified as a messianic figure who would end both Church and state in the End of Days. (Frederick II of Germany was the subject of similar speculation by utopians in his empire.) These connections may have helped protect him during his lifetime, but in 1210, the year of the first ban on Aristotle's works at the University of Paris, his corpse, disinterred by order of the bishop of Paris, suffered the penalty that he had averted while alive.

The penalty gives one some idea of the horror with which the authorities viewed pantheistic ideas and declarations by Christians that they were sinless. Over the next century, a substantial number of heretics would be burned because they maintained that as vessels of the Holy Spirit, they could do no wrong.[52] Of course, the allegations that the Amalricians misbehaved sexually as well as doctrinally may be as false in their case as it was in that of the Cathars. But with the Cathars using Aristotle's writings to support their heretical dualism and masters of philosophy at Paris using the same works to support their heretical pantheism, the bishop of Paris and his confreres at the university concluded that the Philosopher's books were far too dangerous to be read and interpreted by the masters and their undergraduate students. It was this association with obvious heresy that generated the bans of 1210 and 1215, as well as the simultaneous condemnations of David and Amalric. Opinions differ as to the identity of the mysterious Maurice of Spain, whose works were also outlawed, but the most intriguing theory is that the Latin phrase *Maurici Hispanici* really meant "the Moor of Spain," and referred to the famous Muslim Aristotelian, Ibn Rushd, known in Europe as Averroës.

In 1215, then, the year in which Innocent III convened the Fourth Lateran Council, there seemed a clear possibility that Aristotle's works would be identified with heresy and legally banned in Europe, as they had been more informally censored in the Muslim world. But could the authorities prevent students and teachers from reading the most popular works of philosophy ever published in Europe? Moreover, Domingo de Guzmán, the scourge of the Cathars, was clamoring for recognition of his proposed Order of Friars Preachers and insisting at the same time that

Aristotle could be—must be—studied and used by Christian intellectuals in the continuing struggle against heresy. Dominic even demanded that his mendicant friars be admitted as teachers to the theology faculty of the University of Paris, where they proposed to teach Aristotelian philosophy as it should be taught. Resistance to this Dominican incursion by the existing Paris theologians, as well as by most clergymen in Paris, was immediate and sharp. The stage was set for a decisive struggle to determine the future of the new learning at the university.

CHAPTER FIVE

"Hark, Hark, the Dogs Do Bark"

ARISTOTLE AND THE TEACHING FRIARS

GREAT EVENTS, says a Latin motto, come from small causes. Who could have predicted that the fate of scientific education in the West might depend on the outcome of a student riot?

In March 1229, on Shrove Tuesday, Paris's pre-Lenten carnival began at sundown. Despite efforts by Church officials to suppress or at least moderate the bawdy celebration, the city was in its usual Mardi Gras uproar, especially on the Left Bank, where several thousand students lived clustered near the rue du Fouarre. (This was the famous "Street of Straw," so called because the entrances to the schools were straw-covered.) Although some students sported noble titles and reputable connections, many lived on the edge of poverty, hoping to substitute acquired skills for inherited wealth. Rich or poor, most of the young men chafed under the restrictions imposed on their behavior by the Church-run university. Little wonder they looked forward to carnival, when for a few brief hours they could escape the authorities' omnipresent gaze. Behind a Mardi Gras mask, one could take a few drinks too many and make a fool of oneself, indulge in an illicit flirtation, or settle an old score.

During the carnival, some students were drinking wine at a tavern in a suburban quarter known as Saint Marcel, when a dispute arose with the landlord over his bill. "From words, the disputants rapidly proceeded to blows—to pulling of ears and tearing of hair."[1] The landlord called in his neighbors, who beat the students and threw them into the street, but the next day the students returned with reinforcements of their own: "gownsmen armed with swords and sticks, who broke into the tavern, avenged their comrades on the host and his neighbours, set the taps running, and then 'flown with insolence and wine' sallied forth into the streets to amuse themselves at the expense of peaceable citizens, men and women alike."[2] A number of people were injured in the subsequent fighting, and several shops were damaged. Angry complaints were filed with the papal legate and the bishop of Paris, the officials primarily responsible for the administration of the university. As everyone knew, university students were exempt from prosecution by the king's courts, but good relations between the Church and the secular authorities required that something be done.

William of Auvergne, the bishop of Paris, listened gravely to the complaints. He then conferred hurriedly with the papal legate and the university's chancellor and board of regents. Although legally empowered to govern the unruly university community, these officials knew that they were dealing with a corporate body possessing a strong identity and will of its own. They knew, too, that in situations of conflict, the Parisian masters and students tended to unite against all other sources of authority, from the city council to the pope. Some two decades earlier, provoked by an "unjust" administrative decision, they had gone out together on strike, and the regents had been forced to compromise to avert a lengthy, damaging shutdown. Similar battles at other universities had caused schisms and secessions, as when angry students and masters seceded from Oxford to create the new university at Cambridge, and a large group of malcontents left Bologna to form the University of Padua. Normally the outsiders in charge of the university wisely deferred to the insiders' passion for independence. But this time, there was another source of pressure. Blanche of Castile, the ruler of France during the minority of her son, King Louis IX, intervened to demand that the students be punished. The university therefore authorized the city's provost and his mercenary guardsmen—"the savage police of a savage city"[3]—to find and punish the student rioters.

This was a mistake. The guards fell upon the students—according to one chronicler, a group of innocent young men who had had nothing to do with the riot—and killed several of them. The response from the university community was instantaneous. The masters of arts suspended their classes and demanded that the bishop and other university officials punish the murderous guardsmen, compensate their victims, and take steps to protect the students against bullying by hostile Parisians and the police. Representatives of the four student "nations" met in solemn conclave and declared that their members would not return to classes until the university granted their just demands. And if classes remained suspended, they would simply abandon their studies and go home. Notwithstanding these threats, the university officials declined to act. Bishop William made no effort to settle the dispute (a failure which infuriated his patron, Pope Gregory IX), and the regents refused to relent. In fact, they issued a decree suspending all teaching for a period of six years, and forbidding anyone to reside in Paris for the purpose of attending the university.

Most of the liberal arts students then packed up their belongings, left their lodging bills unpaid, and departed the city, joined in their exodus by substantial numbers of masters and students from other faculties.

Some of the Paris strikers found employment or enrolled at other universities, including Oxford, Cambridge, Rheims, Montpellier, and the new universities at Toulouse and Padua. Others went home to wait for the university to come to its senses, or abandoned their plans for a higher education in order to pursue other interests. The faculty of arts at the University of Paris largely ceased operating, although some teachers and students continued to meet during the period of general shutdown and dispersal. The schools of advanced study, including law and theology, remained in operation, but at greatly reduced levels, since their supply of new students had been curtailed and some of their teachers had joined the strike. Other universities, meanwhile, rejoiced at the sudden influx of Paris-trained students and masters, and at the damage being inflicted on their haughty competitor. Some even attempted to take advantage of the ban on Aristotle's scientific works, which remained in effect in Paris but had not yet been extended to other universities. The new University of Toulouse went so far as to advertise that "Those who wish to investigate the inmost parts of nature to their depths may there hear the books on nature that have been prohibited at Paris."[4] And Padua made Aristotelian studies the core of its curriculum.

After two years of diplomatic maneuvering, Pope Gregory IX, himself an alumnus of the Paris theological faculty, decided that enough was enough. On April 13, 1231, he promulgated a solemn decree called *Parens Scientarum* ("The Mother of Sciences"), which has been called the Magna Carta of the University of Paris, since it guaranteed the school a large measure of independence and strictly limited the powers of the chancellor and the bishop of Paris to govern it. The faculty of arts reopened with a flourish, and most of the masters and students ended their self-imposed exile. No doubt, they returned to the Left Bank in a triumphant mood, but they soon discovered that important changes, some of them quite disturbing, had taken place in their absence. The good news was that the ban on Aristotle's "nature books" seemed clearly to be weakening. The bad news (to most masters) was that the Dominican friars—a group resented and feared by many in the university community—had obtained important teaching positions in the school of theology, and that their Franciscan competitors were seeking academic posts as well. What was not immediately apparent was that these two developments— the "invasion" of the university by the friars and the rehabilitation of Aristotelian studies—were intimately related.

Officially, of course, the ban remained in effect. When the pope reopened the university in 1231, he not only renewed the prohibitions of 1210 and 1215 but also made it a punishable offense to discuss scientific subjects in the languages of the common people. Heaven forbid that the common herd should take an interest in such advanced and controversial matters! Yet closing the front door of the schools to the new learning could not prevent it from entering through numerous cracks and windows. From the very beginning, the authorities had demonstrated a reluctance to outlaw Aristotle's books entirely. Thus, it was not illegal to own *Physics* or *Metaphysics* or to read such books alone in the privacy of one's room, only to lecture on them or discuss them collectively. The primary target of the restriction, moreover, was the faculty that had spawned the heresies of Amalric of Bene and David of Dinant: the teachers and students of arts. By the late 1220s, the theologians at Paris must have been discussing Aristotle's ideas openly, since the pope felt obliged to remind them in writing that theology was the "Queen of Sciences," and to warn them not to let the Queen's "servants," philosophy and natural science, reverse the proper order of precedence.[5]

The ban remained in force, yet change was in the air. Students and teachers returning to Paris from Oxford reported that its first chancellor, the well-known (and quite conservative) scholar and theologian Robert Grosseteste, had made the Philosopher's books of natural philosophy required reading. Using Aristotelian methods, Grosseteste himself was said to have discovered the origin of the colors of the rainbow, and advanced work in optics and mathematics was taking place at several Oxford colleges. Could Paris, the "Mother of Sciences," allow herself to fall behind upstart Oxford? When Pope Gregory reopened the faculty of arts, he gave high-ranking clergymen power to absolve the masters and students who had previously been excommunicated for discussing the forbidden books. Most important, in reiterating the ban he added the crucial words "until [the books] have been examined and purged of all suspicion of error."[6] The assumption was that Aristotle's works could be made safe for good Christian students' consumption if they were properly analyzed and "corrected."

Classes began again, and the pope appointed a commission of three respected scholars to begin the analysis, but its chairman died in Rome that same year and the commission idea collapsed. If Aristotle's works were to be discussed freely at Paris, and if the bans recently imposed on Toulouse and several other universities were to be lifted, some new initiative would be needed. What finally caused the breakthrough was not, as one might expect, the students' demands for a scientific education or protests by the masters of arts, but the dramatic appearance on campus of two highly controversial groups of monks: the Dominican Order of Friars Preachers and the Franciscan Order of Friars Minor.

In 1216, Domingo de Guzmán's Order of Friars Preachers had been recognized by Rome as the Church's intellectual shock troops in the war against heresy. The following year, at Dominic's request and in accordance with his followers' own desires, the friars had begun enrolling as students at Paris and elsewhere (although Paris was their favorite university) to begin the process that would make them fully fledged theologians and teachers. They also established their own residential houses, where they could pray and talk together, attend special courses, manage their collective affairs, and maintain their militant esprit de corps. (The Dominicans' house in Paris was the convent of Saint-Jacques, which caused them to be referred to later on as "Jacobins.") Right behind them (in 1219) came Francis of Assisi's Order of Friars Minor, which also established a convent in Paris, enrolled its members as students, and made its presence felt in the university community. When the Dominicans arrived at Oxford two years later, they were again followed at a short interval by the Franciscans, who found the newer university more congenial than Paris to their scholarly and spiritual interests. From this point forward, both orders extended their academic reach until they had established themselves as an important presence in all of the major European universities.

When the masters of arts returned to the classes after settlement of the strike, they were dismayed to discover that the bishop of Paris had taken advantage of their absence to bestow a university chair on Roland of Cremona, a Dominican priest who had recently graduated from the school of theology. One year later, Roland's teacher, John of Saint Giles, entered the same black-robed order, thus giving the Dominicans two theology chairs. The masters bitterly opposed the naming of mendicant friars to university teaching positions. In this they were joined by their usual rivals, the masters of theology, who also objected to having these new colleagues thrust upon them. At first, their objections were easily overridden. The friars had powerful patrons, including the current occupant of the Chair of Saint Peter, who viewed them as his own representatives and strongly approved of their ambition to become influential voices in the universities. Even without this support, however, it would have been difficult to prevent the new orders, both of them strongly evangelical, from recruiting existing students and masters. In 1236, an experienced and well-known master of theology, Alexander of Hales, joined the Order of Friars Minor, thereby becoming the first Franciscan professor of theology at Paris. One of his students, Giovanni di Fidanza, who took the name Bonaventure, would rise to a position of great eminence in the faculty of theology as well as becoming minister-general of the Franciscan Order.

It is not hard to understand why existing teachers would oppose the invasion of their university by these "outsiders." Because they subsisted on charitable donations, the friars were financially independent, with no need for the salaries and fees that supported the rest of the faculty, and none of the economic insecurity that plagued most of the students. Intellectually, their interests were considerably more focused and mission-oriented than those of the other masters, and they pursued them with a fierce passion that many deemed incompatible with the spirit of open, reasoned inquiry. The Dominicans' tigerish dedication to exposing and combating heretics, together with their frequent role as Inquisitors, evoked fear as well as admiration, while the Franciscans' clannish otherworldliness and peculiar scholarly concerns (for example, an intense, almost obsessive interest in the metaphysics and physics of light) also gave offense. Moreover, both orders recruited avidly among the talented liberal arts students, who, once "caught" in their nets, owed their loyalty henceforth to their order rather than to the university. The newcomers were viewed, in short, as agents of outside forces—creatures of the pope who had empowered them, the king who protected them, and the powerful leaders who supervised and controlled their behavior. How could they fail to seem threatening to the members of an academic community struggling to defend its newly won professional autonomy and rights of self-governance? Notwithstanding their powerful sponsors, the struggle against the teaching friars would continue for decades to come.

What this political duel obscured, however, was the vital role played by the mendicant orders in overthrowing the ban on Aristotle's natural philosophy. For years, the masters of arts had insisted that understanding Aristotelian science was the mark of an educated man and studying it the mark of a first-rate university. Heresies like those of Amalric of Bene and David of Dinant were aberrant and avoidable, they argued. Ultimately, the truths of philosophy would prove harmless to religion. One can imagine the skepticism with which the leaders of a Church still engaged in violent warfare against heretics and Muslims must have greeted such entreaties. But the Dominicans did not entreat. Supported by powerful figures from the pope to the bishop of Paris, they insisted that it was precisely this warfare that had made Aristotelian thinking indispensable. They were not academic dilettantes interested in knowledge for knowledge's sake. The Church's intellectual knights needed Aristotle's metaphysical and scientific books— properly interpreted and "corrected," of course—as weapons in their ongoing struggle against the enemies of Christianity.

IT IS ODD TO THINK OF professional heresy-hunters as the advocates for a revolution in thinking, and a scientific revolution at that. From a modern vantage point, one would expect the more secular-minded masters of arts to have been the Aristotelian movement's strongest advocates, and theological zealots its most adamant opponents. But the Dominican and Franciscan theologians were not "fundamentalists" in the modern sense. They were passionate conservatives who believed that the European awakening was irreversible and that the tools of reason, even those developed by pagan philosophers, could be used to advance the long-term interests of orthodox religion. As a result, the most militant and confident defenders of the faith, at this crucial juncture in Western intellectual history, were also the most committed advocates of the new learning. This potent combination of religious fervor and intellectual power virtually guaranteed the acceptance of natural philosophy and "scientific theology" at the University of Paris. From this influential base, Aristotelian ideas and methods would spread unstoppably throughout Europe's other universities, generating new controversies and stimulating new debates.

William of Auvergne, "the first great philosopher of the thirteenth century,"[7] personified the new blend of religious zeal and philosophical innovation. As bishop of Paris, William functioned as the primary liaison between the university at which he had recently taught and the Roman Curia. He was, perhaps, the strongest supporter of the Order of Friars Preachers outside the members of the order themselves. His loathing for the Cathars was so intense that he volunteered to act as an Inquisitor when the Dominicans ran short of men, and his animosity toward the Jews convinced Gregory IX to order the Talmud to be publicly burned.[8] But this intolerant churchman was also a daring theologian. During the 1230s, he wrote several pathbreaking books, including *On the Universe,* a bold attempt to use Aristotle's *Metaphysics* to establish the essential principles needed to defeat the Catharist heresy.

William's key move was to identify the natural world, as Aristotle analyzed it, with the good Creation described by Scripture (such as Genesis 1:31: "God saw all he had made, and indeed it was very good"). What inspired his work was the realization that

Aristotle's account of the natural universe could provide convincing answers to the Cathars' heretical doctrine that good and evil are equally potent forces, with matter constituting the root of all evil and spirit the source of all good.[9] According to the Cathars, matter and spirit were the two basic, contending principles in the universe, each implying a separate First Cause or deity. But Aristotle had argued (opposing the dualists of his own time) that attempts to split the universe along such lines are senseless, since reality does not "contend" with itself in any fundamental sense. The natural universe is a uni-verse—one reality, not two, three, or more. How, then, can it have more than one basic principle or cause?

Of course, Aristotle admitted, there are conflicts within the universe. The lion does not lie down with the lamb, nor do fire and water peacefully occupy the same place at the same time. But these are features of a system that, looked at as a whole, is magnificently integrated. Every part of nature is interdependent with every other part. All opposites in nature imply some common underlying reality, like black and white existing on a common surface. That reality, Aristotle said, is Being, the opposite of which is not spirit, matter, or anything else actually existing, but non-Being. Clearly, matter and spirit are not at war with each other in any fundamental sense, since most natural substances are composed of matter and intelligible form (spirit, if you like), inextricably and harmoniously combined. God, who is pure form, is the most perfectly realized Being of all, but this does not mean that less perfect substances are defective or evil. On the contrary, everything in the universe is in the process of realizing its true form or essence—of becoming as perfect as possible, given the limitations of its structure. In this sense, the natural universe— the world of Being—is not only not-evil, it is positively good.[10]

Aristotle did not have much to say about the problem of evil, as Christians understood it, since the idea of sin—a profound and congenital defect of the human will—played no role in his view of human nature. To him, where humans were most likely to go wrong was in failing to control and regulate some natural impulse, as in eating too much or loving too little. But William could draw conclusions from Aristotle's work that seemed consistent with traditional Catholic views of the sort expressed by Saint Augustine. One conclusion, a bit abstract but comfortably Augustinian, was that evil is not a form of Being at all, but an absence or "privation" of Being. That is, evil is not the product of natural development, in the way that a flower is the product of a seed's development, but the result of a failure to develop naturally. (A rough modern analogy is the psychoanalysts' idea of a "fixation" that prevents a human personality from maturing normally.) A second conclusion is that sin describes something that human beings do in the exercise of their free will, not something inherent in the natural order. The natural universe contains all sorts of things—sexual desire, for example—that are good when used as God or nature intended, but that can be turned to evil when misused by undisciplined or malicious people. Evil is man's work, not God's.

Many modern people might consider this a sensible distinction, but as some medieval critics were quick to point out, it takes a significant step away from the traditional Christian idea that sin is the product of a human nature so corrupted as to require a supernatural Redeemer. To Saint Augustine, the archetypal sin was lust or "concupiscence," a desire for forbidden pleasure that seemed impossible to control without divine assistance. Extending and distorting the logic of his position, the Cathars argued that the lusty, uncontrollably reproducing material universe was evil per se, hence the product of a fallen angel or an evil God. Enrolling Aristotle against the heretics had the unintended effect of undermining the Augustinian view, too, since the Philosopher's defense of nature's essential goodness and autonomy suggested that human nature was not as vulnerable as Augustine had thought. William was unable to deal directly with the tension between the Augustinian and Aristotelian views of evil. The job was therefore passed on to his successors, in particular the Dominican giant, Thomas Aquinas. But the bishop did tackle another problem caused by his reliance on Aristotle's *Metaphysics*: the problem known in the Middle Ages as "the eternity of the world."[11]

Aristotle had described the universe as unitary, integrated, intelligible, and beautiful, but he did not believe that this natural goodness reflected the transcendent goodness of a supernatural Creator. Neither he nor any other Greek philosopher imagined a universe created by a God who made everything from scratch, including matter, form, space, and time—a Creator who maintains everything in existence from second to second, and who intervenes actively in nature and in history. On the contrary, Aristotle asserted quite confidently that the material universe had no beginning and has no end.[12] Nothing is created from nothing—isn't that commonsense maxim borne out by observation and experience? Even Plato, who pictured God as a craftsman, assumed that the basic stuff shaped by the Divine Artificer is as eternal as he is. And Aristotle's God, the Unmoved Mover, is an even more passive figure, conscious of himself but indifferent to man, not really a person (much less three Persons) so much as a force inspiring the regular processes of natural change.

What difference did it make if one considered the universe a reality created by God out of nothing or an independent system co-eternal with God? An enormous difference, according to most of the era's leading theologians. As one modern commentator puts it, "The issue of the eternity of the world was to the relations between science and religion in the Middle Ages what the heliocentric system of Copernicus was in the sixteenth and seventeenth centuries, and what the Darwinian theory of evolution has been since its inception in the nineteenth century."[13] The problem was that the doctrine could lead thinkers in either of two directions. One road led toward pantheism—the confusion of the Creator with his creation. The other led toward secularism—the removal of God from active involvement with the universe. Either of these possible destinations was guaranteed to make the blood of orthodox Christians run cold.

Pantheism, of course, was what had gotten David of Dinant in so much trouble and caused the first ban on Aristotle's works at the University of Paris. If the universe, like God, is unitary, good, and eternal (or "uncreated"), then one may be tempted to conclude either that God is part of the universe, that the universe is part of God, or that they are identical. The first conclusion was essentially that drawn by Aristotle, whose Unmoved Mover is really a part of the natural system he motivates. The second idea—that the universe is part of God—was the heresy of David of Dinant and Amalric of Bene. And the third —the identity of God with the universe—is pure nature-worship, the heresy against which Christians had been contending since the first missionaries were sent to convert the heathen tribes. None of these conclusions was remotely acceptable to William of Auvergne or any other orthodox theologian. Even if the Creator had infused the universe with his goodness and created man in his image, he must never— never!—be confused with his imperfect creation. It was exactly this sort of confusion that had caused Amalric's followers to believe that they could not sin no matter how they behaved, since they were embodiments of the Holy Spirit.

But there was another, equally disturbing implication of Aristotle's doctrine. This was the idea that the things that comprise the universe change and move according to principles or laws inherent in their own nature, not because the Creator made them and chooses continuously to maintain them that way. Instead of bringing the universe too close to God, this line of thinking pushes them too far apart. Not only does the idea of exclusively natural causation eliminate the possibility of miracles, it pretty much eliminates divine providence in any form whatsoever. No creation means no "Second Adam" (as Christ was called), no redemption, and no End of Days. Ultimately, it may mean no God at all other than Aristotle's Unmoved Mover or the eighteenth-century Deists' "Clockmaker God," who winds up the machine of the universe at the beginning of time and then retires permanently while it slowly ticks down. Moreover, medieval theologians worried, if Aristotle's universe is governed by its own inexorable laws, are future events predetermined? If so, what becomes of God's freedom to do absolutely as he pleases? And what becomes of human beings' freedom to choose good or evil?

Both of these dangerous ideas—God intermingled with the universe and God effectively removed from the universe—were expressed in the work of an earlier philosopher who became William of Auvergne's number-one target. This was the great Persian Neoplatonist Avicenna, who maintained that God had created the universe by necessity and through a process of "emanation," or overflow of his God-nature, into successive spheres of Being, beginning with the sphere of pure intelligence and ending with the spheres of the heavens and the earth. Bad enough, said William, that the idea of emanation mixed God into creation, but Avicenna also distanced the Creator from the natural universe by proposing that he had directly created only the first and highest sphere of Being, and that each subsequent sphere had generated the next, lower sphere. This scheme, which seems bizarre to modern eyes, was consistent with the ancient belief that the cosmos was constructed as a set of nested spheres, with each sphere moving the one interior to it, so that activities on earth were controlled, to some extent, by the movements of the heavenly sphere (thus the enormous interest in astrology, which was considered a science from ancient times until fairly recently). But it was also consistent with the more modern notion that God, having originally set the whole universe in motion, was now content to function as the Unmoved Mover, leaving nature to operate according to its own laws.

To all this, William of Auvergne said "No." Creation is not necessary but the result of God's free choice. The world is not a product of emanation, for "what pours out of a spring or fountain is simply what was in there before it came out; no, God *makes* things."[14] Nor does God make things only once, abandoning them thereafter to the working of natural processes. Rather, creation is a continuous process, the work of an omnipotent God who can do anything he pleases, short of creating a genuine contradiction. (For example, since God is absolutely good, he cannot sin.) All this becomes clear, said William, if one reads the "book of nature" aright, understanding that the universe is the product of an Intelligence and a Will that preexist it and remain outside it—in short, that it is "one skill, or work, one discourse or meaning, one sign or designation of Himself, one book or scripture, placed in the sight of the human intellect so that, reading, it may become wise in it and as far as possible learn about its creator."[15] Establishing what would become the Dominican credo, William declared that science and theology are not in conflict, but that the former is radically incomplete without the latter. We cannot understand the universe on the basis of its internal workings alone. The book's deeper meaning can be grasped only by discovering its author's intentions, and for this we need more than Aristotle's natural philosophy. We need divine philosophy, beginning with

the Word of God as revealed in his Holy Scriptures and interpreted by the Fathers of the Church.

WHILE WILLIAM OF AUVERGNE was pouring out his thoughts on
natural philosophy and theology, Aristotle's "nature books" remained banned at the University of Paris, as well as at several
other universities. Even among the Dominicans, there was still
considerable fear of pagan philosophy and science. The statutes
of the order in 1228 forbade the brothers to "study in the books of
the Gentiles and the philosophers, although they may inspect
them briefly."[16] But with the bishop of Paris himself citing *Metaphysics* in support of the Catholic cause, how long could the prohibition last? Clearly, the Dominicans could not be prevented in
the long run from studying the materials that they needed to arm
themselves against the heretics. This they began to do in the privacy of their own convent school, but discussions begun at Saint-
Jacques inevitably continued in the faculty of theology—a trend
that became irreversible in 1242, when a new master, a Dominican
scholar from Swabia, was appointed to a university chair.

Then in his mid-forties, Albertus Teutonicus, as he was then
called, was the first German to become a professor of theology at
Paris. He is remembered today as Albertus Magnus—Albert the
Great. Almost as well known for his blunt, take-no-prisoners
manner of speaking as for his theological insights, Albert was a
vehement opponent of heresy, but his interest in Aristotelian
thought extended far beyond the specific doctrines needed to
conduct disputations with the Cathars or the Joachimites. A man
of enormous energy, he "conceived the almost fantastic plan of
making the complete works of Aristotle, with their wholly new
theory of reality, accessible to the Latin West," and carried it out
by commenting on all of the Philosopher's extant books.[17] Albert's own theological writings were equally voluminous, dealing

with a wide range of doctrinal issues. But some of his most memorable work was Aristotelian in quite another sense, for the blunt Swabian was an extraordinary observer and collector—the most accomplished botanist and zoologist of his day, and a pioneer in the methods of empirical research.

Albert "describes an apple from peel to core," remarks one close student of his work.

> He describes with the greatest precision the "evergreen leathery leaves" of the mistletoe.... He tells which spiders spin webs and where ... and which spiders catch their prey by leaping upon it. He distinguishes between thorns and spikes. He knows, because he has discovered this by tasting, that the sap of trees is bitterest in the roots, and that the bee's abdomen contains a transparent little sac with a subtle taste of honey. He points out that the eel does not live on mud, as Aristotle maintains ... quite often he corrects Aristotle in this way, that is, by referring back to experience.[18]

Especially for a Dominican, this passionate curiosity about the details of nature was something new. Historically, it could be said to grow out of the antiheretical doctrines expounded by William of Auvergne and other defenders of the orthodox faith. Dominicans preaching against the Cathars found it useful to have specific data at their fingertips in order to demonstrate the unity, rationality, and beauty of the material world. For this reason, one of Albert's colleagues, Vincent of Beauvais (who also tutored the children of King Louis IX), compiled a kind of encyclopedia of natural science, metaphysics, and medicine which he called *Mirror of Nature*—a reference work much used by traveling Dominican debaters.[19] But Albert's evident delight in natural phenomena, as well as his insistence on getting the facts right, transcended the order's more utilitarian motives.

Like Aristotle, the German polymath was fascinated by the concrete particulars of nature—the components of structure and process that he felt one must accurately and sensitively observe before deriving general principles from them. With characteristic asperity, he condemned the pseudo-scientists who thought that they could reason from abstract principles to particular facts, or who retailed common myths as common knowledge. "The phoenix is a bird of Eastern Arabia," he remarked acidly, "so we learn from the writings of those who do their researches more in mystical theology than in nature."[20] The universe as a whole, of course, could be derived from the most general principle of all—the Creator—but when it came to understanding the particulars, Albert maintained that "only experience provides certainty."[21] He insisted, therefore, that research into natural processes should proceed without being diverted by irrelevant theological considerations. The material world that we study is, in every detail, the creation of God. But creation means that God gives each created thing its own reality or being. Therefore, our religious duty is to understand things as they really are—a task that cannot be accomplished through the use of scholastic logic. "As far as I am concerned," Albert announced, sounding very much like a modern empiricist, "I abhor logical arguments in those sciences which have to do with things."[22]

Interestingly, this determination to analyze nature as a scientist and divine matters as a theologian led the Dominican theorist to give each realm of inquiry its own proper space and method, hence, to some extent, to separate them. In Albert's view, there could be no conflict between the truths discoverable by empirical research, logical reasoning, and Scriptural interpretation. To him, the idea of a multiplicity of inconsistent truths (like a multiplicity of gods) was inconceivable. But his attempt to disentangle the methods of science from those of religion sometimes produced surprising results. In commenting on Aristotle's book *On the Heav-*

ens, for example, Albert takes note of Aristotle's belief that the sphere of the heavens, like the universe as a whole, is eternal. Nevertheless, he points out matter-of-factly, there are other "opinions" as well:

> Another opinion was that of Plato who says that the heaven was derived from the first cause by creation from nothing, and this opinion is also the opinion of the three laws, namely of the Jews, Christians, and Saracens. And thus they say that the heaven is generated, but not from something. But with regard to this opinion, it is not relevant for us to treat it here.[23]

Albert misstates Plato's position here, but this is of little importance. His statement is remarkable, both because it refers to Aristotle's views and the Judeo-Christian-Islamic doctrine as "opinions," and because he refuses to resolve the issue "here." Now there is no doubt at all which "opinion" he favors. Obviously, he is one of the Christians to whom he refers with such apparent detachment in his comment. But he clearly feels that an essay explaining Aristotle's cosmological views is not the place for a theological discussion. (As Thomas Aquinas was to say much later, somewhat overstating the matter, "I don't see what one's interpretation of the text of Aristotle has to do with the teaching of the faith."[24]) Similarly, when discussing the much debated question of whether there could be more than one universe, Albert concludes, as Aristotle did, "that it is impossible that there be several worlds." But he quickly adds that he is talking only about what is impossible in nature, for "there is a great difference between what God can do by means of his absolute power and what can be done in nature [or by nature]." The proper concern of natural science is not what God could do if he wished, but what he has done: that is, what happens in the world "according to the inherent causes of nature."[25]

This notion of "dual causation"—the idea that a creative God causes the things of the world to operate as causes in themselves—was to become one of the principal doctrines used by Dominican theologians like Aquinas to reconcile science with religion. The idea has had a long life. One encounters it in our own time, for example, when believers in God who also subscribe to the Darwinian theory of natural selection argue that the capacity to evolve life was built into the universe by its Creator.[26] According to others, however, this approach creates more problems than it solves, since it attributes the ideas of human researchers to God, unacceptably distances the Creator from the natural universe, and does not explain how we know the truths of religion, as opposed to those of science. All these criticisms (and more) were voiced by Albert's most formidable critic, who came to lecture in Paris at around the same time that he did. Freshly arrived from Oxford, where he had sat at the feet of the great theologian-scientist Robert Grosseteste, young Roger Bacon soon had the whole university talking about his brilliant and eccentric teaching.

Bacon was probably the first master in more than thirty years to lecture on Aristotle in the faculty of arts—another indication of the gradual fading of the ban.[27] Despite his youth, the English scholar was even more self-assured than Albert the Great, and equally frank. In presuming to lecture on Aristotelian science, he remarked caustically, Albert was attempting to teach what he had not yet learned.[28] Bacon may not have been the greatest genius of his time—that honor is generally accorded to Thomas Aquinas—but he was probably the most learned man in Europe, as well as one of the most imaginative thinkers in history. He believed that one could not understand Aristotle and the Bible without knowing Greek, Arabic, Spanish, Hebrew, Aramaic, and several other languages, all of which he had mastered while still in his teens. He was certain that scientific knowledge would someday give humanity mastery over nature, and envisioned "the technical world of the future: ships without oarsmen, submarines, 'automobiles', aeroplanes, small magical gadgets for releasing oneself from prison, magical fetters (for use on other people) and devices for walking on water."[29] Bacon mapped a sea route from Spain to the Indies, experimented with light, did theoretical work in geometry, and may have dabbled in what some called magic. Until an even younger Bonaventure came of age in the 1250s, he was the leading intellectual voice of the Franciscan movement.

Roger Bacon had come under the influence of the Order of Friars Minor while at Oxford, or perhaps even earlier. (Little is known of his youth, but he may have been raised in a Franciscan convent.) He did not join the order formally until after arriving in Paris, and his relations with his superiors afterward were never easy. Later on, after publishing several essays without receiving the required permission, he was commanded to cease publishing—a ban he violated by sending his *Opus Maius* (*Major Work*) privately to Pope Clement IV at the pontiff's request. Some think that he was punished, perhaps even imprisoned, because of his sympathies for the Joachimite wing of the Franciscan movement, later to be known as the "Spirituals," a radical group that criticized the worldliness and corruption of the Church (including the Franciscan leadership), and that anticipated the coming of the Third Age of the Holy Spirit.[30] Bacon's views on history and society were probably more extreme than those of most of his brethren, but many shared his conviction that the Dominicans were too cerebral and "academic" in their theology, too close to the sources of power in the Church, and too comfortable with the status quo in the university and the world. Bacon's response to the Dominicans' genial worldliness was a typically Franciscan combination of otherworldly spiritual values and "hard science."

Bacon did not oppose Albert's natural philosophy in every respect. He agreed with the German master that in describing the workings of nature there is no substitute for direct experience. He also agreed with Albert's rather un-Aristotelian insistence on the usefulness of mathematics to an understanding of natural processes. What most displeased him was the older man's failure (as he saw it) to achieve a genuine reconciliation of natural science with Christianity. On the one hand, he argued, this was because the Dominicans were not scientific enough. What was needed was analysis, not just description; testable theories, not just sweeping generalities; experimentation, not just observation. On the other hand, the Dominican approach seemed overly intellectual and essentially soulless. The argument that God operated through secondary causes, so that Albert's bees and flowers were naturally equipped to play their parts in the ecological order, might be useful in disputing against the Cathars, but how did it bring Christian believers closer to God? Albert and his colleagues were outstanding intellectuals. Fine. But Francis of Assisi was the first man in history to receive the gift of the stigmata. Two years before his death in 1226, he had experienced Christ personally in the form of a beatific vision that left him with the wounds of nails in his hands and feet, and a bleeding wound on his right side.[31] What use was intellectual inquiry if it did not lead, in the end, to union with God?

For Bacon and other Franciscans, the link between the supernatural and the natural, the realm of religious experience and the world of scientific experimentation, was Light. The "gate and the key" of all the sciences, said Bacon, was "mathematics, which the saints discovered at the beginning of the world . . . and which has always been used by all the saints and sages more than all other sciences."[32] But the treasure chest to be unlocked by this key—"the flower of the whole of philosophy"—was the science of light, later to be called optics but known as "perspective" in Bacon's time. Basing himself in Grosseteste's theory that objects in the universe give off powerful images (or "species") of themselves in the form of rays of light, the young Franciscan developed an accurate understanding of the eye as the receptor rather than the sender of these images.[33] He hypothesized that light rays enter the pupil in straight lines falling perpendicularly on the eye, and reasoned that the speed of light must be finite, although almost unimaginably fast. He also dissected animal eyes and designed optical experiments in an attempt to verify his theories, although the results of these efforts are unknown.

All of this sounds up-to-date enough to have earned Bacon the reputation, in some quarters, of being the first modern scientist. The claim is far from silly, since from the sixteenth century onward, many of Europe's greatest scientists embraced his and Grosseteste's concept of mathematics as the hidden language of nature, their quest to make science more analytical and experimental, and their conviction that the study of light could unlock other secrets of the universe. At the same time, however, it is clear that Bacon viewed science as a quintessentially religious enterprise.[34] He believed that mathematics (by which he meant geometry) gave access to the mind of the Creator, and that light was the purest expression of the Holy Spirit. For Bacon and other Franciscans, this was no mere metaphor. Light was not simply one natural phenomenon among many; it was "God in operation"—the visible manifestation of God's spiritual power. Light was the force that caused the activities of other natural substances, the primary "form" or source of intelligibility, and the divine "illumination" that made human knowledge possible.[35] It was also the wellspring of goodness, for had not God made light before anything else in the universe and declared that it was good? To know light scientifically, therefore, was a step on the road to knowing God personally. Bacon's "perspective" was the intellectual preparation for the mystical ascent to God epitomized by Saint Francis's experience on the mountain.

Were the Englishman's views more "advanced" than those of his opponents? Or were they (as the Dominicans charged) dangerous throwbacks to the pre-Aristotelian past? The answer seems to be "Both." In searching for mathematical formulas that would explain natural phenomena, and in calling for an experimental method, Bacon seemed to be peering into the future. But "experiment" had connotations in Bacon's time that it does not have in our own:

> It is important to remind ourselves that scientific experiment was at this time still deeply entangled in magic and sorcery; experiments were still thoroughly Faustian—trials perhaps, but trials which led to the temptation of good and evil spirits, formulations maybe, but as likely as not ending with magical formulae. This was so in Bacon's time, and things were still much the same in the time of Leonardo da Vinci. Here for example, is Bacon posing a "scientific" problem: "If deer, eagles, and snakes can prolong their lives by using toads and stones, why should the discovery of an elixir of life be denied to mankind?"[36]

More important, from the Dominican standpoint, the Franciscans' spiritualization of light was deeply regressive. It took a large step back from Aristotle, who viewed light simply as a property of certain substances, not as pure form or spirit, and certainly not as a force causing less spiritual objects in the universe to behave as they do. As Albert and his young friend Thomas Aquinas saw it, the theory of light as a universal cause—a mystical belief that could not be verified by experiment or observation—turned science from the study of particular causes into a study of occult relationships. Nor did they agree that human knowledge was the result of divine "illumination." Rather, knowledge was a product of the reason that the Creator had made part of man's natural endowment. Franciscan teachers like Roger Bacon lectured on Aristotle and framed their theories in Aristotelian language, but the essence of their work was Neoplatonic mysticism, which revived the outmoded distinction between matter and spirit. Bacon had accused his opponents of splitting science from religion and removing God from active involvement in the universe. With equal justification, they could accuse him of mystifying science and limiting God's boundless creativity. To divinize part of nature inevitably degraded the rest. The teaching of Aristotle's most precious to Christianity (and the most effective answer to dualists of all sorts) was that *all* of nature bears God's stamp and is worth man's study—even, as Aristotle said, the inner parts of animals.

Although the issues in contention would change over time, the debate between Dominican and Franciscan theologians continued for decades, escalating sharply in the 1270s and even more in the early years of the fourteenth century. One of the most striking features of the conflict, however, is that it did not represent a war between "science" and "religion." Neither side questioned the fundamentals of the Christian faith. Not until the appearance of a group of radical Aristotelians at the University of Paris in the 1260s could a major participant even be accused of being antireligious. Nor did either side take the position, associated with certain modern "fundamentalisms," that scientific inquiry is inherently hostile to religious faith. What each party to the controversy said—and sincerely believed—was that faith must at all costs be preserved. What each proposed was a method of reconciling committed Christians to the material world and the inevitable progress of science. Especially after Thomas Aquinas became the leading Dominican theologian, the Order of Friars Preachers welcomed Aristotle's natural philosophy with open arms, but insisted on putting it in the broader context of a revised Christian theology. Being free to be an Aristotelian made Aquinas "even more of a theologian; more of an orthodox theologian; more of a dogmatist, in having recovered through Aristotle the most defiant of all dogmas, the wedding of God with Man and therefore with Matter."[37] The Franciscans took a less welcoming stance toward Aristotle (and toward matter), but they also insisted that his science could be accepted if its assumptions about nature were revised.

The belief shared by virtually all medieval scholars that, in case of conflict, faith trumped reason clearly had limiting effects on scientific inquiry. For example, one fourteenth-century Schoolman made a good case for the rotation of the earth on its axis, but refused to affirm an idea that seemed to conflict with established interpretations of the Bible (Psalm 92:1: "For God hath established the world, which shall not be moved"). For the most part, however, the attitude of Catholic intellectuals toward scientific research was remarkably sanguine. Although they agreed that the faith must at all costs be preserved, both Dominicans and Franciscans, teaching friars and secular masters, assumed that what the researchers were discovering by using their senses and their reason was real, and that religion would have to come to terms with it. The great issue, in other words, was not whether inquiring into nature's workings was a good thing or a bad thing. It was a good thing, since both reason and nature were from God. The issue was how to define the proper territory and boundaries of the religious and scientific ("philosophical") modes of inquiry, and how to establish a healthy relationship between them. As Aquinas was to say later, it was how to embrace both realms of knowledge fully in one harmonious vision. As a result, no matter how intense controversies within the university became—and they were about to become very intense—there was never any question of abandoning the investigation of nature. "Natural philosophy" was here to stay.

IN 1248, ALBERT THE GREAT left Paris for Cologne, where his order had commanded him to establish a new school. He was joined on his journey by his student Thomas Aquinas, still a Dominican in training, but one already demonstrating a remarkable mastery of Aristotelian thought and a precocious talent for theological speculation. Thomas's gifts were not obvious to everyone. According to one story, the tall, heavy-set young man was so silent in classes that the other students took to calling him the "Dumb Ox." Upon hearing several of his own students use the epithet, Albert is said to have rounded on them, crying, "You call him a Dumb Ox; I tell you this Dumb Ox shall bellow so loud that his bellowings will fill the world."[38]

As the story suggests, the older man's relations with this hulking wunderkind were warm, even paternal. In part, this may have been because Thomas's own family history had been so stormy. His father, Count Landulf, an Italian nobleman with estates in the hill country between Naples and Rome, had sent his clever son to be educated by the monks at nearby Monte Cassino, and then to the university founded in Naples a decade or so earlier by the German emperor (then ruler of Sicily), Frederick II. Ideas flowed freely at the university, which was exposed to the cultural currents emanating from the Arab world as well as from Bologna, Paris, and Oxford, and where Aristotle's works could be freely studied. Thomas's father, who was continually embroiled in imperial and papal politics, expected him to climb the ecclesiastical ladder rapidly — to become an abbot or a bishop and a powerful figure in society. One can imagine his rage upon discovering that the precocious teenager had been "seduced" by Dominican friars at their convent in Naples, and that he was planning to join the mendicant Order of Friars Preachers.

His son — a penniless, wandering, black-robed fanatic? Never! Exercising his fancied rights as a feudal lord and Roman paterfamilias, Landulf demanded that Thomas return home. When the boy demurred, his Dominican ally, John of Saint Julian, told him to saddle his horse and make for the order's convent in Rome, from which he would be taken by the organization's director-general to Paris. Somehow, though, word of the adventure leaked out, and Thomas's parents were forewarned. According to tradition, it was his mother, Countess Theodora, who sent his two brothers (both imperial officers) to capture him before he reached Rome and to bring him to his senses. The brothers ran him down, imprisoned him in one of the family's castles, and held him there for almost two years while his parents waited for him to relent. Thomas later recalled that, in order to break his will, they sent him a "temptress" whose advances, with the help of God, he resisted, driving her away with a burning stick from the fire. He was far more enchanted with the books that his sister smuggled into the fortress, including the Bible, Peter Lombard's *Sentences*, ... and Aristotle's *Metaphysics*. When his family finally gave in to his oxlike will (and to pressure from high Church officials) and released him, he went straight to the Dominicans in Paris, where the brothers at Saint-Jacques swore that he had learned more in prison than they had in their school.

Albert arrived soon afterward. Recognizing the taciturn young man's talent and, perhaps, his need for a trusted protector, the German master took him under his wing. Thomas studied with Albert for eight years, first in Paris and then in Cologne. It was at his master's urging that he returned to Paris in 1252 to complete his studies and begin his own career as a teacher and writer. He knew, of course, that he would be involved in intellectual controversies at the university, especially with the Franciscans, who were then led by a fellow Italian some four year his senior, the redoubtable and multitalented Bonaventure. But he had no idea that he was walking into a violent confrontation that would unite the Franciscan and Dominicans in battle against a host of common enemies.

Aquinas had probably gotten to know Bonaventure during his early years in Paris. He understood that the Franciscan friar, a much more polished and sophisticated theologian than Roger Bacon, wanted to close the gap between Franciscan mysticism and the philosophical discourse of the schools. Bonaventure and his colleagues were especially disturbed by Aristotle's insistence that, although God is the First Cause of everything that exists, natural beings have their own causes and effects that operate without divine participation or intervention. To counteract this doctrine, which seemed to lead toward a godless universe, Bonaventure replaced certain basic concepts of Aristotle with ideas derived from the Neoplatonists, Saint Augustine, and Avicenna. Of course, he denied the eternity of the world, a doctrine which he declared to be logically absurd. (Thomas denied it, too, although he did not think it absurd.) But he also proposed a series of "amendments" to the definitions of form, matter, substance, and causation whose effect was to make God an immediate participant in every natural event—a divine cause operating actively behind each natural cause. For example, while most Aristotelians would attribute the development of an organism—a tree's leaves turning brown, say—to the organism's natural form, Bonaventure maintained that it was the result of "seminal" tendencies built into that particular tree's matter by God. He also asserted that God had created a purely spiritual matter out of which substances like angels and souls were made, and that light was a special substance—not just a medium of sight but of knowledge.[39]

Bonaventure and his English student John Peckham believed that by making philosophical sense of Franciscan beliefs, they could forge a conservative consensus that would take a more cautious approach to Aristotle and avoid a dangerous split between religion and science. To Aquinas, on the other hand, the measures proposed by the Franciscans made for bad religion and bad science.

Aristotle's view of nature was perfectly adequate as far as it went, Thomas insisted, and should not be tampered with by spiritualizing matter, adding supernatural to natural causes, or anything of the sort. Where the Philosopher fell short—seriously short— was in failing to recognize that all created things, with their built-in tendencies to behave or develop according to their natures, owe their entire being to God. God did not create things once upon a time and then step back while nature took over. Creation is constant. As Boethius, Augustine, and Bonaventure himself recognized, it does not take place in time at all. There is simply no inconsistency between God's eternal sovereignty over the entire universe and the potency of natural causes in time. One can therefore study nature as a "pure" scientist while remaining entirely within the tradition of Christian faith.

The great theme that runs throughout Aquinas's epochal work is that "grace does not abolish nature, but completes it."[40] There can be no conflict between religion and natural science, between loving the Creator and understanding his creation, so long as one correctly defines and demarcates both realms of thought. Thomas startled his contemporaries and initially earned the reputation of being a dangerous radical by extending the realm of reason deep into the territory of theology and creating what he called a "natural theology." According to him, there are only three doctrines that cannot be proved by using natural reason: the creation of the universe from nothing, God's nature as a Trinity, and Jesus Christ's role in man's salvation. These truths, which cannot be deduced from experience, depend on faith alone. But other theological doctrines, even the existence of God, as well as the Creator's immateriality, perfection, goodness, knowledge, and other attributes, can be arrived at by using one's reason to analyze and generalize from observed data.[41] Through reason, not just Revelation, we can discover the moral standards that God requires of us in this life and our need for knowledge of Him in the afterlife.[42] Bonaventure meant well, but he did not understand that undermining the autonomy of nature also undermines the autonomy of natural reason. According to Aquinas, this is why compromises such as those proposed by the conservatives produce bad religion as well as bad science.

Thomas had overcome his shyness about speaking out and was just beginning to engage Bonaventure in public debate when the situation at the University of Paris was transformed almost beyond recognition. The change began happily enough, with the end of the ban on studying Aristotle's natural philosophy. Even before Thomas left Paris for Cologne, the prohibition had become a dead letter in the school of theology, and was clearly losing strength in the faculty of arts as well. In the same year that he returned to Saint-Jacques, the masters and students of the English "nation" reorganized the liberal arts curriculum to require all candidates for master's degrees to demonstrate knowledge of several previously forbidden books, including Aristotle's controversial treatise *On the Soul*. Three years later, the entire arts faculty voted to make all of the Philosopher's known works required reading for undergraduate as well as graduate students. Newly translated commentaries, especially those of the Muslim scholar Averroës, were also assigned to eager students. "And now," one eminent historian remarks, "Aristotle is master of the house."

> The old school of liberal arts had long been a very active centre of dialectical and grammatical studies; from now on it was to be a centre of philosophical research in the widest sense of the term. Having been so long debarred from the study of natural philosophy and metaphysics, the members of the Arts Faculty set to work with all the more zeal in order to make up for lost time.[43]

Within a decade, the entry of this new group of masters into the field previously dominated by Dominican and Franciscan theologians would have unexpected and disturbing results. But even before the effects of this change could be felt, a new controversy—or, rather, an old controversy reborn—shook the university to its foundations. We have already noted the tendency on the part of the "secular" masters and doctors (meaning those not in orders) to consider the teaching friars interlopers—representatives of the pope, the king, and other outside authorities inclined to interfere with the independence of the university. For students and teachers to be members of an order with power to regulate every detail of their lives meant that they were part of a different corporate community, one with its own sponsors, its own agenda, and its own sources of funding. There was class antagonism here, since a great many students and teachers were poor and suffered real hardship in order to remain at the university, particularly in the cold winter months. Watching the well-funded, well-fed friars mount the ladder of academic success must have galled them no end. The secular masters and students were not the only group, however, to suffer economic hardship and blame it on the friars. In fact, economic distress among key groups outside the university had helped generate a situation the authorities dreaded and that they ordinarily made every effort to avoid: a conflict within the university linked to a conflict in the society at large.

For a time, the mendicant friars had been heroes, supported not only by popes and princes but also by people of all social classes who sought their counsel and gave them alms. They had, after all, abandoned their property and hopes of worldly advancement and embraced the apostolic way of life in order to do battle against the heretics (in the case of the Dominicans) or to aid the poor and the spiritually impoverished (which was the Franciscans' mission). In the years since Dominic's and Francis's deaths, however, their popularity had waned. While individual

friars remained poor, many were far from powerless, and their orders were becoming quite wealthy. This increase in communal
wealth and political influence did not disturb many Dominicans,
because it could be seen as a fulfillment of that order's mission to
become a powerful force for Catholic education and the extir-
pation of heresy. Many outsiders, however, linked the Order of
Friars Preachers' power to the Inquisition, which had become extremely unpopular in many parts of Europe, or to the papacy,
whose political machinations aroused bitter opposition in regions subject to long-running disputes between popes and secular
princes. (The French, in particular, were frequently at odds with
Rome.) Because of their work with the poor, the Franciscans
were better liked by the public, but their collective wealth and
bureaucratic organization triggered a bitter internal conflict between the order's "Spiritual" and "Relaxed" wings—a dispute
that Bonaventure tried to resolve when he became the Franciscans' minister-general.

Even the Order of Friars Minor, however, became the target
of hatred in some quarters because of a second change in the
mendicants' fortunes—the grant of lucrative privileges previously reserved for the "secular" clergy. The popes not only permitted the friars to preach but also exempted them from the
jurisdiction of local bishops and allowed them to hear confessions
and bury the dead, the last, in particular, an activity that produced
plentiful fees for the clergy. From poor village priests to powerful
bishops, this meant that valuable sources of income were being
drained into the coffers of the orders, and this at a time when living standards in Europe, although slowly rising, were constantly
threatened by a population explosion, bad harvests, and sharp increases in prices, taxes, and debts.[44] It seemed that Peter was being
robbed to pay Paul, and, rather than being humbly grateful for
these privileges, the friars were portrayed (by their enemies, to be

sure) as arrogant and greedy. A popular rhyme perfectly catches
the scorn inspired by these aggressive "Beggars":

> Hark, hark, the dogs do bark,
> The Beggars are coming to town;
> Some in rags, and some in jags,
> And some in velvet gown.[45]

As was so often the case in those days, the immediate trigger of
open hostilities between the friars and the secular masters was a
"town-gown" dispute. There was already bad blood between the
consortium of masters, which excluded the teaching friars from its
membership, and the Dominican order. In 1252, led by the angry
and formidable polemicist (and master of theology) William of
Saint-Amour, the masters insisted that one of the two Dominican
chairs of theology be eliminated. The Franciscans, who had only
one chair, nevertheless saw the demand as a threat to their position
and formed a bloc with the Dominicans, thus incurring Saint-
Amour's wrath as well. In the next term the conflict became considerably more heated. After a fracas in town in which one student was
killed and several others wounded by one of the city guards, the
arts masters passed a statute demanding satisfaction from the city
and threatening to close the university as they had done in 1229.
They brought around an oath of allegiance and solidarity requiring
all teachers to abide by such statutes, even if they were commanded
to strike. Perhaps the secular masters knew that the friars, who felt
obliged to continue teaching in their own schools, would decline to
sign...but decline they did. Protests and demonstrations against
them broke out, with their opponents outside the university joining
the crowds inside. The university went on strike, and angry crowds
forced the friars to suspend their teaching as well.

Warned that matters were getting out of hand, Pope Innocent
IV issued a bull designed to pacify the friars' external opponents
by depriving the mendicants of their preaching, confessional, and

burial privileges. The pope died soon afterward, however, and the first act of his successor, Pope Alexander IV, was to suspend the decree, order the university not to act against the friars, and promise a full investigation of all parties' complaints. It is not clear whether the Dominicans and Franciscans were able to resume teaching at this point, but their leaders must have breathed a collective sigh of relief. They could still count on the crucial support of the pope against their academic and ecclesiastical enemies. But they could not necessarily control their own brethren, especially those of the Franciscan "left"—the Joachimites who believed that the secular clergy were corrupt and would be replaced in the coming Third Age of the Holy Spirit by a purer priesthood, that is, by themselves.

In 1254, the Franciscan master Gerard published a book expressing these views, whereupon William of Saint-Amour preached a sermon before a great crowd of supporters violently denouncing both the book and the arrogant orders that, in his view, had spawned such prideful, irreligious opinions. William followed up his sermon with a diatribe entitled *On the Dangers of the New Times,* charging that evil men had appeared in the universities and in society, as predicted by Saint Paul in his second letter to Timothy:

> People will be self-centered and grasping; boastful, arrogant and rude; disobedient to their parents, ungrateful, irreligious; heartless and unappeasable; they will be slanderers, profligates, savages, and enemies of everything that is good; they will be treacherous and reckless and demented by pride, preferring their own pleasure to God. They will keep up the outward appearance of religion but will have rejected the inner power of it. Have nothing to do with people like that.[46]

In effect, although William did not mention the Dominicans and Franciscans by name, he had accused the friars of being precursors of the Antichrist. He ridiculed their intellectual pretensions, excoriated their clannishness, blasted their morals, and declared that their position as "wealthy beggars" was both hypocritical and anti-Christian. The overwrought document may have inflamed crowds to close the friars' schools again, but it did his cause no lasting good. Aquinas (who was now working in concert with Bonaventure and the Franciscans) answered the tract with one of his own, calmly defending the orthodoxy of the orders. In 1255, Pope Alexander annulled the antimendicant statutes and ordered the university to cease its campaign against the friars on pain of excommunication. The university's answer was to dissolve itself formally, an act that turned out to be an empty gesture. The following year, the pope condemned William's book and convinced the king to exile the irate theologian from France.

Even this intervention did not end the conflict immediately. Saint-Amour would later write an even angrier tract, which both Thomas and Bonaventure answered with essays of their own. But the university was finally forced to bend to the papal will. In 1257, both theologians were accepted by the consortium of masters and (tradition says, on the same day) assumed the position of doctor of theology. During the next few years, through the good offices of the papacy, compromises were worked out, first with the Franciscans and then with the Dominicans, by which the university accepted the teaching friars as part of the consortium of masters but excluded them from teaching in the faculty of arts and limited their participation in university decision making. The privileges that the secular priests and bishops had objected to were curtailed by Pope Boniface VIII in 1300, and the university's oath of obedience was finally accepted by the teaching friars in 1318.

After the crisis of the 1250s, a period of relative calm descended on the University of Paris. Thomas Aquinas had no idea, of course, that he would not live to an old age, but he wrote and lectured as if time were fleeting, producing the great body of work that would one day earn him the title of "Angelic Doctor" and a reputation, even outside the Church, as the most powerful Western thinker between Saint Augustine and Sir Isaac Newton. Bonaventure left Paris in the year of his academic promotion to become minister-general of the Franciscan order, but he and Thomas would continue to engage in sharp debate modulated by deep friendship and mutual respect. According to one story, Thomas and several companions came to visit Bonaventure in later years, when the future "Seraphic Doctor" was writing his biography of Saint Francis. Finding his friend in his study in a state of ecstatic contemplation, Thomas turned to his associates and indicated that they should postpone their visit. "Let us leave one saint to write about another," he said.

Early in the 1260s, the situation at Paris had apparently returned to normal. Aquinas had made several trips to Italy at the pope's request, and he and his associates were keeping up the debate over Aristotle with Bonaventure's successor, the future archbishop of Canterbury, John Peckham. But appearances are deceiving. The masters of arts, most of whom had never cared much for either Bonaventure or Aquinas, were reading Aristotle with eyes of their own, and paying particular attention to the commentaries of the Muslim thinker Averroës. At around the same time that Thomas was coming into his own as a teacher of theology, a new student joined the Picard "nation," composed of young men from the Low Countries, and began to assert himself as a leader in the ongoing turf battles between the Picards and the French. The student was Siger de Brabant, and he soon turned his attention from student squabbles to something far more significant: the growing controversy over a new, radical interpretation of Aristotle. Suddenly everyone at the university was taking sides in a struggle even more acrimonious than the battles involving the friars. In a little while, Siger's involvement in this controversy would plunge Thomas Aquinas into the most difficult fight of his life.

CHAPTER SIX

"*This* Man Understands"

THE GREAT DEBATE
AT THE UNIVERSITY OF PARIS

EVERYONE HAS heard of Saint Thomas Aquinas. Many people recognize the name of his great adversary and friend, Saint Bonaventure. But hardly anyone remembers Siger de Brabant, although his role was as important as that of the two saints in the struggles that shaped Western attitudes toward faith and reason.

According to one distinguished historian, Siger "was gifted with undeniable intellectual ability; he was a profound thinker, a tried logician, and an assiduous reader of the philosophers; he loved clarity and precision. . . . A manuscript of the ancient college of the Sorbonne calls him *Sigerus Magnus* [Siger the Great], and Dante places him in paradise in the company of the twelve sages, by the side of St. Thomas."[1] Since Siger was assuredly no saint—in fact, many considered him the most dangerous heretic in Europe—the praise that Dante gives him has long mystified readers of *The Divine Comedy*. On his poetic tour of Paradise,

Dante imagines Saint Thomas introducing him to eleven great souls, including Albert the Great, Solomon the Wise, Boethius, Saint Isidore, and . . . Siger de Brabant. Of Siger he says:

> This one, to whom you now turn your glance,
> Is the light of a spirit whose lofty thinking
> Made death seem slow to arrive.
> It is the eternal light of Siger,
> Who, lecturing in the Street of Straw,
> Deduced much-envied truths.[4]

Some commentators have speculated that this verse reflects Dante's radical streak—his love of unfettered reasoning and his impatience with papal censorship. Others have tied the praise to Siger's repeated professions of Christian faith (there are no heretics in Dante's Paradise) and his reported reconciliation with Saint Thomas, or even to his tragic early death. The poet's motives remain opaque, but what is quite clear is the great weight that he accords to Siger's ideas and personality in a world struggling to define the relationship between Aristotelian science and Christian orthodoxy.

When we first meet Siger, however, it is not as a philosopher in heaven but as a leader of students at the University of Paris, and as a bit of a thug. Born in 1240, the future controversialist came from a French-speaking region in what is now Belgium, near the city of Liège. There he received his early education, and, at a certain point, became a canon of the city's cathedral. When he began his studies in Paris sometime around 1260, Siger joined the Picard nation, which was composed of students and masters from the Low Countries and certain other lands not included in the French, Norman, or Anglo-German nations. Combining the elements of a college, a fraternity, and a street gang, each of these associations offered its members courses, comradeship, mutual aid, and protection against the not inconsiderable dangers of life in the big city. Relations between the four nations were always tense and often rowdy, but they seem to have deteriorated sharply during the 1260s, perhaps because mitigation of the conflict with the friars deprived the liberal arts students of a common enemy.

The French nation, the largest and best organized of the groups, was a favorite target of the "foreigners." In 1266, the French admitted a student who was also claimed by Siger's nation, prompting a gang of Picard toughs to raid the French residential quarters, kidnap the young man, and beat up his would-be hosts rather badly. The latest of a series of such incidents, this was the last straw for the French, who broke off relations with the other nations, "seceded" from the university, and attempted to elect their own chancellor. An alarmed pope dispatched his legate to hear grievances on all sides and mediate a resolution of the conflict. Siger is mentioned in these complaints as a Picard leader who participated in an earlier kidnapping and in other disruptive acts (for example, breaking up a memorial service held by the French), but, aside from a warning, no action was taken against him, and peace was restored to the campus. The story does not demonstrate that Siger was a bad character, as some of his detractors have suggested. Student life was rough in Paris, and few young men escaped involvement in the nations' endless "wars." It does provide evidence, however, of a certain passionate combativeness that would later color Siger's tone in debate, a disinclination to be overawed by authority, and a personal magnetism that drew substantial numbers of comrades and supporters to his side.

Siger's first books began to appear in the late 1260s, after he became a master of arts, along with writings by other young masters who seem to have shared his views. The names of the "Sigerists" most often mentioned are those of Boethius of Dacia, Goswin of la Chapelle, and Bernier of Nivelles. Interestingly, many of these hard-edged, more uncompromising rationalists hailed from the Netherlands, northern Germany, and Scandinavia. It is as if the interpretation of Aristotle were moving away from the soft Mediterranean lands that first nurtured a blending of Greek, Arab, and Christian ideas, and toward those starker northern regions whose motto, in a phrase coined six centuries later by the ascetic Dane Søren Kierkegaard, might well be "Either/Or." Siger had a good many co-thinkers, but he was clearly their leader. The hallmark of his teaching was to present Aristotle's ideas about nature and human nature without attempting to reconcile them with traditional Christian beliefs. In fact, Siger seemed to relish the discontinuities between Aristotelian *scientia* and Christian faith. Among other things, he and his colleagues taught their students that, according to the Philosopher and his Arab interpreter Averroës, the world and the human race are eternal, the behavior of natural objects is governed by the laws of their nature, man's free will is limited by necessity, and all humans share a single active intellectual principle, which is a substance separate from their individual bodies.

The radicals' presentations were for the most part subtle and well reasoned. They frequently stated, with apparent sincerity, that if the conclusions of philosophy should conflict with those of faith, the doctrines of the Church must prevail.[3] Siger wrote:

> One should not try to investigate by reason those things which are above reason or to refute arguments for the contrary position. But since a philosopher, however great he may be, may err on many points, one ought not to deny the Catholic faith because of some philosophical argument, even though he does not know how to refute it.[4]

Boethius of Dacia agreed that "we incur foolishness by seeking a proof where none is possible or incur heresy by refusing to believe what ought to be held on faith."[5] Of course, a philosopher must be free to philosophize about every disputable issue, since his job is to teach "the natures of things." But there are not many occasions when science will clash with religion, since each mode of inquiry has its own proper sources and methods. "For the teaching of the philosophers depends upon demonstration and sure reasons possible in matters about which they speak, but faith depends upon any miracles and not on arguments."[6]

To the modern ear, this might sound reasonable, but it was the conservatives' nightmare come true. Siger and his comrades taught a number of doctrines that seemed to contradict the fundamental teachings of Christianity . . . and then they stopped. The question raised by angry critics like the Franciscan theologians William of Baglione and John Peckham, was what the Sigerists meant by this. What did it mean to teach pagan philosophy and then to stop? If the universe, including all the species in it, is eternal, then there never was a Creation or an Adam and Eve, nor can there be a Last Judgment. If all natural activities are governed exclusively by natural laws or tendencies, this leaves no room for divine providence and ordinary miracles like the Eucharist, much less the once-in-an-eternity miracles of Christ's incarnation, atonement, and resurrection. The doctrine that all people share one intellect (an idea associated with Averroës, and known as "monopsychism") seems clearly to negate the immortality of individual souls. And if free will is an illusion, what becomes of sin, grace, and the rewards or punishments of the afterlife? The conservatives were horrified by the idea that these propositions, backed by the enormous authority of the Philosopher, were being taught by members of the liberal arts faculty as scientific truth, with the truths of faith relegated to the realm of irrational belief. One can imagine them looking sidelong at Thomas Aquinas, shaking their heads, and muttering, "We *knew* that this would happen when Aquinas argued that Aristotle's doctrines were perfectly fine as far as they went. What if they are as far as anyone goes? What happens to Christianity then?"

The radical Aristotelians grouped around Siger and Boethius of Dacia were almost certainly a minority of the arts masters, although one historian writes that they had the support of "the most striking personalities and the most remarkable thinkers" on the faculty.[7] But their response to the theologians' attacks was not calculated to calm conservative fears. The radicals replied (with some justification) that they were not theology professors but teachers of the arts and sciences, which now included the entire Aristotelian corpus. They were neither qualified nor permitted to determine theological questions. Therefore, they simply taught Aristotle, along with the most significant interpretations of his natural philosophy and ethics by leading commentators, most of whom happened to be Arabs and Jews. The theologians could make whatever they wished of these doctrines; the job of the masters of arts was simply to present them.

As might be expected, this evasion further infuriated the critics. Why would the masters teach these doctrines if they could not vouch for their truth? Hadn't they, in fact, asserted repeatedly that they *were* true? In one of his essays, Siger answered the scholastic question, "Would the statement, 'man is an animal,' be true if there were no men?" by declaring that the question is absurd, since the human race, like the rest of the universe, is eternal. "This conclusion must be firmly held," he wrote, "since when it has been pondered, the intellect acquiesces and subsides. Away with verbal vanity in this matter lest it impede knowledge!"[8] Similarly, the radicals pointed out that natural science provides no evidence that bodies once dead can be resurrected, or that souls, even if immortal, can experience pain and pleasure in the afterlife. To the charge that such statements denied the fundamentals of

Christian belief, they repeated that while Aristotle's worldview accurately described the workings of nature, those who taught it had no intention of contradicting the higher truths of faith. Boethius of Dacia put it like this:

> There are many things in faith which cannot be demonstrated by reason, for instance that a dead body returns to life as the same individual and that a thing which is generated returns without generation [references to the Christian doctrine that the body is resurrected at the end of the world]. On the one hand, he who does not believe this is a heretic; on the other, he who seeks to know it by reason is a fool. . . . And since there are many points in these matters which faith posits and which cannot be investigated by human reason, therefore, where reason falls short, faith supplies the defect.[9]

In light of such statements (which recall Peter Abelard's impassioned "I would not wish . . . to be an Aristotle if it cuts me off from Christ"), most modern scholars acquit Siger and Boethius of the charge that they taught the scandalous doctrine of Double Truth. But their opponents were not so sure. Double Truth meant that a proposition could be true scientifically but false theologically, or the other way round, and that there was no way of using one type of truth to falsify the other type. This second point was crucial, since even Aquinas, the apostle of reason, admitted that a few unshakable doctrines of faith, such as the incarnation of God as man, were scientifically undemonstrable, and a few apparently reasonable this-worldly doctrines, like the eternity of the universe, were falsified by faith. But if both kinds of truth were equally true—if neither kind trumped the other in cases of conflict—Christian thinking would be in crisis. Not only would Double Truth produce logical contradictions (the same statement could be true and false simultaneously), in practice it would force people to choose between faith and reason. Shorn of their reasonableness, traditional religious doctrines might command the allegiance of the uneducated masses, the priesthood, and a few conservative intellectuals. But a great many educated Christians, trained to use their reason and to trust its results, would abandon or greatly modify their faith.

On the one hand, Double Truth threatened to produce rank secularism, or religion whittled down to a vague deism. On the other, it implied an orthodox religion echoing Tertullian's ancient credo—"I believe because it is absurd." This sort of split did take place in European society five centuries or so after the struggle described here.[10] Fearing that it was about to happen in their own time, some of Siger's contemporaries accused him of advocating the Double Truth doctrine. Pleased that it did eventually happen, a few modern writers have made the same attribution as a way of praising him. To one such historian, Siger is "the unequivocal champion of the autonomy of reason" who taught that "Religion was necessary for the masses, but not for educated people. Dogmas were beneficial for faith, but reason often taught the contrary."[11] According to the distinguished French medievalist Étienne Gilson, however, the radicals taught no such thing. "Not a single one among those men [Siger and company] would have ever admitted that two sets of conclusions, the one in philosophy, the other in theology, could be, at one and the same time, both absolutely contradictory and absolutely true."[12]

It seems, on reflection, that both authorities are right. The radical masters did not teach the doctrine of Double Truth, but there were tendencies in their thinking that led in that direction, and that, in one instance, at least, induced either Siger or one of his followers to cross the forbidden line. In 1270, Thomas Aquinas entered the fray with an attack on Siger's theory of the soul called *On There Being Only One Intellect*. At the very end of his essay,

Thomas quotes an unnamed radical as writing these words: "Through reason I conclude necessarily that intellect is numerically one, but I firmly hold the opposite by faith." This statement throws the normally unflappable Dominican into a rage. "Therefore," Aquinas snorts, "he thinks that faith is of things whose contrary can be necessarily concluded [that is, proved]. Since the only thing that can be necessarily concluded is a necessary truth whose opposite is false and impossible, it follows from this statement that faith is of the false and impossible, which not even God can bring about and the ears of the faithful cannot bear."[13] Thomas might have been equally irritated by Boethius of Dacia's statement that philosophy depends on reason, but faith on miracles. After all, wasn't the whole theological enterprise based on showing that faith was not "blind" but could be supported—most of the time, at least—by science and reason?

Gilson is undoubtedly right to say that the radicals saw the danger of Double Truth and ordinarily steered clear of it. But the very ambiguity of their position, combined with the fierce suspicion of their intentions evoked by their brash, youthful style and a growing conservative nervousness about the Aristotelian revolution in thinking, drove churchmen less judicious than Thomas to accuse Siger of actually advocating the most pernicious tendencies of his doctrine. A modern analogy comes to mind. After World War II and prior to the start of the Cold War, some Western liberals advocated a number of "progressive" policies that they thought would conduce to world peace and global justice. They proposed turning nuclear weapons and materials over to the United Nations, giving economic aid to the Soviet Union, taking a neutral position toward the combatants in the Chinese Revolution, and so forth. Some conservatives thought from the very beginning that these proposals were "Communist inspired" or that they revealed "Communist tendencies," but when the

Cold War actually began, it became common practice to accuse the former progressives of having advocated policies that were objectively pro-Communist, if not deliberately treasonous. When the progressives answered that they had not intended to strengthen Stalinism but only to eliminate the causes of war, they were accused of having been willfully blind to the destructive implications of their own doctrine. They had been "soft on Communism," which was now taken to be the same thing as being pro-Communist.[14]

By a similar logic, Siger and his comrades—even his liberal opponents—were considered to be "soft on secularism." In the thirteenth century, of course, secularism was not yet a coherent doctrine, much less an immediate threat to Christianity. The Catholic Church had no competitor in Europe (at least, not after the Cathars were destroyed), nor was there much risk that a handful of radical Aristotelians could provoke a major rebellion against established doctrines even if they had wanted to do so. Even so, high-ranking churchmen were extremely sensitive to the potentially subversive implications of the new learning, especially when the class on which their influence increasingly depended— the clerical intelligentsia—seemed vulnerable to heterodox teachings or inclined to split along doctrinal lines. The war against the Cathars was still a vivid memory; the Franciscan movement was deeply divided between its own radicals and conservatives; the secular masters remained hostile to the mendicant orders; and now the liberal arts masters (a substantial minority, at least) were developing ideas inimical to those of the theologians. It is not so surprising, therefore, to find officials like Stephen Tempier, the bishop of Paris, reacting very strongly—almost out of panic—to the development of radical currents in the arts faculty.

The ban on Aristotle's scientific works was by now a dead letter. Resurrecting it would only provoke disobedience and further inflame dissension at the university. But it might not be too late to ban specific doctrines based on those works by Siger and his "Averroistic" friends. Perhaps a healthy rebuke might be administered even to Thomas Aquinas, who had gone so far toward pure Aristotelianism that many considered him the father of this bastard doctrine. With such thoughts in mind (so far as we can determine them), Bishop Tempier convened a commission of conservative theologians to discuss how to respond to the radical threat. In December 1270, he made what he hoped would be a decisive move. For the first time in more than half a century, the bishop of Paris banned the teaching of certain Aristotelian and Averroist doctrines at Europe's greatest university.

The Condemnations of 1270 threw down the gauntlet to Siger de Brabant and his radical colleagues in the faculty of liberal arts. Tempier listed thirteen propositions that he condemned as false and heretical, declaring that anyone who taught them "knowingly" or "asserted" them as true was ipso facto excommunicated.[15] It went without saying that anyone who persisted in advocating the forbidden propositions would be subject to the processes and punishments of the Inquisition. The banned propositions reveal the major doctrines most offensive to the conservative theologians.[16] Some were associated with Averroës' theory of the soul and the doctrine of monopsychism: for example, "That there is numerically one and the same intellect for all humans," and "That this [statement] is false or improper: humans understand." It was now forbidden to maintain "That the soul separated [from the body] by death cannot suffer from bodily fire," or "That God cannot grant immortality and incorruption to a mortal and corruptible thing."[17] Other condemnations were directed against the Aristotelian theory of God as a passive Unmoved Mover: "That God does not know singulars"; "That God does not know things other than Himself"; and "That human acts are not ruled by the providence of God." Several were related to the doctrine that humans' free will is limited by necessity, either astrological or psychological.[18] And two, "That the world is eternal" and "That there never was a first human," were associated with the doctrine of the eternity of the world.

Which of these statements were "taught knowingly" or "asserted" by teachers at the University of Paris? It is impossible to say. Clearly, the radical masters taught that Aristotle had asserted a number of controversial propositions—for example, the eternity of the world—and they may also have argued that certain of these propositions were true, at least by the standards of natural philosophy. One can imagine discussions at the university in which topics like the meaning of soul's immortality and freedom of the will were debated. But it is inconceivable that Siger or any other teacher would deny God's providence or assert that "God does not know things other than Himself." Any master at the University of Paris presenting Aristotle's Unmoved Mover as the true God would find himself not only out of a job but very likely serving as fuel for one of the Inquisition's bonfires.

More problematical still was the legal effect of the condemnations. Since Aristotle's works remained the core of the liberal arts curriculum, the masters would be required to teach his ideas "knowingly," at least in the form of "According to the Philosopher, such and such is true." The real prohibition, then, was probably against asserting them as true, except with some appropriate qualification. With respect to the resurrection of the dead at the Last Judgment, for example, a master could teach that the proposition "Dead bodies cannot be regenerated" is true as a matter of mundane natural philosophy, but that the teachings of the Church reveal a higher truth: the coming of a Judgment Day at which this law of nature (among others) will be abrogated. The problem with masters making this sort of statement, however, was not only that it put them into the theology business but that such stock phrases might seem to offer little more than lip service to an established dogma. One could teach Aristotle and the commentators as before, simply adding lifeless formulas understood by both master and students to be necessary to avoid the wrath of the authorities, but not to be taken seriously.

To use another modern analogy, some masters may have handled Tempier's condemnations in the way that many scholars in the Communist nations handled prohibitions against discussing democracy or human rights during the 1970s and 1980s; that is, by making the required verbal bows to Marxism-Leninism while delivering messages whose subversive content was quite clear to their fellow teachers and students. We know little about how Siger and his followers adapted to the Condemnations of 1270. The best evidence that they did not abandon their prior beliefs entirely is that the controversy continued. In fact, the 1270s turned out to be the stormiest decade of the conflict, bringing new issues into dispute and new parties into the struggle. Another chapter in the conflict began with the dramatic return to the university of Thomas Aquinas.

WHEN THE IDEAS of Siger de Brabant became a cause célèbre in the mid-1260s, Aquinas was no longer at the University of Paris. He had left his teaching position a few years earlier to serve his order in Italy and had been busy establishing a new center for theological studies in Rome, completing his four-volume *Summa Contra Gentiles*, and beginning his *Summa Theologica*. Late in 1268, however, he received a summons from the Dominican director-general ordering him to return immediately to Paris to reassume his chair at the faculty of theology. There were several reasons for this unexpected (and very likely unwelcome) change. For one thing, the alliance between the Franciscans and

Dominicans engendered by their joint defense against the secular masters was breaking down. For another, powerful figures at the university, not only the Franciscans but also secular masters and even a few Dominicans, were saying that Siger de Brabant was merely spelling out the unorthodox implications of Aquinas's own theology. To these conservatives, the eruption of radicalism among the masters of arts proved that Aristotle's natural philosophy, embraced too enthusiastically, represented a serious threat to Christian orthodoxy. While they focused their main fire on Siger, their attention turned increasingly to the figure many held ultimately responsible for the radicals' excesses: the leader of the liberal Aristotelians, Thomas Aquinas.

Thomas returned to Paris to defend not only his own reputation but also that of the Dominican order, which considered him its theological champion. Unfortunately, he proved a far better theologian than an academic politician. As a master of theoretical disputation he had no peer, but in the Byzantine tangle of university politics, with its competition among liberal arts masters and theologians, mendicants and secular clerics, various student "nations," and the mendicant orders themselves, his tactical skills left something to be desired. One would not expect a man of his character and convictions to temporize or play a crafty game, but he seems to have bulled ahead without much regard for the consequences of his behavior. An example: Shortly after Thomas's return, the master of arts Gerard of Abbeville launched a bitter attack against the Franciscans on the grounds that their refusal to own property communally was unscriptural, "holier than thou," and foolish. Bonaventure and John Peckham, the new Franciscan professor of theology, vigorously defended their order's position, but Thomas had little sympathy for their views and said so. Adopting Aristotle's definition of practical virtue as a balance between extremes, he criticized the Franciscans' aversion to community property as excessively ascetic. Poverty does not make one holy, he insisted. Wealth is morally neutral; it all depends upon how one uses it.[19]

To men like John Peckham, this criticism was doubly infuriating. Not only did it break ranks with brother friars and lend support to the antimendicant forces at the university but it illustrated what many conservatives had been saying about Aquinas for some time: that he preferred Aristotle's worldly ethics to those of Saint Augustine and therefore tended to blur the all-important boundary between the sacred and the profane. No wonder radicals like Siger de Brabant felt that they could philosophize about nature without worrying about the consequences of their teaching for the faith!

Controversy swirled around Thomas's allegedly "unchristian" attitude toward worldly happiness. Traditionally, the Church had taught that man is born to suffer in this world, and that his only real hope for happiness is in heaven. But Aristotle had asserted that our earthbound existence offers many opportunities for joy, the most lasting and reliable of which is the joy of using our reason to learn and understand.[20] According to Thomas, the problem with this formulation was not that it was wrong but that it was incomplete. Since the human perspective is so limited, we can never hope to learn more than a tiny fraction of what there is to know, and we apprehend even that bit of knowledge "through a glass, darkly." We have a basic need to understand, and our inability to satisfy it by knowing more and knowing it fully makes us unhappy. Worldly happiness is therefore real but relative. Genuine happiness, which Aristotle, being a pagan, could not comprehend, means knowing God, the ground of all Being, and thereby seeing things as they really are. That is the knowledge for which we ultimately yearn, which we cannot obtain in this life, but which people of faith may finally achieve in heaven.[21]

How disconcerting for the traditionalists, to have Aquinas arrive at their own theological destination by such a worldly route. Instead of offering mankind the hope of heaven as a solace for earthly suffering, Thomas pictured an afterlife of which we have already had a foretaste, thanks to the relative happiness available to us right here. To Christians of the ascetic type, the idea must have smelled suspiciously like the Muslims' Garden of Allah. But to Thomas, it was the essence of Christianity to assume that human nature, like nature generally, moves by its own inherent principles of development toward God. Our destiny (Thomas would say, our "final cause") is heavenly, but our earthly home is not the realm of tears, vile bodies, and intellectual illusions described by Augustinian pessimists. The natural world is not in any respect evil. Ultimately, it is not even incomplete, since the nature of all things is to move continuously and harmoniously toward their completion in God.

Thomas applied this same reasoning (Aristotle corrected by Christianity, Augustine corrected by Aristotle) to the vexed questions of ethics and free will. Despite Adam's fall, he maintained, our natural reason and our free will equip us, with God's help, to act morally.[22] Even human social institutions, of which Augustine despaired in *The City of God*, are capable of becoming decent houses for the human spirit, since, as Aristotle says, "man is by nature a political animal."[23] And—here is where Thomas joined battle with both Siger and the Franciscans—the human being is not merely a soul temporarily inhabiting a corrupt and insignificant body. We are a fusion of soul with body that outlasts even death.

It is not surprising that the human soul should have become the most sharply disputed question of the decade, since the subject stands squarely on the boundary line between science (or natural philosophy) and religion. For Aristotle and his medieval readers, the soul was a perfectly suitable subject for scientific inquiry, since the Philosopher's *anima* was not merely some sort of ethereal "spirit," but included all the faculties that we would study under the headings of human physiology, psychology, and cognitive science: a capacity for nutrition, growth, and reproduction; a capacity to register and process sense impressions; and a peculiarly human capacity to understand things and to will them.[24] Aristotle's goal in his difficult and elusive treatise *De Anima* (*On the Soul*) was to explain the human soul on the basis of the same principles that apply to other subjects of natural philosophy. His interpreters, including Siger de Brabant, Thomas Aquinas, and Bonaventure, shared that ambition, but disagreed profoundly about the meaning of his work and how to coordinate it with Christian doctrine.[25] Siger's explosive commentary on *De Anima* appeared in 1269 or early 1270. Thomas answered with a closely reasoned, sometimes angry denunciation of the radicals' theory called *On There Being Only One Intellect*.[26] And that same year, John Peckham challenged Aquinas to defend his own theory of the soul before the massed students and teachers of the University of Paris.

What this tripartite dispute was *not* about was the question of whether human beings possess an immortal soul. All agreed that while some functions of the *anima* are too closely connected to the senses to survive the death of the body, a person's "rational soul" or intellect does survive. Interestingly, they asserted this not as a matter of religious dogma but because it seemed confirmed by reason. Even Aristotle, who was no Christian, had observed that "mind ... seems to be an independent substance implanted within the soul and to be incapable of being destroyed."[27] The Philosopher's conviction that there was something super-sensual and indestructible about the intellect was shared by virtually all medieval theologians, who were as enchanted by reason as he was. The problem was how to explain this scientifically, seeing that the thinking that we do, and whose effects in other people we observe, is always the activity of a living person. What is the intellect's relationship to the person who exercises it? And if it belongs to the person, what is the nature of its immortality?

Aristotle bitterly opposed the idea that the soul is an immortal substance trapped in an alien body, and that matter and spirit, body and soul, are at war with each other. He insisted, on the contrary, that the soul is the "form" or animating principle of the human being, which means that body and soul together form one integral substance. It is not the soul that thinks through the man, he declared, but the man who thinks through the soul.[28] Yet the man dies and the soul does not. How to explain this apparent anomaly? The radical answer came from Siger de Brabant, who borrowed much of it from Averroës. Essentially, Siger saved the unity of man's body and soul by redefining immortality as a collective, not an individual, end state. The intellect can survive while the man dies, he maintained, because it is not an integral part of the individual soul but a capacity external to us, although it acts within each person in a way that makes it seem to belong to that person. We understand easily enough that there is such a thing as "matter," although matter ordinarily appears in the shape of individual things. Why not admit that there is also such a thing as a nonindividualized "mind"—a common faculty that we exercise individually while we live, but that lives eternally as part of a single species-intellect after we have gone.[29]

It was this monopsychic doctrine, above all, that drove the conservative theologians wild, for its obvious implication was that there was no individual immortality, and thus no possibility of reward or punishment for individuals in the afterlife.[30] But Thomas leaped into the fray as well, since he detested the idea of a collective mind that thinks through individuals, although it does not belong to them individually. This is nonsense, Thomas declared, since it goes against our most basic intuitions, our experience, and our common sense. Siger's theory must be wrong—in fact, any theory must be wrong—if it robs the individual of his or her intellect and prevents us from saying, "*This* human being understands."[31]

In *On There Being Only One Intellect*, Thomas defended the Aristotelian principle that body and soul together make one individual person. Against the radicals, he argued that the *anima* was not a collective mind. Now turning to the conservatives, he argued that it was not some sort of alien presence temporarily inhabiting a human body. Of course, if the intellect's only function were to animate a particular body, it would become extinct when that body ceased to exist. But, said Thomas, it is possible to harmonize the ideas of individuality and immortality without separating the soul entirely from the body. The key is to recognize that the intellect is not just an ordinary form fused with matter but something capable of independent subsistence, a form that is like a substance, similar in this respect to the "intelligences" that Aristotelians thought moved the heavenly spheres. The soul is capable of surviving on its own, but it does not inhabit a body like a "ghost in the machine."[32] On the contrary, it is only by uniting with a human body that it becomes individualized, obtaining an identity that persists even after the body dies. Imagine some material, like molten metal, poured into a mold to make a sculpture. When the mold is broken, the metal survives, but it owes its permanent shape to the experience of being in the mold. What survives, in the case of human beings, is not some abstract, depersonalized soul, but the form of a real individual person.[33]

Siger de Brabant apparently found Thomas's analysis persuasive. The radical leader soon abandoned his monopsychism and adopted the position outlined in *On There Being Only One Intel-*

lect.[34] But conservatives like John Peckham were more convinced than ever that the Dominican's views were dangerously unchristian. At bottom, "Thomas was maintaining and Peckham denying that the body is part and parcel of the nature of man."[35] To Aquinas, this emphasis on the sanctity of the body had a peculiarly Christian meaning, considering that God had sanctified the human body of Christ.[36] Conservatives steeped in the Augustinian tradition, however, saw the idea as more Greek than Christian—another piece of evidence that Thomas, like the radicals, had been drinking too deeply of Aristotelian wine. Of course the soul and the body were at war! To lose sight of this fact would be to turn one's back on a thousand years of Christian asceticism. Their conviction that the Dominican's thinking was a menace to religious orthodoxy deepened when another controversy erupted at the university and Thomas adopted a position that seemed unforgivably radical.

This debate was about the eternity of the material world. We can summarize it by stating that Thomas managed to take a position on the issue that offended virtually everyone except his own followers. Siger and the radicals insisted that from the point of view of reason the universe is without beginning or end. Rational thinking, Siger said, demonstrates that the world has always existed, since science shows us that all effects have causes which are the effects of prior causes.[37] Of course, he added, if faith demands that we believe in Adam and Eve or in the world's creation ex nihilo, then we must accept this, not because it is reasonable or provable, "for faith can be neither science nor opinion," but because it rests on sacred authority.[38] The conservatives replied to this in a number of ways, some of them quite subtle.[39] There was no need to rest the belief in a new creation on blind faith, they insisted, since Siger could be defeated by scientific and logical arguments. Thomas took the position that it was impossible to prove either position in this debate by scientific reason.[40] Clearly Siger was wrong to say that the eternity of the world was the better argument, but he was quite right to say that the Christian doctrine of creation is a matter of faith, not something that can be proved by reason.

This argument was a red flag for Bishop Stephen Tempier and his allies on the faculty of theology. Aquinas pretended to oppose Siger and his cohorts as vigorously as they did, but when one looked under the surface, weren't he and the radicals really saying the same thing? Nature was governed by natural laws that worked without God's intervention. Men and women could be happy in this life, despite their fallen state. The soul received its individuality from the body. And now, at least as a theoretical possibility, the material world could be co-eternal with God. Thomas, like Siger, had recently developed a large following among the masters of arts, and had even drawn under his banner mendicant scholars like the capable Augustinian Giles of Rome—another development that convinced the conservative theologians that Thomas was a dangerous enemy in disguise.[41] One authority on medieval philosophy compares his position to that of the Western liberals accused of being Communist fellow travelers during the Cold War.[42] But Thomas's situation was more perilous than theirs, for while most liberals adjusted their political views to accommodate the prevailing consensus, he boldly insisted that the cure for abuses or misapprehensions of Aristotle's ideas lay in a better understanding and more aggressive application of those same ideas. A moderate by disposition, Thomas reasoned like a revolutionary, inflaming the dispute despite his own preference for peace.[43]

A storm was rising in Paris. Thomas, however, would not be there when it broke. In 1272, for reasons that are not clear, he returned to the priory in Naples where he had begun his religious career, and where he was now expected to establish a new Dominican college. Perhaps he was fatigued by the endless controversies at the university. Perhaps his Dominican superiors felt that his usefulness there was at an end. Thomas may simply have felt compelled to finish his *Summa Theologica*, or—who knows?—sensed that God wanted more of him than his skill in academic disputation. Even before leaving Paris, we are told, he had begun to have unusual experiences. Several times he was found in church in an apparent trance or "ecstasy." After completing a difficult essay on the Eucharist that his university colleagues had requested, he laid it on the altar, whereupon, according to friars who were present, the figure on the crucifix came down, stood on the scroll, and said, "Thomas, you have written well of the sacrament of my body." Then, according to the same witnesses, Thomas rose several feet into the air and remained there for a few minutes, suspended. Another incident was said to have occurred after he returned to Naples. One night, at the Church of Saint Dominic, a voice from the crucifix praised his work and offered him any reward he chose. "I will have Yourself," he was said to have replied.

These experiences, however, were only preludes to something that happened to Thomas in 1273, while he was celebrating mass at Saint Dominic's. What the nature of this experience was one can only guess, but when the service ended, he said to his friend, a friar named Reginald, "I will write no more." Later, when Reginald pressed him to continue his work, he said, "I can do no more. After what I have seen, everything that I have written seems like straw." Thomas stopped writing and would have stopped traveling as well, except that the pope asked him to attend a general council of the Church at Lyon which was to deal with Rome's relations with the Greek Orthodox Church, a subject on which he was an expert. He stopped north of Naples to visit his sister, but fainted in the street in her village. After recovering consciousness, he asked to be taken to a nearby monastery, because, he said, it would be better for God to find him among monks than among laypeople. His last act was to have the Song of Songs read to him by the brothers and to discuss it with them as far as he was able to. He was forty-nine years old when he died, leaving the *Summa Theologica* unfinished.

As it happened, Thomas's old friend Bonaventure was also in poor health. The Franciscan leader was able to attend the council at Lyons, but died that summer during the proceedings. As a result neither man was present when the controversy that had engaged them so deeply in Paris came to an unexpected climax.

CONSERVATIVE POWER at the University of Paris was on the rise. The emergence of Siger de Brabant and the radical masters had thrown a bad scare into the liberal arts faculty as well as the theologians, and Aquinas's interventions had not served to clear his own followers from the suspicion that they were radicals in disguise. In 1272, an election for rector of the arts faculty—a powerful position in the university—turned into a major contest between the contending factions. Alberic of Rheims, a French master, apparently represented the anti-Siger forces, and Siger himself, still a leader of the Picard nation, is thought to have been his opponent. We know very little about the conduct of the election campaign, except that it was unusually bitter and hard-fought, and that Albert ended with a clear majority of votes.[44] Siger's supporters, charging foul play, refused to accept the Frenchman's victory and elected a rector of their own.

The reasons for this desperate move seem clear. The rector of the arts faculty had the power to adopt statutes binding upon all masters. Since the 1260s, all masters other than members of the mendicant orders had taken an oath swearing to obey these rules, or else be declared "perjured and rebels."[45] To disobey would therefore mean, at the very least, the end of one's university career. Immediately after the election, Alberic's regime adopted new statutes forbidding the arts masters either to reach theological conclusions in their lectures or to "teach against the faith" in philosophical matters. The second prohibition was broad, requiring interpretation in each case. It would obviously be interpreted against the radicals, and violating it would result in their expulsion from the university. With their backs to the wall, the dissidents refused to recognize the legitimacy of the statutes, and for the next three years, the liberal arts faculty became, in effect, two faculties, each with its own administration, teachers, student body, and rules.

The situation could not last. In 1275, after several attempts to mediate the dispute, the papal legate, Simon of Brioni, came to the university, held hearings, and imposed a settlement on the arts faculty that favored the conservatives. During the period of the split, the radical masters may have moved the discussion of controversial topics from public forums to private quarters, for the following year a new decree of the university forbade any teacher from lecturing in private on matters other than logic and grammar.[46] For the radical leaders, the game was over. Siger, Goswin of la Chapelle, and Bernier of Nivelles returned to their homes in the city of Liège, where they held positions as canons of Saint Paul's cathedral and Saint Martin's church. There, on November 23, 1276, they were summoned by the Inquisitor of France, the Dominican cardinal Simon du Val, to appear before him at Saint-Quentin to answer unspecified charges of heresy.

According to older histories, Siger and his friends were in Paris when the Inquisition moved against them, and they fled to Italy to avoid the citation and to appeal for justice to the papal court.[47] More recent research suggests that they obeyed the summons, came to

Saint-Quentin, and were acquitted of heresy, either because the evidence against them was weak or because the bishop of Liège pressured the Inquisitor to release them. Bernier of Nivelles returned to Paris in the 1280s and taught theology at the Sorbonne College, which he could not have done if he had been convicted of heresy.[48] Siger and Goswin of la Chapelle probably remained in Liège for a time, but did go to Italy several years later—a strange journey, as we will see.

The conservatives had won . . . or had they? The problem not yet recognized was what it meant, under these circumstances, to "win." Ever since the papacy of Innocent III, the Church had opened its mind to the Aristotelian ideas percolating through the universities, as it had opened its arms to mass evangelical movements of the sort led by Francis of Assisi. There were limits to this openness, of course. It did not include toleration of schismatic movements or obviously heretical teachings. But the policy of flexibility deliberately ran serious risks for the sake of maintaining the unity and cultural supremacy of the Church in a time of rapid change. Permitting scholars fascinated by natural philosophy to study Aristotle and to speculate about scientific matters did present a danger that their findings would throw doubt on traditional Christian doctrines. This was exactly the sort of danger that the Islamic authorities had decided to avoid by isolating the Muslim Aristotelians and preventing them from teaching in Muslim universities. What if Europe's natural philosophers were driven from the Catholic universities? Another sort of risk would be posed if the dialogue between faith and reason that had taken place inside Christian institutions ended, and an intelligentsia without religious ties developed under the patronage of secular rulers.

Bishop Stephen Tempier and his allies did not give this problem much thought. What they found especially disturbing was not that the radicals preached heretical doctrines openly (which, for the most part, they did not do) but that their teachings and writings reflected an attitude threatening to traditional Christian values. The radicals were not heretics, but they were fascinated "with the truly amazing potentialities of human reason to acquire new knowledge and insight." For them, "in the face of this new plethora of knowledge about the natural world, theology simply became uninteresting."[49]

This shift in attitude helps to explain why conservative opposition to the radical Aristotelians intensified even after the radicals lost the election of 1272 and their leaders fled Paris. The Sigerists continued to imply, even if they did not say so directly, that the truths of Aristotelian science were at least as compelling, if not more so, than the old doctrinal verities. As arts masters, they were not supposed to teach theology. And so they would not. But simply by focusing on natural philosophy without exploring its implications for the faith, they put the truths of theology in the shade—a development that must have infuriated their opponents, since they gave them so little to attack in the way of directly offensive or heretical statements. But how does one compel scholars to find a subject interesting, or stop them from thinking about things that fascinate them? An Innocent III might have recognized that this was a losing battle—that if Christian theologians did not engage the natural philosophers, as Thomas and Bonaventure had done, the study of nature (including human nature) and the study of divine things would go their separate ways. Stephen Tempier, however, was no Innocent III. With the radicals weakened by the loss of their leaders, the bishop and his cohorts could not resist the temptation to smash their movement completely, and, as a significant bonus, to bring the Thomists into disrepute.

On January 18, 1277, Pope John XXI, a former theology professor at the University of Paris, wrote Stephen Tempier stating that he had heard reports of teaching at the university "prejudicial to the faith" and asking him to investigate the charges. It is likely that the bishop had already begun his own investigation, and that the pope's letter was written at his request.[50] In any case, Tempier immediately convened a panel of sixteen theologians and "other wise men" to assist him. Although the only member whose name is known was the secular master Henry of Ghent, it is likely that all were handpicked conservatives, probably including the chancellor of the university.[51] The panel did its work quickly. The bishop had learned from his experience seven years earlier, when his attempt to proscribe a few of the radicals' most egregious errors misfired. His aim this time was to outlaw an impious, secularist attitude, and this meant banning every dubious Aristotelian proposition advanced by the radical masters, as well as those possibly implicit in their teachings and those that some future scholar might presume to teach on the basis of Averroës' work or that of other commentators. He cast his net wide. This time it was not thirteen teachings that were banned but 219.

Tempier's letter introducing the list of condemned propositions accused certain unnamed masters of teaching and discussing the "manifest and execrable errors" listed in the attachment. He then charged them with teaching "that these things are true according to philosophy but not according to the catholic faith, as if there were two contrary truths, and as if the truth of sacred Scripture were contradicted by the truth in the sayings of the accursed pagans."[52] Finally, he ordered them to stop teaching these false propositions and stated that anyone teaching or even listening to them will be excommunicated unless within seven days he surrenders himself for appropriate punishment to Tempier himself or to the chancellor of the university.

As in 1270, it is likely that few of the condemned propositions were ever taught or advocated in the form stated by Tempier. Certainly the radical masters did not openly advocate the doctrine of Double Truth, even though their critics considered that a logical consequence of their teaching. The Condemnations of 1277 added a number of new categories of proscribed statements to those named seven years earlier. A major source of concern was Aristotle's teaching that the best life is the life of philosophical contemplation, which could be interpreted to favor natural philosophy over theology. It was now forbidden to teach that "there is no higher life than philosophical life," or that "theological discussions are based on fables," that "the only wise men of the world are philosophers," or that "Christian revelation is an obstacle to learning."[53] Since nobody at the university would have dared to uphold such principles openly, these proscriptions were either intended to stop people from expressing them in private or (what amounts to the same thing) to stop them from being thought. Other outlawed propositions were gross misrepresentations of radical teachings—misrepresentations so egregious as to suggest that they were part of a deliberate "smear campaign." As one modern critic remarks, speaking of the propositions relating to the eternity of the world:

> The picture which emerges . . . is one of able and devout Christian philosophers and theologians being attacked for largely non-doctrinal reasons, and condemned by a dishonest and vengeful committee of theologians . . . who had the ear of a fairly unintelligent, through fearful and conservative bishop.[54]

There is much justice in this charge. At the same time, at least some of the teachings condemned by Tempier had been advanced by radical masters either as scientific truths or as hypotheses needing to be discussed. The most troublesome issues, interestingly enough, involved the relationship between God's power and the regularities of nature. Nobody questioned God's ability to suspend the normal operations of nature. Indeed, without accepting that principle, it is hard to see how any Christian could believe in Christ's birth of a virgin or in the other events recorded in the Gospels. The problem was that the principle was becoming increasingly abstract as intellectuals came to believe that God did not want to suspend the laws of nature and would not do so, especially where the laws in question were fundamental to the structure and operations of the cosmos. Could God prevent the sun from rising in the morning? In theory, certainly. Had he ever done so? No; his one interference with the sun in its course is reported in the Book of Joshua (10:12–15), when he delayed the sun's setting for "almost a whole day" to enable Joshua to win a battle. Would he ever do so? At the end of time, perhaps; but until then one could safely count on the morning sunrise, and study it as a scientific phenomenon.

This tendency to assume that nature's workings could be described and even predicted on the sole basis of what Aquinas had called "secondary causes" produced a series of condemnations that were really warnings against considering natural laws absolute, and thus replacing God with Nature. Among the propositions condemned in 1277 were several statements based on Aristotle's *Physics*: that God could not make several worlds or universes; that he could not move the spherical heavens or earth with a rectilinear motion, since this would produce a vacuum; and that he could not make an "accident" exist without a "substance" or make two bodies exist simultaneously in the same place.[55] The great irony of these condemnations, as we now know, was that insisting on God's power to violate the laws of nature, as Aristotle understood them, helped later natural philosophers to discover a number of non-Aristotelian natural laws. (It turned out, for example, that nature does not "abhor a vacuum.") But the stimulation of scientific speculation was not Bishop Tempier's intention. His purpose was to reassert the supremacy of traditional Christian doctrines and attitudes over natural philosophy—a task that led inevitably to an attack on the "natural theology" of Thomas Aquinas.

Tempier's first move against Thomas's theology was somewhat ambiguous. Not many of the 219 propositions that he condemned were obviously Thomist, although the conservatives believed (as do some modern scholars) that several were aimed at the Dominican's teachings.[56] In any case, less than two weeks after Tempier issued his list, Aquinas's doctrine of the soul was specifically condemned at Oxford by Robert Kilwardby, the new archbishop of Canterbury (and a Dominican), along with more than twenty radical propositions.[57] These condemnations would be repeated and augmented by the Franciscan theologian John Peckham when he became archbishop of Canterbury in the 1280s. Meanwhile, Tempier initiated another high-speed investigation, this time of Thomas's leading disciple at the faculty of theology, Giles of Rome. At the end of March, Tempier censured fifty-one propositions taken from Giles's work, and the Augustinian was forced to discontinue his teaching at the university. Several weeks later, the bishop opened a new investigation of false teaching at the faculty of theology, with the aim of censuring Thomas's views. It appeared as if the Thomists might follow the radicals into ecclesiastical oblivion. Mysteriously, however, the investigation was terminated. John Peckham alleged that the powerful Dominican lobby in Rome used its influence to cancel the planned proceedings, and he might have been right.

With the radicals in full flight, the controversy over Thomas's teachings had become a sectarian battle between the Franciscans and the Dominicans—one in which the Franciscans no longer enjoyed a marked advantage. Stung by Kilwardby's assault, the Dominicans mobilized immediately, adopting internal rules that provided for the punishment of any member of the order who, like the English archbishop, criticized Aquinas's views publicly. A war of treatises ensued, with leading Dominicans and Franciscan theologians denouncing each other with abandon. In 1279, William de la Mare, Peckham's successor in the Franciscan chair of theology at Paris, published an unsparing critique of Aquinas called *The Correction of Brother Thomas*, a collection of allegedly deviant Thomist propositions which the Franciscans promptly made a part of the curriculum in their schools. The Dominican theologian, John of Paris, answered with a ferocious blast at de la Mare called *The Correction of the Corruption of Thomas*. The high-water mark of Franciscan influence was probably reached at Oxford in the mid-1280s, when Archbishop Peckham condemned a master of theology for teaching Thomas's views on the soul, and an ex-Franciscan pope, Nicholas IV, upheld the condemnation. After that debacle, the Dominicans, who made Thomas's theology the basis for the curriculum in their own schools, steadily gained ground. In 1323, less than fifty years after his views were condemned at Oxford, the controversial Italian was canonized by Rome. Two years after that, in a most unusual document, the bishop of Paris retracted the Parisian condemnations that "concerned or are claimed to concern the doctrine of Blessed Thomas," thus clearing the Thomists of any suspicion of heresy.[58]

In their own time, the Condemnations of 1277 triggered a furious, continent-wide debate. Although their legal effect was limited to the University of Paris (and, in the case of Kilwardby's condemnations, to Oxford), the issues that they raised were discussed in universities throughout Europe. According to some historians, the repressive atmosphere they created in Paris restricted the free discussion of natural philosophy at that university for several decades.[59] But the notable fact is that the condemnations had so little effect, even in the short run, on the development of Thomist theology, rationalist thinking, or scholarly interest in natural science. Even in the flood tide of repression there was no attempt to revive the ban on Aristotle's works. The Philosopher's natural philosophy, along with the works of Averroës, Avicenna, and other controversial commentators, remained the core of the European liberal arts curriculum. Theologians continued to debate the major issues raised by the Aristotelian worldview, from the doctrine of secondary causes to the eternity of the world and the nature of the soul. And Thomism, which had been struck a "glancing blow," recovered its status as a respectable blend of philosophy and theology.[60] Several centuries later, it would become the preferred philosophy of the Roman Catholic Church.

More surprisingly, perhaps, the radical current of thought associated with Siger and his companions, although forced underground for a time, quickly reappeared. In the 1320s, the well-known radical John of Jandun gained a large following in Paris by teaching the separation of reason and faith, church and state, and by collaborating with Marsilius of Padua on the treatise *Defensor Pacis*, a notorious attack on the doctrine of papal supremacy.[61] Radicalism never conquered at Paris, but it became a strong influence at Bologna and a dominant force at the University of Padua. Once unleashed on European society, the idea that the truths of natural philosophy deserved as much attention and credence as those of theology could not be suppressed. The oddest consequence of the condemnations, perhaps, was the impetus that undermining certain key assumptions of Aristotle's unwittingly gave to empirical science. One leading historian notes that the affirmation of God's unlimited creative power by conservatives "led to an avalanche of speculative or hypothetical natural philosophy in the fourteenth century in the course of which various principles of Aristotelian natural philosophy were clarified, criticized, or rejected."[62] In the end, the entity most affected by Bishop Tempier's crusade was the Church itself, which turned from its earlier enthusiastic embrace of the new natural philosophy to a position that was far more critical and suspicious. After

1277, the split between reason and faith that everyone but the radicals had attempted to avoid seemed to develop with a force of its own. As Étienne Gilson puts it, the "honeymoon of theology and philosophy had . . . come to an end."[63]

And what of Siger de Brabant, the provocateur whose inflammatory ideas and writings lit the fuse for this intellectual explosion? We know that his liberal opponent, Thomas Aquinas, was declared a saint not long after his death, and that his conservative nemesis, Bonaventure, later joined Thomas in that elite company, Bonaventure's canonization having been delayed by strife between the Franciscan factions. The only form of sainthood that Siger enjoys, however, is a reputation among certain historically minded leftists for martyrdom in the sacred cause of Reason. Siger's last days are shrouded in mystery. All we know (from an Italian poem) is that he was in Orvieto, Italy, early in the 1280s, possibly seeking to restore his reputation at the nearby papal court in Viterbo. With him was his "secretary," a fellow cleric whom some believe was Goswin of la Chapelle. Was Siger lobbying the curia to clear his name and regain his teaching privileges? Was he under house arrest in Orvieto? Amid the fog of rumors, only one fact is well attested. Sometime between 1281 and 1284, Siger de Brabant was murdered, stabbed to death by his secretary, who had allegedly gone mad.[64]

Today, no doubt, so shadowy an end to a controversial life would produce a careful forensic investigation, if not an official fact-finding commission and any number of speculative books on "the Assassination of Siger." The radical leader's friends, however, were lying low, and his enemies seem to have greeted his demise with a collective sigh of relief. Nobody demonstrated any great desire to poke among the embers of a ruined career. The "mad secretary" story may or may not be true, but until new evidence is uncovered, it will have to suffice.

CHAPTER SEVEN

"Ockham's Razor"

THE DIVORCE OF FAITH AND REASON

POPE BONIFACE VIII declared the year 1300 a Jubilee Year and invited all Christendom to celebrate it with him in Rome. A staggering number of pilgrims and visitors poured into the ancient capital— so many that to admit the teeming crowds new openings had to be cut in the city walls. The visitors included most of Europe's heads of state as well as Christian clerics and laypeople from every region and social class. Their number was estimated at 200,000 each day, and this in a city whose normal population was well under 100,000. The festivities and ceremonies continued virtually nonstop, filling the air with the smoke of roasting meats and aromatic incense. Nothing like it had been seen in Rome since the days of the emperors and the "triumphs" celebrating their legions' victories. But this celebration was deceptive. It was not so much a triumph as a way of diverting attention from a series of defeats. Behind the façade of papal magnificence and religious unity lay an increasingly divided, troubled, and violent society.

Boniface presided over the Jubilee like an emperor reborn: as pope he was not only head of the Catholic Church, with its vast landed wealth and legions of clerics, but also Europe's supreme moral and political authority. One historian calls the celebration "perhaps the first example of the manipulation of the masses for a political end, in this case the demonstration of the power of the papal theocracy and the full authority of papal rule over all Christian people."[1] Boldly, the pope declared himself the final arbiter of conflicts between princes and a fountain of justice to the common folk—a leader whose will in disputed cases must be obeyed, since he was Christ's representative on earth. This was not a new idea, of course. It had originated with Boniface's great predecessors, Gregory VII and Innocent III. But times had changed far more than the pope cared to recognize. His misguided attempt to incarnate the great architects of papal supremacy brings to mind Karl Marx's statement that when history repeats itself, it does so "the first time as tragedy and the second as farce."[2]

The reign of Boniface VIII had begun inauspiciously, to say the least. In 1294, bedeviled by internal disputes and hoping to restore public confidence in Rome's leadership, the College of Cardinals had elected as pope a saintly recluse named Pietro da Morrone, who went directly from his hermit's cell in the Italian mountains to the gorgeous offices of the Vatican. There the hapless man took the name Celestine V before proceeding to demonstrate both the sweet otherworldliness of his nature and his incompetence to hold the most challenging administrative office in Christendom. Cardinal Benedetto Caetani, as Boniface was then known, had advised him initially not to accept the election. Five months later, he supported the ex-hermit's unprecedented decision to abdicate the chair of Saint Peter. Caetani was then elected pope in his own right, but his advisers warned him not to leave his eighty-year-old predecessor at liberty, since the Franciscan Spirituals, then agitating against corruption and worldliness in the Church, might use him to foment opposition to the established order. Twice the old man was arrested and detained by the pope's agents. Twice he escaped from his captors, but his second escape, a flight by sea, was thwarted by a shipwreck. Recaptured on the Italian coast, Morrone was imprisoned in a dank, narrow cell in the fortress of Fumone at Ferrentino, where he died miserably after ten months of suffering.

Boniface shrugged off the criticism of his behavior. After all, he was everything that the hermit pope was not: a wealthy aristocrat, an expert in law and finance, and a tactician who had flourished in the arcane, contentious world of Vatican politics. Surely he would be able to solve the problems that the simple hermit had been unable to comprehend. The most serious of these was the alarming increase of violent warfare among Europe's noble families. Across the continent, the aristocratic solidarity that had been nurtured for centuries by diplomatic marriages, codes of courtly behavior, and crusades was giving way to a struggle for power more intense and uninhibited than anyone had believed possible. From Sicily to Scotland, plots and counterplots, wars and rebellions were the order (or disorder) of the day. France, long the home of learning and *courtoisie*, had emerged under Philip the Fair as the most centralized and powerful monarchy in Europe. Edward I's England was undergoing an analogous concentration of power in the hands of the great nobles. Just as Boniface was taking office, the two nations began their Hundred Years War— a desperate struggle for European supremacy fought largely by mercenaries, in which both monarchs were compelled to tax the Church to defray their military expenses.

Here, as at other sites of conflict, the Catholic authorities were caught between Scylla and Charybdis, compelled either to serve "their" king (as the French bishops tended to do), or to safeguard the rights of the Church and face the secular ruler's wrath. The difficult situation was exacerbated by the fact that the pope was also a feudal lord, so that loyalty to his interests might well seem like treason to the local sovereign. Unfazed by such complexities, Boniface threw the power of his office and his personal prestige into a series of attempts to resolve the conflicts that were turning Europe into a rancorous collection of warring principalities. To restore peace and protect the Church's interests, he intervened in Italy, Spain, Scotland, Hungary, Poland... and, of course, England and France. In virtually every case, however, his actions proved either fruitless or counterproductive. Boniface imagined that he could impose his will on disobedient princes by issuing decrees backed by his power to excommunicate and depose them. But the effectiveness of these measures in the past had always depended on the secular rulers' awe of the papal office and their fear of local rebellions against their own authority. Papal threats were of no avail against monarchs as powerful, popular, and unscrupulous as Edward I and Philip the Fair.

"My master's sword is of steel," said one of Philip's ministers, "the pope's is made of verbiage."[3] Words were Boniface's stock in trade, but they were also his undoing. The pope has been described as "a man of scant tact and of easy manners, whose insensitive actions and pungent remarks brought him many enemies."[4] Scholars at the University of Paris remembered when, as Cardinal Caetani, he forbade them to challenge the privileges of the Dominican and Franciscan friars. "You masters of Paris have made all your learning and doctrine a laughing-stock," he wrote imperiously. "To us your fame is mere folly and smoke.... Rather than revoke this privilege [the mendicants' right to hear confessions], the Roman Curia will utterly destroy the University of Paris. We are called by God not to acquire wisdom or dazzle mankind but to save our souls."[5] Clearly, this pope lacked the mature judgment and diplomatic skills of an Innocent III. Given the changes taking place in European society, however, it is unlikely that even a pope with Innocent's abilities could have brought peace to the Christian community.

The political strife that so concerned Boniface was but one symptom of a profound social crisis. The optimistic, expansive, increasingly integrated Western community of the High Middle Ages was giving way to a society prone to "natural disasters and social dislocations."[6] More than two centuries of economic growth had ended in depression and stagnation, inflaming conflicts between lords and peasants, great and petty nobles, mercenary soldiers and civilians, townspeople and country folk. The population boom had ended as well, with growth declining to near zero.[7] Even the climate went bad, as Europe entered a "little ice age" of cold winters and short growing seasons. Boniface would not live to see the bubonic plague—the Black Death— devastate the continent, but he was aware that the relatively peaceful and unified society he had known as a youth was vanishing. The common people, more exposed to the vicissitudes of change, felt this transformation especially keenly, although they understood it not at all. The turn of the century saw an upsurge in apocalyptic prophecies and expectations, a new growth of "enthusiastic" spiritual movements (some of them flirting with heresy), and a revival of mysticism involving laypeople as well as the clergy. The same forces that had challenged the Church in the reign of Innocent III had reappeared with a vengeance, but this time against the backdrop of a society in decline.

Against these enemies Boniface proved powerless, despite his bold political ambitions. When he preached a new Crusade to reunite Europe and reclaim the Holy Land from the Muslims, his proclamations were simply ignored. When he demanded that Edward I of England leave Scotland in peace, the king's response was to seize a substantial portion of the English clergy's revenues. The pope's efforts to bring Philip the Fair to heel were even more disastrous, since the French bureaucrats had little fear of him, and no scruples at all about using their plentiful resources to undermine his authority. In response to a papal decree demanding that Philip cease taxing the French clergy to pay for his wars, the king simply cut off the supply of French money and treasures to Rome. When Boniface published a new bull calling for reform of the French regime, Philip's ministers burned it and issued a scurrilous forgery in his name. The legate he sent to protest these actions was seized by the French interior minister and imprisoned. Finally, in 1302, the beleaguered pope issued his famous bull, *Unam Sanctam,* claiming the power to depose disobedient kings, and stating, "We declare, proclaim, and define that subjection to the Roman Pontiff is absolutely necessary for the salvation of every human creature."[8] Philip's response was to convene a council in Paris attended by French clerics loyal to him, which promptly branded Boniface a heretic, robber, simoniac, and practitioner of black magic, and accused him of the murder of Celestine V.

Boniface struck back with the only weapon at his disposal: an order asserting his plenary power over the French clergy and excommunicating the French king. It was too late. Before the decree could be published, Philip's minister, Nogaret, arrived in Italy and, with the help of the pope's hereditary enemies, the Colonna family, raised an army of two thousand mercenaries for an attack on the papal palace in his home city of Anagni. Resistance was useless. The pope's retinue of cardinals deserted him, and he was captured alone, decked out in the papal regalia, and seated on the throne in his palace. Nogaret, who was under orders to bring him back to France for a show trial, is said to have narrowly prevented the head of the Colonna clan from killing him. While drunken mercenaries looted the palace, Nogaret imprisoned the pope in the dungeon without food or water—an ordeal that ended three days later, when friendly townspeople freed the prisoner, scattered the remnants of the mercenary band, and sent the minister packing back to France. They then dispatched Boniface to Rome in the custody of the Orsini, another hostile aristocratic clan. A few months later, his health and morale broken, he died in the Eternal City. It was barely three years since the false dawn of the Jubilee.

The unprecedented brutalization of a sitting pope was a sign that the balance of power between secular and ecclesiastical forces in Europe was undergoing a tectonic shift. This became obvious when Boniface's successor, Clement V, moved the papal headquarters to Avignon and permitted the French monarchy to establish effective control over the Church's finances and politics. While Philip the Fair smashed the order of Knights Templar, Rome's principal financiers, and expropriated their considerable wealth, the pope appointed scores of French cardinals, and England began the process of slow withdrawal that would eventually take that nation out of the Roman orbit altogether. In the mid-1300s, Catholicism endured the scandal of the "Great Schism," in which Avignon and Rome each housed alleged popes in whose eyes the competing pontiff was an imposter or "antipope." Especially for an office whose legitimacy always depended far more upon awe and reverence than upon force, such goings-on could be fatal. Little more than one century later, a German monk named Martin Luther, utterly disenchanted with the papacy, would initiate a far greater schism—one that ended the unity of the Church and plunged the continent into a century of religious warfare.

With the organized Church in disarray and unprecedented disorders looming just over the horizon, it is no wonder that many historians speak of "the end of the Middle Ages" in elegiac tones. To Catholics especially (but not only to Catholics[9]), the thirteenth century, the age of reforming popes and scholastic saints, is the "great century," while the fourteenth century is fraught with violent events and evil omens. But this is far from being the whole story. True, the medieval consensus was beginning to disintegrate. One did not have to be a prophet to foresee that the consequences would be painful and bloody. Yet the same subterranean forces that shook the edifice of Christian unity were opening up radically new perspectives in thinking. The Western intelligentsia was still almost entirely Christian, of course, and it was still thoroughly Aristotelian. But Aristotle's children had now spawned independent-minded progeny of their own—daring innovators who would take the master's thought in unexpected new directions.

As is so often the case, conflict was the midwife of new ideas. At the dawn of the new century, the Franciscan friars found themselves embroiled in conflicts on two fronts. Internally, the disagreement between the order's "Spiritual" wing and the more conservative "Conventuals" had intensified, reflecting the new wave of religious enthusiasm then sweeping Europe.[10] The radicals believed that their order had lost touch with the ideals of Saint Francis. According to spokesmen like the charismatic monk from Narbonne, Peter John Olivi, the Friars Minor had relaxed the founder's prohibition against holding communal property, and were drifting with the rest of the Church toward the values of materialism, legalism, and power politics. As an antidote, the Spirituals advocated communal as well as individual poverty, spontaneity, and spiritual inwardness. Some flirted with Joachimite ideas about a coming Third Age of the Holy Spirit when the religious establishment would become irrelevant. Others deplored Rome's involvement in European politics, questioned the pope's authority in doctrinal matters, and favored the empowerment of secular kings and princes. The Catholic leadership had responded by condemning Olivi's writings and by mounting an increasingly repressive campaign against other troublemakers.[11] But there was a disquieting tendency among the radicals to view the repression as further evidence of the hierarchy's corruption and illegitimacy.

At the same time that their internal unity was fracturing, the Franciscans were involved in a new round of philosophical disputes with their old adversaries, the Dominicans. The atmosphere in Rome had changed greatly since the Condemnations of 1277. Thanks to the Dominicans' ferocious advocacy of their champion, Thomas Aquinas, as well as a shift in the European political climate, Rome recognized that Thomas's thinking was not nearly as radical or threatening as had been feared. "It is better to marry than to burn," Saint Paul had declared. Now that it was clear that the lust for knowledge was as irrepressible as carnal desire, the authorities could appreciate how cleverly Thomas had harnessed that craving to the sacred doctrines and institutions of the Church. The Dominican theologian deserved canonization not only because of his spiritual gifts but because his "baptism" of Aristotle had yielded two great apparent benefits. It did for scientific enterprise what Innocent III had done for popular evangelism—that is, it brought a potentially hostile force inside the Church-run universities, where it could be watched, controlled, and used for the greater glory of God; and, by creating a "natural theology," it gave sacred doctrines the prestige and persuasiveness of scientific truth.

Thomas's Aristotelian/Christian perspective had not yet achieved the supremacy in Catholic circles that it did later on, but it had clearly become quite respectable. This did not impress the Franciscans—especially those of radical bent—who saw Thomism as the theological expression of a Church too much at home in the world, too far removed from the core of religious experience, and too confident of its ability to understand and enforce God's will on earth. How like the Dominicans, backbone of the Inquisition, to embrace a theology that purported to bundle up all knowledge in one neat package. Earlier critics such as Bonaventure and John Peckham had accused Aquinas of glorifying reason at the expense of faith, and had prescribed a strong dose of Plato as a corrective. But the new criticism, voiced by powerful thinkers like John Duns Scotus and his remarkable student, William of Ockham, took a far more radical tack.

The Franciscan innovators had little interest either in glorifying reason or debunking it. The problem, as they saw it, was that the older generation of theologians, both Dominican and Franciscan, had misconceived what we know and how we know it, and had therefore drawn an improper boundary between faith and reason. What was urgently needed, in their view, was no mere correction of Thomism, but an entirely new map of knowledge. And the way to create such a map was to turn Aristotle against himself: to use Aristotle's methods of reasoning to examine and criticize the conclusions commonly thought of as Aristotelian.[12] Scholars throughout Europe would soon be calling this the "modern" approach (*via moderna*), as opposed to the "old school" approach (*via antiqua*) represented by both Thomas and Bonaventure. Those old friends and adversaries would have been appalled, no doubt, by the "modernist" tendency to separate the realms of theology and science, but their influence in the universities was waning. Out of the crisis of medieval society, a new way of thinking was being born.

JOHN DUNS SCOTUS was not a rebel by temperament, but his short life was full of revolutionary significance. Born around 1265 in a village just north of England's Scottish border, he was teaching in Oxford by the late 1280s.[13] Just after the turn of the century, he went to lecture in Paris. As a result of Philip the Fair's struggle with Pope Boniface, Duns Scotus and other friars loyal to the pope were forced to leave the university in 1303, but he returned the following year and was named Franciscan regent master in the school of theology in 1305. Three years later, he went to Cologne to direct a Franciscan school and died there of unknown causes. The touching description on his gravestone in the Minority Church in Cologne reads, "Scotland bore me, England received me, France taught me, Cologne holds me fast."[14] Unlike William of Ockham, who was associated with the Franciscans' Spiritual wing, Duns Scotus seems to have stayed out of the order's internal politics, and his theological writing, while bold and innovative, stopped short of taking positions that might be regarded as heretical. (William seldom stopped short of anything.)

Like Thomas Aquinas, Duns Scotus was an Aristotelian, especially when it came to describing and analyzing the operations of the natural universe. But he disagreed strongly with Thomas's attempt, heroic though it was, to leap in one bound from Aristotle to Christ. Thomas believed that by understanding the laws governing nature, we perceive, even if dimly, the creative intentions of God. According to Duns Scotus, this was a serious mistake. Our minds have some powers of which Thomas was unaware— for example, the power to understand the form of individual things intuitively, without mechanically "abstracting" their general characteristics from sense impressions.[15] But we cannot look into the "mirror of nature" and reach valid conclusions about God's intentions, desires, or plans. Nor, on the basis of what we observe in the natural universe, can we deduce the truths of religion. Thomas thought that by reasoning from natural data, we could prove doctrines like the omnipotence of God, the distinction between good and evil, and the immortality of the soul. Another mistake. That sort of knowledge, the Franciscan insisted, can only be acquired through faith.

Thomism's underlying error, in Duns Scotus's view, was its doctrine of necessity. Basing himself on Aristotle's distinction between "necessary" being (that which absolutely *has* to exist) and "contingent" being (that whose existence is dependent upon other factors), Thomas had argued that God is necessary being.[16] Strictly speaking, everything else is contingent, since its existence depends upon God, and very likely upon other factors as well. But, said Thomas, God is the creator of the universe, and since he chooses most of the time to operate through secondary causes, he transfers some of his own necessity to the natural world. Since he creates species, for example, a human embryo necessarily develops into a human being, if it develops at all, not into a horse, a fish, or a flower. The thrilling thing about this is that it permits us, even if in a limited way, to discover the intentions and will of God. For the patterns we apprehend in nature—in particular, what Thomas called "intelligible species"—represent the designs of the Creator. And it is also through his will that we gain certain knowledge of them through the power of our "active intellect."

Up to a point, Duns Scotus could accept this reasoning. He agreed that God is necessary being (although he preferred to call him infinite being). He also agreed that we can know some things with certainty, although his standards for certain knowledge, based on the model of mathematics, were more difficult to satisfy than Thomas's.[17] What he found entirely unacceptable, however, was the implication that God's power is self-limited by being channeled into the "secondary causes" that we see operating in nature. Since God is absolutely free to do as he wishes, Duns Scotus insisted, everything that he does is contingent, not necessary, and he is not bound in the slightest by the natural laws that humans discover. These natural regularities are dependent every instant on God's spontaneous will; indeed, the time and space in which they operate are themselves contingent on his will. If he wished, God could retroactively unmake everything that he has made, as well as make a human embryo develop into a fish or a flower. (This is not entirely theoretical, of course, since he *has* made miracles, as well as creating a universe from nothing.) Nothing exists necessarily except God himself. But if this is true, everything that science discovers must be provisional. God's absolute freedom makes the laws of nature merely probable rather than certain.

How strange to see a Franciscan philosopher-theologian arrive at a conclusion essential to scientific thinking by asserting the freedom of an omnipotent God to do as he wishes. Using hindsight, one can see Thomas Aquinas supplying the first part of a scientific worldview by emphasizing the existence of knowable causal patterns in an integrated, interdependent natural universe. Duns Scotus supplies a second element: the recognition that our understanding of how these causes operate must always be provisional. A third component—what might be called the metaphysical simplification of the universe—was the achievement of William of Ockham, although Duns Scotus initiated the movement in this direction.

Like Duns Scotus, Ockham taught first at Oxford and then at Paris.[18] Twenty years younger than his famous predecessor and considerably more tempestuous by nature, he was notorious for his slashing, uncompromising critiques of the "old school's" theological errors. One error that particularly annoyed him was the tendency of Aquinas and other representatives of the *via antiqua* to assume the existence of metaphysical "entities" originally derived from Aristotle, such as a "potential intellect" that permits humans to receive and store information, and an "active intellect" that permits them to analyze it. Receiving information and reasoning about it are two functions of a single mind, he argued. Why suppose that there must be a separate mind-entity for each function?[19] Similarly, Ockham vehemently denied the independent reality of hypothetical entities like "man" and "animal." These "intelligible species" are merely mental concepts or linguistic terms abstracted by humans from the primary objects of knowledge: real existing individuals.[20] God is the final cause of everything, the Franciscan declared, but unnecessary metaphysical complications (assigning separate "final causes" to every substance in the universe, for example) do not help us to understand the natural world. In fact, they are obstacles to clear understanding.

This tendency to simplify reached a climax in "Ockham's razor"—the famous doctrine that holds that conceptual entities ought not to be multiplied unnecessarily.[21] The real difference of opinion here, however, was over the meaning of "unnecessary." For Thomas, entities such as the active intellect, intelligible species, and final causes were necessary to construct a system of thought linking the operations of nature explicitly to the creativity of God. Ockham's razor, on the other hand, implied that the task undertaken by Thomas—the attempt to construct a unitary system capable of explaining both natural and divine things—was impossible. Behind his call for simplicity, in other words, lay a conviction that natural science and theology must go their separate ways. On the science side, there are concepts and methods derived from experience and processed by reason that help us to understand the natural world and the world of human society. On the theology side, there are doctrines revealed by Scripture or the Church that help us to understand God and what he requires of us. From Ockham's point of view, Thomas had made a hash of things by conflating the two realms of understanding. His system had mystified nature. Worse yet, by claiming that we could reason our way to an understanding of God's attributes and intentions, it had demystified God. The job of the new school of philosopher-theologians, as William saw it, was to reverse this mistake—that is, to demystify nature and re-mystify God.

With the work of Duns Scotus and William of Ockham, the Aristotelian revolution took a radically new turn. The Franciscan innovators greatly admired Aristotle's genius, but they rejected certain ideas of his that Aquinas had considered indispensable and focused attention on others that he had downplayed or ignored. Where there had been one Aristotle recognized by medieval Christian thinkers, there were now two. The result was a split in the Aristotelian movement which opened a great gap between faith and reason, religious experience and scientific endeavor.

The Aristotle that Aquinas found so compelling was the philosopher who discovered reason in nature. His hero was the cosmologist who observed the motions of the heavenly spheres and deduced a Prime Mover; the biologist who found evidence of inherent purpose in the patterned development of living organisms; the psychologist who detected a fundamental harmony between man's reason and the objects of its understanding. To Thomas, the universe itself, interpreted through Aristotelian lenses, provides evidence of God's existence, goodness, and creative intentions. This, however, is exactly what the Franciscans denied, for how can humans, using human concepts, possibly understand God's will, except as God has revealed it through sacred writings? The Aristotle that inspired Duns Scotus and William of Ockham was the philosopher who taught that what we really know of nature are individual things or facts rather than general ideas.[22] The relations between these things or facts, which we describe by using general concepts like "cause" and "species," cannot be proved to exist in the same way that individual things exist.[23] God creates the universe, said William of Ockham, but the patterns that we discover by reasoning abstractly about created things are the products of our mental processes, not evidence of divine intentions. Reason is not inherent in nature, which obeys God's unfathomable will, but in our own minds.

With this thunderclap, modern empirical science was born—or, at least, conceived. For the natural relationships that people can describe using their powers of observation and reason are not unreal in the sense of being illusory or meaningless. Not at all. They are simply probable rather than certain, "contingent" rather than necessary, limited to explaining natural processes rather than capable of explaining God. William of Ockham had severed the link postulated by Thomas between our minds and God's. "For Ockham, the human link to God can only come through faith, since the only link we have is God's power to create *any* universe and not just this one."[24] Moreover, the result of recognizing this limitation is not necessarily depressing but liberating. Freed of the burden of making theological sense of scientific findings, "we can approach nature with a new optimism, a new strength, and a new technique."

> Creation presents itself as a gift to us. The gift, however, bears no connection to the giver—except in the tautological sense that a gift must be given. Therefore, nature as creation can be unpacked. And since we are cut off from God except in the act of faith, we might as well unpack that gift and make ourselves at home here.[25]

Christian thinkers interested in natural science might take comfort from this conclusion. The "Ockhamist" school in Paris produced a burst of creative scientific activity on the part of natural philosophers there. But what of those motivated chiefly by their desire to know God? At the same time that Ockham's critical thinking was clearing the way for empirical science, a great spiritual yearning was sweeping Europe, generating another wave of popular movements dedicated to personal communion with

Christ. What did it mean to these believers to say that God can be known not through reason but only through faith?

Traditionally there were three recognized paths to the knowledge of God: revelation, reason, and the sort of experience often described as "mystical." That is, one could read and believe what was said of God in the Bible and other holy books; one could deduce his existence and attributes either from the principles of logic (as Saint Anselm tried to do[26]) or from the "nature of nature" (the quest of Aquinas); or, more rarely, one could have the same sort of experience that biblical figures and certain mystics had of hearing God's voice or experiencing him directly in some other way. There was general agreement, however, that whichever path or paths one followed, God's infinite superiority and otherness relative to human beings meant that our knowledge of him must be extremely limited. The twelfth-century Jewish theologian Moses Maimonides set out the extreme position by declaring that we can know God only negatively—that is, we can know what he is not, not really what he is.[27] Of course, the sacred writings describe him as good, just, wise, all-powerful, merciful, and so forth, but this raises a further question: What does God's goodness or justice have to do with ours? Maimonides felt that to impose human definitions of such attributes on God was a sort of idolatry, and many medieval Christian thinkers agreed.[28]

This created an obvious problem. If God is completely "other," we may have no way of understanding him at all. Even his existence may be questioned (as Maimonides noted), since it can be asserted that God does not "exist" in the same sense in which we exist.[29] On the other hand, to assume that the terms used to describe him in sacred writings are to be taken literally—so that God is merciful or just, angry or vengeful in a recognizably human sense—denies the Supreme Being's transcendence. This produces a dilemma. "Either God appears to be something of a

Greek god or a Superman, just like us but more so, or he is so distinct from us that we cannot speak of him at all."[30] One of the outstanding features of Aquinas's theology was its use of analogy to escape from this trap. There is some "likeness" between the Creator and his creatures, Thomas argued, in a way analogous to the relationship between the sun and the objects that it warms. The sun is the source of heat; the objects that it warms are only the recipients; but there is still something (heat) that they have in common. Similarly, the "names" of God (such as goodness and wisdom) are true of God not literally, but "only according to likeness and metaphor."[31]

The usefulness of this approach is still debated, but Ockham would have none of it. Either a term like "goodness" means essentially the same thing in different contexts, he said, or it means different things. Either God is good in a human sense, or he is good in some sense that we cannot understand. Between this either/or "there is no room for analogy."[32] Ockham's razor had struck again, with the result that the sources of knowledge of God were reduced to two: sacred writings (as interpreted by the theologians) and mystical experience. To the Franciscan, this conclusion no doubt seemed eminently orthodox. Wasn't it implicit in the Condemnations of 1277 and in conservative attacks on Aristotle going back to Saint Augustine? But the assertion that we cannot know anything of God through nature or unaided reason sent a shudder through the Catholic establishment, since its effect would be to drive a wedge between thinking and believing. Ultimately, it threatened to narrow the business of the Church to praying, theologizing, and administering the sacraments.

Ockham's razor threatened to cut loose natural science, social thought, and all other branches of philosophy from their Christian moorings, and even to eviscerate theology, since the aim of that discipline from the time of Boethius had been to "reconcile faith and reason." This would spiritualize the Church all right, but it would also tend to de-intellectualize it and cut it off from the world, while secular governments, already employing hordes of bureaucrats and lawyers, became Europe's great patrons of scholarship. And how would the Catholic faith flourish and spread if its advocates could not appeal to natural reason as well as tradition and authority? If Ockham had softened the presentation of his ideas and stayed out of ecclesiastical politics, these implications might not have been noticed. If he had offered them at another time, he might not have provoked enemies in high places. But he was a controversialist and an activist by nature, and the men who would judge his thought were now strongly influenced by the Thomist thinking that he had so bluntly disparaged. For both the philosopher and his Church, the way ahead was likely to be stormy.

IN 1323, THE YEAR that Thomas Aquinas was recognized as a saint, William of Ockham was summoned to appear before a papal commission in Avignon to answer charges of heresy. His accuser was John Lutterell, the former chancellor of Oxford, a belligerent Thomist who had earned a reputation for treating Franciscan theologians as harshly as they had once treated the Dominicans. Lutterell sent fifty-six extracts from Ockham's writings to Pope John XXII with a recommendation that they be censured. The pope immediately appointed a commission to investigate the charges, ordered William to come to Avignon, and told him to remain there until the commission was ready to hear his testimony.

What lay behind this summons? At least part of the answer can be given in one word: politics. For almost fifty years, the Franciscans had attempted to discredit the followers of Aquinas, many of whom were Dominicans. Now the Thomists were in the ascendant, and men like Lutterell (whom the Oxford faculty had deposed as chancellor because of his intolerant treatment of Franciscan scholars) saw their chance to even the score. Worse yet, the Franciscan movement had spawned a powerful radical wing—the Spirituals—that many Christian leaders now considered a greater danger to the Church than any Sigerist sect. Ockham made no secret of his sympathy for the radicals, who abhorred Rome's entanglement with property and political power, and who insisted that the Catholic hierarchs stop behaving like feudal kings and barons. In some ways, his views resembled those of Arnold of Brescia, since the obvious consequence of disempowering the Church (in worldly terms) would be to strengthen the rising power of ambitious secular princes. Ockham was not an insurrectionist like Arnold, and he had not yet challenged the pope's infallibility in matters of Christian doctrine, but he was considered dangerously independent. This impression was not mitigated by his activities in Avignon. While waiting in the city for his summons to testify—a wait that would last four years— he befriended Michael of Cesena, the Franciscans' secretary-general, who was awaiting his own trial on charges of Spiritualist heresy.

The friendship did not go unnoticed by the pope's agents.

But there was another factor operating as well. Even now, reading William of Ockham is like watching a high-wire artist operate without a safety net. Philosophically speaking, the abyss that yawns beneath him is a permanent divorce between faith and reason. Politically speaking, it is the pit into which the Inquisition was prepared to hurl brilliant theorists who carried their ideas too far. For although William was as devout a Christian as Duns Scotus or any other theologian of his time, the direction in which his thinking pointed was strangely similar to that for which Siger de Brabant and his followers had been condemned in 1277. Like Siger, William did not adhere to the doctrine of Double Truth.

He had no doubt that the truths revealed by God were uncontradictable. But, again like Siger, his thoughts seemed to lead toward the conclusion that there were two sorts of truth: one for investigators of nature, the other for theologians and worshipers of God. Moreover, there was something about the way in which Ockham expressed his ideas that almost invited prosecution. A modern analyst might say that he wanted to generate a crisis that would force him to choose between his commitments to the organized Church and to the Church as the people of God.

In part, the provocative character of the Franciscan's work was the result of his fierce insistence on clarity of thinking, which meant avoiding comfortable ambiguities of the sort he thought marred Duns Scotus's writing.[33] But he also seems to have been one of those innovators (one thinks of Marx and Freud) whose intention is to shock his audience into considering a new mode of thought by polarizing groups of followers and opponents. An example: William argued strongly, as Duns Scotus had, that God's absolute freedom could not be limited by the so-called laws of nature, or even by God's prior action in history. All of God's actions were free and spontaneous. None were compelled or necessary. To illustrate this, Ockham chose an example designed to make respectable jaws drop. Although God chose to redeem us by becoming man, he declared, it was not necessary for him to have taken this particular action. If he had chosen to, he could have redeemed us in some other way—for example, by becoming a stone, a tree, or an ass.[34]

Prior theologians had gone to some lengths to demonstrate that even if God's actions in the world were not necessary, they were not, in human terms, absurd. For clarity's sake, and also, perhaps, for shock value, William had no interest in this sort of demonstration. He liked to argue that God could, if he wished, condemn the innocent and reward the guilty, or make two solid objects occupy the same place at the same time. The point was to demonstrate that God's absolute freedom and power are not limited by our notions of justice or common sense. God does not declare things to be good because they are good; they are good because that is what he declares them to be. And he does not observe the laws of nature because they are laws; they are laws insofar as he chooses to observe them. All this might, under other circumstances, have given rise to an interesting discussion in the schools, but the pope's commissioners in Avignon were not there to lead a scholarly discussion. They were summoned to judge a man who had written that our Redeemer might as well have been a donkey as Jesus Christ.

Perhaps because shocking formulations of doctrine are not necessarily heretical, the commissioners spent almost four years processing the case against William, while the latter wrote his *Summary of Logic* and talked politics with Michael of Cesena. Finally, in 1327, they issued fifty-one articles of censure describing his ideas (depending upon the treatise being examined) as "heretical," "false," "dangerous," "erroneous," "rash," or "contradictory."[35] Normally, the next step would be for William to retract the condemned statements and promise to sin no more, a common practice among academics fallen afoul of Church authority. A variety of sentences might then have been imposed, ranging from the termination of his academic career to milder forms of reprimand or punishment.[36] Another possibility, of course, would be to refuse to recant or to insist upon maintaining the proscribed views publicly, a course of action that could lead, ultimately, to the stake. William declined to pursue either of these alternatives. His new friend, Michael, had also been condemned by a papal commission, in his case for refusing to accept the pope's decree declaring that the Spirituals' refusal to own property collectively was heretical. (Property ownership of any sort was a positive virtue, declared John XXII.) Together with Michael, William decided to take advantage of a new alternative created by the unrelenting warfare between the pope and certain secular rulers: flight to the territory of a hospitable, antipapal prince.

King Ludwig of Bavaria was just such a ruler—one of the new breed of princes not at all impressed by the pope's power to excommunicate his enemies. For almost ten years, Ludwig and Frederick of Austria had battled ferociously for the title of German king—a dispute settled in Ludwig's favor on the field of battle in 1322. But victory left the Bavarian monarch with an even more implacable enemy: the same Pope John XXII. Like German rulers before him, Ludwig controlled a considerable amount of territory in northern Italy. His ambition was to be crowned Holy Roman Emperor and to succeed where Frederick II had failed in extending his hegemony over the Papal States as well. In order to thwart him, the pope recognized Frederick of Austria as the legitimate king of Germany and demanded that Ludwig come to Avignon to surrender his crown.

Unsurprisingly, Ludwig refused to comply. Instead, demonstrating the new power being wielded by secular rulers over the churchmen in their kingdoms, he summoned a general council of German bishops to support his claims. Pope John then excommunicated Ludwig, and the German ruler retaliated by having "his" bishops declare that the pope himself was a heretic who should be deposed. (Pope John had, in fact, made some very odd doctrinal statements that exposed him to this counterattack.) Ludwig formed an alliance with his old enemy Frederick of Austria, came to Rome, and had himself crowned Holy Roman Emperor by the same aristocrats who had once kidnapped Pope Boniface VIII.

In April 1328, cardinals loyal to Ludwig elected a pope of their own and seated him at the Vatican. Once again, scandalously, the

Church had two popes, one in Avignon and one in Rome. Ludwig left for Pisa, which is where William of Ockham found him. Ockham, Michael of Cesena, and another Franciscan accused of heresy had fled Avignon rather than await their sentences. Ludwig, who very likely arranged their escape, was delighted to welcome such famous, learned, antipapal figures to his court. He embraced them, promising to take them to his capital in Munich and protect them from the pope's wrath. Ockham was equally enthusiastic about the new alliance. "You defend me with your sword," he is supposed to have replied boldly, "and I will defend you with my pen."

If this was actually his vow, William was true to it. Munich had become a favorite place of exile for émigré philosophers who readily agreed to assist the German king in his struggle against Pope John XXII. The Franciscan fugitives, soon to be excommunicated for fleeing to the enemy camp, discovered in Munich a community of scholars who disagreed strongly among themselves, but who were united in opposing papal claims to infallibility in matters of doctrine and absolute obedience in matters of Church law and politics. The radical Averroists John of Jandun and Marsilius of Padua were in the city writing their tract against papal authority, *The Defender of Peace*. Leaders of the German spiritual brotherhood, the Beghards, could be found there, as well as followers of the controversial Dominican mystic Meister Eckhart. Hurling himself into political and ecclesiastical writing, William abandoned speculative theology and spent the next ten years in Munich writing in defense of the Spirituals' position on poverty and on the freedom of the Church. He died there in 1349, very likely a victim of the disease whose devastation marked the end of an era: the Black Death.

William of Ockham's ideas about the Church in the world were, in their own way, as radical as his theology. He upheld the

Franciscan ideal of a poor clergy, denied the pope's power to rule over secular sovereigns, and argued that the ultimate source of religious authority was the people of the Church rather than the hierarchy. Popes and cardinals were merely men. They could (and did) sin, err, and fall into heresy. For that reason, William considered his own excommunication by a "heretical" pope a nullity. Some have called William the first Protestant, yet he remained intensely Catholic. Unlike Marsilius of Padua, he had no interest in subjecting the Church to secular absolutism or in denying the pope's legitimacy as head of the Church, so long as the pontiff acted in accordance with divine law. Unlike Martin Luther and the Protestants of the next century, he believed that the Church, as well as the Bible, was a source of revealed truth, and that it should never be divided. William has been well described as "a man at once strangely modern and yet altogether medieval."[37] In politics as well as in theology, he belonged as much to the future as to the past.

THE SAME THING could be said of a contemporary of Ockham's who, like him, was a victim of the Church's narrowing vision. In the same year that the papal commission condemned Ockham's fifty-one propositions, the great German mystic Meister Eckhart appeared in Avignon to defend himself against twenty-eight counts of heresy.

At first glance, one would have considered Eckhart to be Ockham's antithesis. In the first place, Eckhart was a Dominican—the first and most highly placed member of his order to endure an inquisitorial proceeding. His loyalty to the pope was unquestioned, he was not a controversial theorist, and he had never been accused of advocating heretical views. Before being summoned to Avignon, he had been the Order of Friars Preachers' chief administrator in northern Germany and its vicar-general in Bohemia.

Twice he had held a chair in theology at the University of Paris and had served as senior professor at the Dominican house of study in Cologne. Now in his late sixties, he was also one of the most respected preachers in Germany, where his sermons in the vernacular were considered masterpieces of the German language. Although a scholastic theologian with numerous treatises to his credit, Eckhart lacked Ockham's transcendent logical brilliance. (In fact, after his arrival in Avignon, the outspoken Franciscan is said to have called his teachings ridiculous.[38]) His consuming interest was a different sort of transcendence altogether. Eckhart's favorite theme was the ability of Christian believers to know God personally, and it was his effort to explore that mystical theme in theological language that had landed him, near the end of a distinguished career, in the defendant's chair at Avignon.

The two men's differences were glaring, yet they were far from polar opposites. Both Ockham and Eckhart were "Aristotle's grandchildren"—post-Thomist thinkers who rejected the idea that people could reason their way to God by finding evidence of his intentions in nature. Both distinguished sharply between the mental concepts arrived at by abstract thinking and the "really real" entities or relations knowable through intuition or faith. And both gave a dramatic new emphasis to the importance of experience to the process of human learning. But there was a world of difference between how each man defined and employed "experience." The experience that interested Ockham was the immediate sensory and intellectual apprehension of natural things—the data that subjected to rational analysis can yield probable truths about the natural universe, but not about God. To Eckhart, on the other hand, what experience meant, above all, was the immediate, intuitive knowledge of God—a "datum" that could be used, like the data of natural science, to test and reinter-

pret accepted doctrines.[39] Eckhart accepted the distinction between things knowable by reason and through faith, but by redefining faith to include religious experience, he greatly reduced
the importance of reason. As reckless, in his own way, as Ockham, he even seemed to suggest that the doctrine of the Holy
Trinity was merely a mental concept that did not express the more
fundamental unity of the Godhead experienced by mystics. "Who-
ever sees two or distinction does not see God,"[40] he declared—an
idea that mystical adepts might understand, but which was bound
to offend analytical theologians.

The great preacher's troubles seem to have begun in 1325 during the order's general meeting in Venice, at which charges were
made that "the utterances of certain German Dominicans risked
leading their hearers astray."[41] A preliminary investigation ordered by Pope John XXII cleared him of suspicion of heresy, but
the reprieve was short-lived.[42] Eckhart soon found himself facing
the implacably hostile Heinrich of Vineburg, the archbishop of
Cologne. Known for his penchant for burning local heretics,
Heinrich was considered by Eckhart's sympathizers to be a cold,
conniving Church politician jealous of the Dominican leader's
reputation for learning and spirituality. The description may be
accurate. Certainly, Heinrich seemed determined to bring Eckhart down by any means necessary. But he may also have feared
the impact of the preacher's teachings in the inflamed German
atmosphere. Northern European cities were seeing a rapid prolif-
eration of pietistic groups known as Beghards (men) and Beguines
(women)—communal associations of laypeople who practiced
apostolic living, preached a gospel of spiritual perfection, and
sometimes lapsed into various forms of mystical heresy. The hierarchy's great fear—realized in later years by John Wycliffe in
England, Jan Hus in Bohemia, and, finally, Martin Luther in Germany—was the emergence of a charismatic "insider" like Eckhart,

a member of the educated elite, at the head of a massive, independent religious movement.

Whatever Heinrich's motives may have been, he refused to accept the investigator's report exculpating the Dominican leader. Instead, he established a commission in Cologne to inquire further into Eckhart's orthodoxy. The inquisitors found well over one hundred of his statements to be either heretical or questionable. In the autumn of 1326, Eckhart made several appearances before the commission in which he defended his teachings passionately, and sometimes with asperity. Most of them, he argued, were perfectly orthodox. Some might be considered unorthodox if they were wrongly interpreted, but the language in which they were expressed was intended for the educated clerics to whom he preached, not for uneducated people likely to be misled. (Eckhart's principal audiences consisted of cloistered nuns.) In any case, he added, he had no intention of making doctrinal errors and would correct them if they were called to his attention. "They regard as error whatever they fail to understand," he said of his accusers, "and also regard all error as heresy, whereas only obstinate addition to error constitutes both heresy and the heretic."[43]

The commissioners were unimpressed. Months passed without a decision, and Eckhart finally appealed to the pope, for the sake of the Dominican order, to settle the matter himself. He also preached a sermon in the Dominican church in Cologne solemnly declaring that he hated heresy and would recant any statement that was later held to be erroneous. But the doors of tolerance were closing. Eckhart's file was transferred to Avignon, and, although in bad health, he traveled there in order to plead his case before a papal commission.

What had the unfortunate man written or said to cause such a strong reaction? One sample of his preaching illustrates both the beauty of Eckhart's language and its hazards. The sermon in

question is "See What Love," in which the preacher comments on
Saint John's statement, "See what love the father has given us; we
are called Sons of God and we are."

> Notice by what we are the Son of God; by having that same
> being that the Son has. How then are we the Son of God, or
> how does one know that one is the Son of God, since God re-
> sembles no one? For this is assuredly true. Indeed, Isaiah says,
> "To what have you compared him, or what image do you give
> him?" (Isa. 40.18). Since, then, it is of the nature of God not to
> be like anyone, we are compelled to conclude that we are noth-
> ing, so that we may be transported into the identical being that
> he is himself.
>
> When this is achieved, when I cease projecting myself into
> any image, when no image is represented any longer in me,
> and when I cast out of myself and eject whatever is in me, then
> I am ready to be transported into the naked being of God, the
> pure being of the Spirit. All likeness has to be expelled from it.
> Then I am translated into God and I become one with him—
> one sole substance, one being, and one nature: the Son of God.
> And after this has been accomplished, nothing is hidden any-
> more in God which has not become manifest or mine. Then I
> become wise and powerful. I become all things, as he is, and I
> am one and the same being with him.[44]

The subject of this passage is an experience long cherished by
the spiritually gifted, and, in Eckhart's time, avidly sought by
many ordinary believers: the experience of personal communion
with God. What makes the preacher's statement both moving and
dangerous is that it operates simultaneously on three levels: it is
biblical exegesis interpreting the words of Saint John; it is a poetic
description of the "emptying" or "annihilation" of the ego that
many spiritual adepts believe precedes and permits the "filling" of
the self by the Spirit; and—here is where the main source of

trouble lay—it is also scholastic theology, which was considered a science, not a poetic art.

Eckhart analyzes the experience of mystical rebirth and union using the same Aristotelian terms ("being," "substance," etc.) employed by Saint Thomas, Duns Scotus, and other theologians to explain the relationship of the created universe to the Creator. In answer to Maimonides' question about the possibility of knowing a deity who is transcendently "other," he maintains that we can know God experientially, even if we do not know him intellectually. This idea is not necessarily unorthodox; carefully and "academically" stated, it might have been received respectfully even by those who disagreed with it. But when Eckhart proclaimed, "We are compelled to conclude that we are nothing, so that we can be transported into the identical being that is [God] himself," his scholastic critics immediately smelled heresy. "We are nothing" suggests that God is the only reality and that Creation is an illusion—an ancient error. And the idea that humans can actually become God in this life would immediately remind the papal commissioners of current popular heresies like those of the Beghards. It was one thing for a cloistered nun to say that in experiencing union with God, "I become wise and powerful. I become all things, as he is, and I am one and the same being with him." It was quite another for some lay preacher to proclaim that those who experience the mystical union transcend their normal human limitations and become incapable of sinning.

In Avignon, Eckhart defended himself in person before the commission, arguing that statements such as this might seem questionable if taken literally, but that they should be interpreted poetically, as he had intended. He might have saved his breath. Since he was a sophisticated theologian with a background in university teaching, the papal commissioners felt justified in treating him as a scholastic philosopher and taking his words literally.

Reading Eckhart's sermons, of course, one finds them anything but academic. The great preacher seems to have intended them neither as pure scholasticism nor as poetry, but as something in between—the kind of quasi-poetical philosophy that one encounters much later in figures like William Blake and Nietzsche. In the fourteenth century, however, it was potentially fatal to describe the "spark" of the soul as something "uncreated" that knows God exactly as God knows himself,[45] or to maintain that the just man is transformed into God in the same way that the bread is transformed into the body of Christ in the Eucharist.[46] In 1329, the commission condemned both of these doctrines "as stated" along with twenty-six of Eckhart's other teachings. A distinguished career in God's service was drawing to its tragic close.

In a papal bull issued a year later, Pope John XXII softened the verdict somewhat. Seventeen of the challenged statements were heretical, he said, but the remaining eleven, although likely to mislead the unwary, were capable of an orthodox interpretation. Perhaps the pope sensed that the Dominican leader had been treated too harshly. He might have worried (although he probably did not) that the loss of great souls like Eckhart together with great intellects like William of Ockham might not bode well for the future of the Church. The defendant, in any case, did not live to read the papal decree. Eckhart died shortly after giving his testimony, either on the trip back from Avignon or after arriving home in Germany. Disgrace blotted out the funerary details. Neither the time, the date, nor the place of his death is known.

At around the same time that Meister Eckhart left Avignon to die in a place unknown, William of Ockham escaped the papal city to join other refugees at King Ludwig's court in Munich. The two defendants were neither friends nor enemies. So far as we know, they never met. If they had, it is difficult to imagine what they would have said to each other, considering the fact that they inhabited such different worlds of sensibility, talent, and concern. In these two scholastics, the Dominican preacher and the Franciscan logician, we can see the split emerging that would henceforth divide Western culture into two divergent currents: a culture of the heart and a culture of the head—a personal faith validated by religious experience and an impersonal science validated by explanatory power. Eckhart's disciples in Germany contributed to a great flowering of mystical evangelism in the Rhineland.[47] The activities of the devout Germans loosely known as the "friends of God" give a strong foretaste of the coming Protestant movement, with its inwardness and evangelical zeal, its communities of "saints," its intense focus on Scripture, and its relative lack of interest in scientific reasoning. At almost the same time, Ockham's successors in Paris engineered a revival of natural philosophy that served as a gateway to the discoveries made later by scientists like Copernicus, Galileo, and Newton.[48]

So began the divorce between faith and reason—the emergence, in fact, of the Double Truth that had so troubled the dreams of medieval scholars and churchmen. Eight centuries earlier, Boethius had implored his friend Pope John I to reconcile faith and reason "if possible." The question was always to what extent a genuine reconciliation was possible between the visions of an autonomous, self-sufficient universe and a universe dependent upon a personal God. Aristotelian Christianity did not resolve the conflict between these perspectives, but it had held them in creative tension. With the passing of the Aristotelian tradition, Western culture—and the individuals who created it—would find itself increasingly torn between the ideals of the reasoning head and the questing heart.

CHAPTER EIGHT

"God Does Not Have to Move These Circles Anymore"

ARISTOTLE AND THE MODERN WORLD

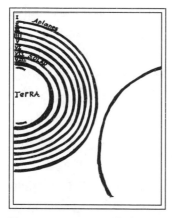

ONE OF THE EARLIEST history lessons that I can remember is the tale of Christopher Columbus's discovery of the New World.

Time out of mind, the teacher said, people had believed that the earth was flat. European sailors avoided venturing too far out into the Atlantic lest they sail off the edge of the world. But inquisitive Columbus, a man of science as well as action, thought that the earth was round and asked the Spanish queen to finance a bold experiment. By sailing west, he would arrive at the rich lands of the East and repay the monarch in Indian treasure. Financially, the venture was a disappointment. Isabella was repaid in West Indian breadfruit, not East Indian gold. But scientifically, it was a triumph. By verifying the hypothesis of the spherical earth, Columbus put an end to centuries of medieval ignorance.

Here is another man of science writing about the shape of the earth and the possibility of circumnavigating the globe:

The evidence of the senses further corroborates [the sphericity of the earth]. How else would eclipses of the moon show segments shaped as we see them? As it is, the shapes which the moon itself each month shows are of every kind ... but in eclipses the outline is always curved; and, since it is the interposition of the earth that makes the eclipse, the form of this line will be caused by the form of the earth's surface, which is therefore spherical. ... Hence one should not be too sure of the incredibility of the view of those who conceive that there is continuity between the parts about the pillars of Hercules [the Straits of Gibraltar] and the parts about India, and that in this way the ocean is one.[1]

The writer, of course, is Aristotle. These words appear in his treatise *On the Heavens,* written more than 1,800 years before Columbus left Cádiz aboard the *Santa Maria.* First translated into Latin from the Arabic in the twelfth century by Gerard of Cremona, they were quoted approvingly and commented on by numerous scholastic philosophers, including Pierre d'Ailly, a fifteenth-century theologian and scientist. An annotated copy of d'Ailly's *Image of the World* was found in Columbus's library.[2] During medieval times, the common folk may well have believed that the earth was flat, but virtually no educated European credited the flat-earth hypothesis.

How did we come to believe the fable of medieval ignorance? How did Aristotle's ideas, lost to the West for six centuries after the fall of Rome, vanish again from our historical consciousness? The idea of a medieval "dark age" is a corollary of the origin myth of modern science: the notion that scientific research could not emerge as a respected and productive activity until it had liberated itself from the clutches of a dogmatic, authoritarian faith. The dramatic theme is rationality versus religion, with religion playing the role of the oppressive censor or persecutor, and selected scientists and freethinkers that of the hero or martyr. One recalls Copernicus's writings placed on the Roman Catholic Index of Forbidden Books; Giordano Bruno burned and Galileo persecuted by the Inquisition; Anglican bishops ridiculing Darwin's theory of natural selection; and ministers of every faith denouncing Freud's "despicable" psychoanalytical theories.[3] These were real disputes, of course, and they are far from obsolete.[4] What is mythical is the idea that faith and reason have always been implacable enemies—an idea that implies that any other relationship between them is impossible.

Two names are sufficient to explode the myth of medieval ignorance: Jean Buridan and Nicole Oresme. Both men were teachers at the University of Paris in the mid-1300s, a time when the Ockhamist school dominated natural philosophy in Europe.[5] Buridan taught in the arts faculty at Paris, served as the leader of the Picard nation, and was elected rector of the university three times.[6] Oresme, a theologian, was originally his student, and ended his life a bishop and counselor to King Charles V. Given the origin myth of modern science, scholastic scholars like these should not have achieved any sort of major scientific breakthrough. In fact, like bold scientific thinkers ever since, they took an existing paradigm (the Aristotelian theory of motion) as their starting point, and ended by revolutionizing it.[7]

Buridan wrote on a dizzying variety of topics, from philosophy and logic to ethics and politics, but he is chiefly remembered for discovering a new way of thinking about motion. Like every other philosopher of his time, he accepted the ancient idea that the heavenly bodies were attached to nested spheres that moved east to west in circular orbits around the fixed earth. The question was how they moved, or rather, what moved them, since, according to Aristotle, nothing moves or changes without some sort of force operating continuously on it. In the case of the heavenly spheres, Aristotle thought that each sphere was moved by an "Unmoved Mover," or by what some philosophers called an "intelligence," with God, the Prime Mover, responsible for keeping the whole system in motion.[8] Buridan's remarkable insight was to recognize that one could do without these "intelligences" if one simply assumed that things once set in motion remain in motion unless they meet resistance. The tendency of moving objects to remain in motion he called impetus.

The idea of impetus was far more surprising than it may seem, since it turned what everyone had thought of for centuries as an effect (something done to objects) into a cause (something that objects do naturally by themselves). It is almost as if we were to learn, after centuries of teaching children to read and write, that reading and writing were activities children could learn alone once a book was placed before them. Buridan was clearly concerned about the potentially unorthodox implications of his breakthrough. Aristotle's theory seemed almost Christian, since it made motion dependent upon a sort of divine intervention (the "intelligences"), while Buridan's post-Aristotelian approach seemed...well...godless. The Parisian scholar was quick to point out, therefore, that the Bible has nothing to say about Unmoved Movers or intelligences, and that there was no religious necessity for such entities. On the contrary, he wrote:

> One could rather say that God, as he created the world, imparted to each heavenly circle a movement according to his pleasure. He impressed upon each one the impetus which has moved it ever since in such a way that God does not have to move these circles anymore except in the general sense in which he bestows on all activity his constant assistance.[9]

Another factor that made the theory of impetus explosive was its universality. Buridan did not limit his discussion to the heavenly spheres, which had always been considered radically different in their structure and operations from the earthly (sublunar) realm. On the contrary, he applied the concept to earthly motion as well. Aristotle had argued that when a projectile is thrown on earth, what keeps it going after it has lost contact with the thrower is a replacement of the air behind it, which pushes the object ahead with decreasing force until it falls to the ground. But Buridan referred to simple experiments that seemed to disprove the Aristotelian theory. A spinning top moves without leaving its place, and without evidence of air replacement. A magnet draws an iron object toward it by its own force of attraction.

> A ship drawn swiftly in the river even against the flow of the river, after the drawing has ceased, cannot be stopped quickly, but continues to move for a long time. And yet a sailor on deck does not feel any air from behind pushing him. He feels only the air from the front resisting.[10]

In short, the heavens and the earth did not necessarily obey diametrically opposed laws. Impetus was a characteristic of moving objects in both realms. And the concept could even be quantified by multiplying the velocity of the moving object by the amount of its matter—a formula that is virtually the same as the modern formula for momentum.[11]

Theories this daring made Jean Buridan's name known throughout Europe, but Nicole Oresme outdid even his master. Oresme's work in mathematics developed methods of geometrical representation which anticipate modern graphing techniques and the development of analytical geometry.[12] Applying these techniques to the science of motion, he arrived at a proof of the "mean speed theorem" that is substantially the same as that used by Galileo in the seventeenth century.[13] But his most colorful and revealing achievement may be that contained in his last book, *The*

Book of the Heavens and the Earth, written at King Charles's request in 1377.

The subject was the rotation of the earth. Oresme and Buridan had both written earlier on the question, concluding after much ingenious reasoning that the traditional view was correct: the earth remained immobile at the center of the universe. Near the end of his life, however, Oresme changed his mind. He did not announce that the earth rotated while the heavens stood still, but declared with astonishing aplomb that the case for a rotating earth was as good or better than the case for immobility. The initial basis for this was a thought experiment that supported his conclusion that all motion is relative to the position of the observer. He wrote:

> One cannot demonstrate by any [experiment] whatever that the heavens move with diurnal motion. Whatever the fact may be, assuming that the heavens move and the earth does not or that the earth moves and the heavens do not, to an eye in the heavens which could see the earth clearly, it would appear to move; if the eye were on the earth, the heavens would appear to move.[14]

Jean Buridan had also done the same "eye in the heavens" experiment, and had agreed that the relativity of motion makes it impossible to decide the question by observing the heavens from earth. But Oresme's old master argued that other evidence proved that the earth stood still. For example, he said, an arrow shot straight up on a windless day falls back to its starting point, which it would not do if the earth were rotating. Not at all, Oresme replied. For if the whole earth rotated, an arrow shot up would combine its own vertical motion with the horizontal motion of the atmosphere, and would therefore return to its starting point. The situation, he said, was exactly like that of motion on board a moving ship, where "there can be all kinds of movements—horizontal, criss-cross, upward, downward, in all directions—and they seem to be exactly the same as those when the ship is at rest."[15] Moreover, he argued, the concept of a rotating earth was far more elegant and economical than the Aristotelian paradigm involving multiple rotating spheres. Applying Ockham's razor to this problem, one would have to favor the simpler, less cluttered explanation.

This was heady stuff, particularly in light of the fact that Oresme was a bishop, and that there was biblical language suggesting that the earth stood still. Even so, as a Catholic theologian, he understood that many passages in Scripture are not to be taken literally, but represent an accommodation to "the customary usage of popular speech."[16] If the arguments for a rotating earth were clearly superior to the arguments for a stationary earth, Oresme would probably have interpreted sacred writings like Psalm 92:1 ("For God hath established the world, which shall not be moved") figuratively, or as a manner of speaking understandable to common folk. But this was not the case. Based on the available evidence, neither hypothesis was clearly preferable to the other. The only reason to favor the paradigm of a rotating earth was its simplicity. In this case, he decided, one ought to interpret the Bible literally. Under the circumstances, the best thing to do was to accept the traditional view of the unmoving earth.

Historians have made much of what one distinguished scholar calls "Oresme's apparent turnabout,"[17] but this misses the point. For a world-renowned philosopher to have raised the hypothesis of a rotating earth to a level of scientific acceptability was a revolutionary act. Once Oresme had broken with Aristotle by asserting that the earth's immobility could not be proved by reason, the cat was out of the bag. In a flash, the stationary earth also became a mere hypothesis that could be proved or disproved by later evidence. Moreover, as Copernicus (who was familiar with Oresme's work) later recognized, the same principles used to support the idea of a rotating earth could also be used to support the revolution of the earth and other planets around an immobile sun. And further evidence might show that the sun itself was a moving body, one star among others in a vast, mobile universe.

Oresme's breakthrough, in other words, was as much psychological and cultural as it was scientific. The idea of a fixed earth seemed to be proved by the sort of commonsense observations on which all Aristotelian science rested. But Oresme and Buridan had shown that what was common sense to an observer at one location in a moving system might be non-sense to an observer at another location. Even though they left the earth at the center of the universe, the effect was "decentering," especially when the earth's rotation was admitted to be a distinct possibility. Like children thinking about their parental home, people were used to thinking of their earthly home as the heartland of all meaning—not just one place among others but a unique location from which one could observe the rest of the universe objectively; not an object spinning dizzily in space like some gigantic top but a place satisfyingly at rest. Admitting the possibility of a rotating earth not only challenged these emotion-laden assumptions but began the process by which the earth (and, later, the celestial bodies) would be considered inanimate "things" rather than the living beings of Aristotelian cosmology. When Oresme allowed the earth to rotate, it was only a matter of time (and further cultural change) before someone else would allow it to revolve.

With the remarkable work of the Parisian Ockhamists, the Aristotelian revolution reached its limit and began to self-destruct—or, to speak more accurately, to self-transform. The impulse to make sense of the material universe that had led the scholars of twelfth-century Spain and Sicily to recapture the ancient knowledge remained alive—more so than ever. But the new discoveries made in Aristotle's questing, this-worldly spirit, while using some of his basic concepts, now tended to undermine many of his conclusions: the centrality of the fixed earth and the absoluteness of motion; the distinctions between form and matter; the "four causes"; and, most important, the purposeful, animate structure of the natural universe. Out of the interplay of Aristotelian science, Christian doctrine, and new developments in European social life, something new was being born: a science increasingly alienated from religion, and a faith seeking a foothold in "a mechanical world of lifeless matter, local motion, and random collision."[18]

The relationship of Aristotelian thought to Christianity in the Middle Ages was always uneasy.[19] The great changes in European society that were intensifying people's this-worldly interests and inclining them to value the pleasures of life on earth brought the two worldviews closer together. But instead of fusing, or one perspective eliminating the other, they existed from the twelfth century onward in a state of creative tension. Close enough to permit each worldview to "read" the other with understanding and to accept some of its ideas, they were far enough apart to generate continual dialogue and self-reflection. The Aristotelian tendency was always to emphasize the autonomy of nature and human history, while the Christian tendency was to insist on God's personality and providential activity in the world. But both tendencies were present in the minds of the same individuals— men like Bonaventure and Aquinas, Duns Scotus and William of Ockham, Jean Buridan and Nicole Oresme. The great scholastics did not see this as an either/or choice. Their passionate preference was for both/and.

Christian thinkers of the medieval renaissance could not rest content with the idea either that the world was a puppet show with God pulling the strings or that it was a godless machine. Nor could they accept the choice between a human nature totally depraved and entirely dependent upon God's arbitrary will or one totally free and self-determining. Their attempts to resolve these contradictions were inevitably unstable, producing further dialogue, criticism, and revision. And this very instability was the key to further progress. While differing strongly among themselves, the scholastics maintained the idea of an integrated, explicable, and interesting universe that they had extracted from Aristotle. They also affirmed the Judeo-Christian idea of a creative, caring, all-powerful God who is free to remake the universe at will. This combination—a sovereign God who gives his creation both meaning and autonomy—provided fertile soil for the development of new scientific and religious ideas. It produced many theologies, not just one. Bonaventure's "seminal reasons," Aquinas's "secondary causes," Ockham's theory of knowledge, and Buridan's theory of impetus were all attempts to reconcile an omnipotent personal deity with a universe operating (for the most part) according to its own internal logic.

Viewed in this light, the famous Condemnations of 1277 seem not so much an attempt to reverse the Aristotelian revolution as an effort to keep faith and reason from spinning off into separate orbits. In retrospect, at least, the project seems to have been doomed to fail.[20] The scholarship of the universities reflected the interests and aspirations of an intelligentsia formed and nurtured by the Church in order to maintain its intellectual and moral leadership at a time of dramatic social changes in Europe. But now a transformation far more profound and disruptive than the medieval renaissance was on the horizon. The next two centuries would see a vast increase in the urban population and in capitalist enterprise, the invention of printing and the spread of printed books, an unprecedented outburst of artistic activity, the development of new forms of warfare based on firearms, the rise of sovereign nation-states, the first great voyages of exploration, a revolution in science triggered by the work of Copernicus, and the development of a dissenting religious movement led by the former Augustinian monk Martin Luther.[21] Under the pressure of these transformative changes, the unity of the Christian intelligentsia fractured. The scholasticism of the universities, increasingly brittle and dogmatic, became a target for ridicule and bitter criticism by a new generation of philosophers and scientists.

Aristotelian Christianity had maintained a stormy, productive dialogue between faith and reason. But what if this encounter ended? What if the methods, interests, and basic concepts informing the thought of rationalist thinkers and people of faith were to become so separated—and on each side, so self-contained—that each party considered the other's worldview irrelevant? Rationalists and believers might then feel free to ignore each other's views and concerns, except where competing claims to the same intellectual territory made conflict inevitable. In the modern period, faith and reason would enter upon a new relationship—no longer a turbulent marriage, but a fractious divorce in which the alienated parties, greatly changed by their separation, meet periodically to argue about the terms of their separation, and, on rare occasions, to take inspiration from each other. Understanding why this divorce occurred may throw some light on the possibilities of future reconciliation.

THERE IS A longstanding debate—by now, I think, a rather silly one—about whether the work done by scholars like Oresme and Buridan was "real" science.[22] A French historian started it early in the twentieth century by maintaining, contrary to much current opinion, that there was strong continuity between medieval and modern science.[23] Others disagreed, insisting that the work of the scholastics was not really like modern science, because their methods and metaphysical assumptions differed so greatly from ours. I call the debate silly, not because there is anything wrong with trying to determine the extent to which scholastic *scientia* and modern science resemble each other but because the question whether they are essentially the same or different is so "medieval" and masks other concerns.

It is in the nature of science to develop and change radically from generation to generation. The curved and relativized space-time continuum of Albert Einstein probably differs more dramatically from the universe conceived of by Isaac Newton than Newton's universe differs from that of Buridan and Oresme. In fact, Einstein's methods (emphasizing "thought experiments") and his overall conception of science are closer in some ways to the scholastics' than to those of his immediate predecessors. What could be more Aristotelian in spirit than these remarks of Einstein's?

> The very fact that the totality of our sense experiences is such that by means of thinking . . . it can be put in order, this fact is one which leaves us in awe, but which we shall never understand. Scientific research can reduce superstition by encouraging people to think and view things in terms of cause and effect. Certain it is that a conviction, akin to religious feeling, of the rationality or intelligibility of the world lies behind all scientific work of a higher order.[24]

No one doubts that there were scientific revolutions after the Middle Ages, but why deny that what the scholastics did was also science? Imagine Einstein declaring that because Isaac Newton was a deeply religious man who believed in absolute space and time, he was no scientist! The historian Edward Grant has it right when he remarks that "the habit of applying reason to resolve the innumerable questions about our world, and of always raising new questions" is "a gift from the Latin Middle Ages to the modern world." He is also right to add that for the past four centuries, this gift has been "the best-kept secret of Western civilization."[25] Why this should be so—why even scientific thinkers have blanked out their medieval heritage—is a puzzle whose solution may help us to understand the modern separation of faith and reason.

In one sense, it is no surprise to see the scholars of the early modern era rejecting Aristotle's authority. No thinker dominated Western intellectual life so completely and for such a long time as did the Philosopher. Medieval students did not have to agree with him on every point—in fact, on some points, Christians were expected to disagree—but for four centuries, one could not begin a discussion of metaphysics, natural science, logic, theology, ethics, aesthetics, or politics without referring to Aristotle's views and dealing respectfully with them. One can understand why this weighty authority, which reflected the interests and values of the old Roman Catholic intelligentsia, would have felt burdensome to innovative thinkers confronting the problems of a new society. From a scientific point of view, furthermore, Aristotle and his followers had made some serious mistakes. The scholastic thinkers themselves challenged a number of his basic concepts, including his theories of light, motion, and knowledge. By the seventeenth century, critics such as Francis Bacon had broadened the attack to include Aristotle's metaphysics and methods (especially his emphasis on formal logic as a way of discovering scientific truths), and were ready to declare Aristotelian science obsolete.[26]

As I say, the new philosophers' desire to liberate themselves from Aristotelian authority is understandable. They were right to recognize that with vast changes reshaping European society at every level no ancient philosophy could claim to provide the key to universal knowledge. But this still does not account for the extraordinary vehemence with which thinkers like Bacon rejected scholastic thought—a vehemence amounting to a denial that Aristotle's ideas and those of his medieval interpreters played any progressive role at all in the course of human enlightenment. It was not just a question of criticizing the Aristotelians strongly, as modern democratic theorists, for example, might criticize the defenders of authoritarian government, but something more like the rewriting of history that we associate with Stalinism in the Soviet Union—the "airbrushing" out of figures and events embarrassing to the current regime. Leading philosophers of the early modern period did not merely attack Aristotelian Christianity, they dismissed it. Here is Francis Bacon, for example, on the subject of scientific progress:

> Out of twenty-five centuries with which the memory and learning of men are conversant, scarcely six can be set apart and selected as fertile in science and favorable to its progress. For there are deserts and wastes in times as in countries, and we can only reckon up three revolutions and epochs of philosophy. 1. The Greek. 2. The Roman. 3. Our own.... Nor need we mention the Arabs, or the scholastic philosophy, which in those ages, ground down the sciences by their numerous treatises, more than they increased their weight.[27]

The medieval renaissance, in this view, becomes a "desert and waste." By the time that Bacon wrote, of course, scholastic thinkers had discredited themselves by reasoning pseudo-scientifically about matters of faith and opposing any new natural discoveries that ran counter to Aristotle's conclusions. If Galileo's telescopic observations suggested that the sun lay at the center of the planetary system, the telescope must be defective, since the Philosopher believed in an earth-centered cosmos. Despite his prosecution by Church authorities spouting this sort of nonsense, Galileo himself distinguished between healthy scholastic science and decadent dogmatism. He remarked:

> If Aristotle should see the new discoveries in the sky, he would change his opinions and correct his books and embrace the most sensible doctrines, casting away from himself those people so weak-minded as to be induced to go on maintaining abjectly everything he had ever said.[28]

Unlike the magnanimous Galileo, however, Bacon and his co-thinkers condemned all Aristotelian thinking back to Aristotle himself. For them, it was not bad science but no science at all.

The denial that Aristotelian thinking had played a creative role in Europe's intellectual life was not limited to natural philosophers. The two leading Aristotle-haters of the early modern period were its greatest religious leader and an equally brilliant atheist philosopher. Martin Luther, who detested scholastic theology in general and Aristotle in particular, put his feelings succinctly: "In a word, Aristotle is to divinity, as darkness is to light."[29] And, "It is an error to say that no man can become a theologian without Aristotle. Indeed, no one can become a theologian unless he becomes one without Aristotle."[30] The secular political philosopher Thomas Hobbes was, if anything, more dismissive:

> And I believe that scarce any thing can be more absurdly said in natural philosophy, than that which now is called *Aristotle's Metaphysics*; nor more repugnant to government, than much of what he hath said in his *Politics*; nor more ignorantly, than a great part of his *Ethics*.[31]

What accounts for this ferocious hostility? In the Prologue to this book, I suggested that cultural chauvinists of every stripe want to believe that their civilization is entirely self-created, rather than being a product, even in part, of "alien" ideas. To obliterate the Aristotelian revolution has the advantage of disguising the West's enormous debt to a more advanced Islamic civilization.[32] But there are other ways in which obliterating the past served the interests of Europe's new leaders. Aristotelian Christianity was an obstacle to all those who wished to break the power of the Catholic Church and to end its monopoly of educational resources: the rulers of secular nation-states, the leaders of Reforming churches, the rising business class, and the scientific intelligentsia. But—this is where the embarrassment comes in—it was not just Rome's political and ecclesial authority that these elites were casting off but the moral restraints that the Church had tried to inculcate and impose through the use of concepts like natural law and the Just War. The merchants and traders of the new Europe did not want to be hemmed in by medieval notions of the "just price" or restrictions on investing at interest. The leaders of new churches and sects were not prepared to modify their passionate convictions for the sake of maintaining a transnational moral community. And the new secular rulers wished to be free of any limitations whatsoever on their legal authority and military power.

The most brilliant spokesman of the new ruling class was Thomas Hobbes, who argued in his masterwork, *Leviathan,* that man's fundamental right is the right to self-preservation.[33] For the sake of their security, people must yield up all their other rights to the state, thereby granting it a monopoly of force and unlimited legal power over its citizens. The law of the state is *the* law, he declared; all other laws, like the natural law, moral law, and international law asserted and defined by the Church, are laws in name only, without binding effect on the subjects of sovereign states.[34] In all this, Hobbes's great philosophical enemies were Thomas Aquinas, who held that a law of the state contrary to the natural or moral law has no binding force,[35] and Aristotle, whose treatise *Politics* is a defense of the principle that politics is a branch of ethics, and that the purpose of the state is not just security but justice.[36]

Hobbes's views of politics were not entirely indefensible. By the time he wrote *Leviathan*, the Church was long past the point that it could guarantee Europeans either security or justice, and many people believed that empowering the sovereign state was necessary for the preservation of civil society. But one cannot help noting the extent to which his work insists on separating power from principle, law from morality, and the realm of facts from the realm of values. Hobbes is the arch-"realist"—the first in a long line of thinkers ending with the modern advocates of *raison d'état* and "My country, right or wrong." In opposition to Aristotle and Aquinas, who believed that the purpose of law is to assist naturally sociable people to be good, he assumes that people are driven by a self-interested will and need to be frightened into submission. ("Man is a wolf to other men," he famously declared.) Similarly, while Aristotle held that the validity of any form of government depends upon its conformity with right reason, Hobbes glorified the will of the sovereign, which is sufficient by itself to make valid laws. Will and power alone are real. Reason and morality are dangerous fantasies. Thus speaks the prophet of the modern state.

One striking feature of this philosophy is how much it has in common with the thought of the Aristotelians' most implacable religious opponent, Martin Luther. Of course, I do not mean to equate the two men. Luther, who lived a century earlier than Hobbes, would have been horrified by the Englishman's political amorality, and Hobbes considered the rebellious Puritans of his own time a menace to public order. Nevertheless, just as Hobbes fought to free the secular state from Catholic political and moral claims, Luther struggled to establish the autonomy of the sanctified congregation. For the Reformer, as well as for Hobbes, Aristotle's optimism about human reason was a dangerous delusion.

Since people were incurably willful and disobedient, the only solution was to subject them to the dictates of a far greater will: that of
a sovereign God. Hobbes opposed the Church's attempt to exert
worldly power over sovereign princes. Luther agreed. More important, he excoriated its efforts (as he saw them) to limit God's
absolute power by offering to mediate between sinners and their
Judge. To Luther, the Catholic Church's "economy of salvation,"
with its system of tithes, penances, and other good works, was
little more than a con game designed to keep benighted believers in
a state of subjection to a worldly institution. Men and women
could be saved, if God decided to save them, only by faith, not
through any sort of law.[37] Let the state take care of legal matters; a
church's concern should be its members' eternal salvation.

With Luther's theological revolution, the separation of faith
and reason foreshadowed by William of Ockham's philosophy
and Meister Eckhart's religious practice was realized.[38] One is
not surprised to discover that Luther and John Calvin opposed
Copernicus's sun-centered astronomy as vehemently as did the
Catholic Holy Office. The Protestant leaders had determined that
the individual's relationship to God need not be mediated by
popes and priests; that "Scripture alone," not the authorized interpretations and doctrines of the Roman Church, represented
God's unalterable word; and that the papacy was neither authoritative in matters of law nor infallible in matters of doctrine. By
the time they finished stripping away "non-apostolic" customs
and doctrines, there would be little left of the Church as a public
institution. Moreover, the attack on scholastic theology would
tend to put questions of belief beyond the realm of rational argument. Luther "knew" that man is justified by faith alone because,
while reading the *Epistle of Paul to the Romans,* he came upon
Paul's quotation from Habakkuk, "He who through faith is righteous shall live," and was illuminated.[39] Suddenly, he understood

the relationship of faith to salvation. Because of this experience, his sermons took on a new character. As a classic biography of the Reformer puts it:

> It was not an eloquent rhetorician or a pedantic schoolman that spoke, but a Christian who had felt the power of revealed truths, one who drew them forth from the Bible, poured them out from the treasures of his heart, and presented them all full of life to his astonished hearers. It was not the teaching of a man, but of God.[40]

This was all very well if one agreed with Luther's interpretation of the passage from Romans, but many other Christians (including most Catholics) did not. How to determine, in such cases, which interpretation was correct? Eliminating the Church as the sole authorized interpreter of Scripture opened the door to the fundamentalist approach, which asserts that such-and-such is the literal meaning of the text, not an interpretation at all, or that a particular interpretation is divinely inspired, and therefore unquestionable. In Luther's time and afterward, Christians fed up with fanciful, allegorical interpretations of the Bible that reflected the prejudices of the interpreter were inclined to embrace this type of literalism, especially if it was accompanied by the sort of illumination that Luther himself had experienced. Fundamentalist literalism, in other words, was not a feature of the medieval worldview from which modern rationalists had to be "liberated." It came into the world as a result of the same attack on Aristotelian-Christian thinking that produced secular science. One can imagine this as a sort of intellectual nuclear fission. Bombarded by its early modernist opponents, Aristotelianism implodes, generating a coldly objectivist science and a passionately subjectivist religion.

Of course, fundamentalist literalism was not the only method of interpreting the Bible and other authoritative texts. But in the

absence of an authorized interpreter of Scripture and an "infallible" arbiter of doctrinal disputes, serious doctrinal disagreements would have to be settled either by permitting a schism (and
schisms within schisms) to occur within the Church, or by imposing some "authorized" set of beliefs on nonbelievers by violence.
Violence—more than a century of atrocious religious warfare—
was Europe's initial response to the new subjectivism, although
it would not have been as widespread and intense had not ambitious secular rulers seen the crisis as an opportunity to aggrandize
themselves and their nations. Schisms within schisms, supported
by an ethic of religious toleration, followed this fruitless attempt
to impose religious conformity by force. But the regime of toleration under which most Westerners now live presupposes a general agreement that while religious groups are free to proselytize
and to seek (within limits) to influence public policy, faith is essentially a private matter involving the individual's relationship
with God.

Aristotle was discredited, in part, because the Catholic
Church had used his ideas to maintain its cultural hegemony in
Europe—a supremacy that many Westerners considered oppressive, and that was now obsolete.[41] But the Aristotelian revolution
was "forgotten" for other reasons as well. Although most of us
would not want to reconstitute the medieval order even if we
could, the era's ideals and achievements stand as a continuing re-
proach to the deficiencies of modern culture. For a time, the West
opened itself up to revolutionary new ideas from non-Western
sources and from fervent mass movements in the streets. For a
time, rationalist thinkers and people of faith engaged each other
in an intense, continuous dialogue productive of new insights for
both sides. For a time, religious fundamentalism and power politics were subordinated to the quest for a universal morality capable of inspiring people to act as members of a transnational

community. One does not have to be nostalgic for the Middle Ages to recognize that obliterating this part of our past makes the present seem eternal, and obliterates alternative futures.

The West's destiny, it seems clear, is to become part of a diverse, yet integrated global civilization. Many of the institutions and ideas once thought to be the hallmarks of modernism, such as the sovereign nation-state, "value-free" science, and "reason-free" religion, now seem obstacles to the achievement of global community. As we are drawn into ever-closer contact with other peoples and cultures, the search for more inclusive norms of truth, goodness, and justice takes on a new urgency. The Philosopher's ideas have always seemed most relevant to those inhabiting an age of expanding trade, increasing intercultural connections, and rising expectations for human development. The Aristotelian project, which seemed irrelevant in an age of political and religious fragmentation, may serve in the next phase of human history as an inspirer of creative, integrative thought.

ONE THEME OF the cultural propaganda that bombards us unremittingly is the message that we live in the age of science—a time when the methods of inquiry, modes of argument, and standards of proof used by "hard" scientists have become virtually universal, and all objective knowledge (as opposed to merely subjective belief) rests on an appeal to reason. The origin myth of modern science tells us that this era was born out of the scientists' struggle against dogmatic, obscurantist religion, and that its result was the replacement of faith by reason, at least in the sphere of public discourse. As one commentator puts it, "Science replaced religion as preeminent intellectual authority, as definer, judge, and guardian of the cultural world view."[42]

The subsequent story, commonly told, is one of the steady aggrandizement of reason and marginalization of faith. As rationalist methods and concepts came to provide the basis for social science, law, politics, and even ethics, religious faith, increasingly cut off from a scientific understanding of nature and society, became a private affair—a satisfier of personal emotional needs rather than a source of knowledge.

> The domains of religion and metaphysics became gradually compartmentalized, regarded as personal, subjective, specula-tive, and fundamentally distinct from public objective knowl-edge of the empirical world. Faith and reason were now definitively severed.[43]

But the story does not end here. Since modernization is an ongo-ing process, Reason continues to expand her dominion, pushing into previously undiscovered territory (including the realms of psychology and ethics), while Faith's territory continues to shrink. God becomes what some call a "God of the gaps"—a principle used to explain mysteries that science has not yet gotten around to unraveling.[44] This tale of science triumphant ends somewhere in the future with the final victory of secular rationalism and the "death of God."

Clearly there is something wrong with this narrative. As this book goes to press, the president of the United States, a believing Christian closely allied with other believers of various faiths, has committed his nation to war against an Iraqi regime that he has repeatedly defined, in Augustinian religious terms, as "evil."[45] One can consider this mere rhetoric designed to mask other more "rational" interests, but, if so, it is rhetoric that resonates strongly with millions of the leader's constituents. The underlying fallacy, it seems to me, is the notion that because scientific rationalism has gained intellectual preeminence in certain fields, it must therefore be hegemonic in culture. This might be true if people's heads could be separated from their hearts, if reasoning subjects could be clearly distinguished from reasoned-about objects, and if there were genuine sciences of ethics, politics, and social relations. All these "ifs" were assumed by early modern thinkers to be facts or, at least, realizable trends.[46] But none has been realized or is likely to be realized in the foreseeable future. As a result, the realm of "merely" subjective personal beliefs retains a viability, power, and expansionist potential that the standard modernist narrative ignores.

Most modern political leaders would not consider consulting religious authorities for advice in solving scientific or technical problems. But American presidents from Abraham Lincoln to George W. Bush have talked with their spiritual advisers—and sometimes with their God—before committing the nation to war. The reality obscured by the idea of scientific triumph is the persistence of faith in modern society—faith not as a marginal activity but as an essential feature of Western social life, and not as reason's docile junior partner but as a mode of thought hostile in many ways to rationalist claims. The narrative of science triumphant sees the "privatization" of religion as a weakness, exposing the realm of Faith to increasing encroachment by Reason. This seems to me a serious error. Privatizing faith conserved it rather than extinguished it. As society modernized, science did infringe with some regularity on religion's traditional "turf." Darwin's account of the origin of species, for example, forced many theists to revise their interpretation of the story of creation in Genesis. But faith entrenched in private life, and presenting itself as a satisfier of basic psychic and spiritual needs, has been in a position to infringe just as strongly—perhaps even more so— on the territory claimed by reason.

This development is rooted in the collapse of the Aristotelian consensus. When the Reformers, secular politicians, and natural scientists dismantled scholasticism, religion gave up its claim to control the terms of public and commercial discourse. Indeed, it had little choice but to do so, since military power was gravitating into the hands of secular princes and economic power into those of the business class. But, in a way not generally recognized, modern science was also forced to redefine itself. Scientific rationalism emerged from the wreckage of scholasticism strengthened in technique but greatly impoverished in scope—unable to command the fields of metaphysics, ethics, and politics as Aristotle had done; unable to answer the "why" questions about the universe that his doctrine of "final causes" had supplied; and unable to encompass philosophical issues like the eternity and intelligibility of the universe. Certain of these fields—metaphysics and theology, in particular—were left to be dealt with privately by people in their individual capacities. But others, including ethics, politics, and social relations, fell into a no-man's-land claimed by both sides. The result has been continued conflict of a sort unforeseen by the celebrants of scientific "preeminence."

The major sites of current conflict are not those dramatized by the origin myth of science. In fact, disputes between scientists and religious authorities over the findings and theories of physical science have seldom been necessary, from the point of view of theology.[47] Where a sacred text seems to say one thing about the physical world and natural science another, the issue can usually be resolved by revising one's interpretation of the text (as Jewish and Catholic authorities, among others, did for centuries), or by getting the scientists to admit that their knowledge is uncertain. The Catholic Church was no more compelled to oppose Copernican cosmology than Protestant churches were to oppose Darwinian evolution. Given the leeways of textual interpretation, the reasons for such opposition often lie more in a religious organization's social and political commitments than in Holy Writ itself. As the historian John Hedley Brooke points out, many conflicts said to be between science and religion are really clashes between opposed scientific theories or religious views.[48] Even now, theologians and scientists converse without great asperity about issues such as the theological implications of the big bang theory of the origin of the universe and the ethical implications of genotypic mapping.

But what about the region lying in the borderland between religious and scientific thought—the area one might call "human studies"? How can we reconcile theological and scientific truths about questions of human motivation, ethics, social relationships, and politics? How can we derive norms of inquiry and conduct that cut across deep cultural divisions? This is precisely the area in which modernist distinctions between a private, emotional religion and a public, rationalist science have proved most debilitating, and in which our Aristotelian heritage may be most useful.

Frequently, conflicts over issues like homosexuality, abortion, divorce, and gender equality take the form of "culture wars" between forces described as progressivist, secular, or rationalist on one side, and traditionalist, religious, or fundamentalist on the other.[49] These labels are seldom useful and in many cases can be positively misleading. On either side of any of these issues one will find people whose views are founded on some principle of religious faith or fundamental ethical commitment. People on both sides argue rationally about the nature of human beings and the likely impact of their behavior on society. These disputes are not between faith and reason but between alternative visions of the good person and the good society that have roots in both modes of thought. What makes them potentially destructive (among other things) are claims that one party's views are purely rational and scientific, while the other's rest on pure faith. Such claims eliminate the possibility of dialogue, since, according to modernist conceptions, rationality relies on inductive logic and objective evidence, while faith is validated by other means entirely.

"Homosexuality is genetically determined; religion and ethics have nothing to do with the matter," say some advocates of gay and lesbian rights. But the argument from genetics (whose scientific validity remains in question) masks an ethical commitment that places a higher value on love between consenting adults than on policies and customs promoting heterosexual behavior. "Homosexuality is condemned by the Bible; that's all there is to it," reply some of their "fundamentalist" opponents. But the argument based on biblical literalism (which involves selecting some commands for enforcement, while ignoring others) masks non-biblical concerns for the maintenance of the traditional heterosexual family and the avoidance of promiscuity and disease. Similarly, where abortion is concerned, science does not tell us when, if ever, a fetus is entitled to the protection accorded a newborn child, nor can the issue be settled simply by quoting Saint Thomas on "ensoulment" and natural law. Agreement on such matters may not be possible between people holding strong convictions on either side. But a humane dialogue can take place between those committed, as the Aristotelians were, to the search for norms that are both ethical and reasonable.

Because disputes in the area of human relations are so explosive, Westerners have attempted for several centuries to resolve them jurisdictionally. Some matters (especially those involving faith and ethics) are left to determination by individuals in their private capacity, while others—the "public issues"—are to be decided by scientific and political authorities. But the conflicts just discussed demonstrate that the attempt to maintain a hard boundary line between private religious concerns and public policies cannot succeed. That abortion or divorce should be a private matter to be determined by individuals on the basis of their own interests and moral principles is a fine idea—unless one believes that abortion is a form of murder or that divorce is a form of spousal and child abuse. That questions of peace and war should be left to the political authorities also seems reasonable—until one is asked to support what one believes to be an unjust war. Disputed questions of this sort cannot be settled jurisdictionally, since their assignment to the private or public sphere is a function of the scope and intensity of one's ethical and rational beliefs. This becomes clearer if we recognize that "public issues" frequently involve the same mix of religious, ethical, and rational concerns as contested "private issues." When is warfare or violent revolution justified? What are our moral and political obligations when faced by extremes of wealth and poverty? How should we respond to deprivations of human rights? What diverse cultural practices should we tolerate, even if they seem illiberal or "uncivilized" to us?

None of these questions can be answered simply by citing a biblical verse or an ethical principle. Nor, despite their public nature, can they be determined by quoting the results of some scientific study or assigning them jurisdictionally to the realm of power politics. Answers that make sense require the sort of dialogue between a rationally influenced faith and an ethically interested reason that took place a few centuries ago in the medieval universities. Especially in a rapidly globalizing world, where people everywhere seek to satisfy basic human needs for subsistence, identity, security, dignity, justice, and purpose, the Aristotelian project seems more relevant than at any time since the High Middle Ages.

The fundamental thrust of the scholastic movement, stimulated by Aristotle's concept of a purposeful universe, was to "reconcile faith with reason." Intelligent people committing themselves to certain religious beliefs or ethical values wanted reasons to do so in addition to those mandated by tradition or the command of some charismatic leader. They wanted to know why they should make these commitments rather than others, and how those they made were reflected or affirmed by developments in nature and society. At the same time, scholars investigating nature and society wanted to understand the relationship between the facts and patterns they uncovered and the realm of beliefs and values. That is, they needed to be able to evaluate the impact of their discoveries and to determine how they could be used for human betterment. The end of the Aristotelian era left us with these urgent needs unsatisfied. Science, deprived of its connection with religious faith, has become increasingly technical and "value-free," while religious commitments, cut loose from their natural-istic moorings, seem increasingly a matter of arbitrary "instincts" or tastes. Worse yet, with global economic and military power concentrating at an unprecedented rate in the hands of a few powerful elites, both faith and reason tend to become tools in the hands of raw, self-aggrandizing power.

Under these circumstances, the partners to this former mar-riage, turbulent though it was, cannot help dreaming of a possible reconciliation. Reason could transform the earth, if only science and technology were inspired and guided by a new global moral-ity. Faith would expand and mature, if only the world's religions addressed themselves to long-term trends in society and nature, and helped to create that global morality. And—since the split between faith and reason divides each of us against himself—we could become more loving and useful to each other and more sat-isfied with ourselves, if only we could integrate these fundamen-tal aspects of our being.

Integrate, not "fuse." For it is the creative tension between faith and reason that we dream of restoring, not some false iden-tity. Just as the shattering of the Aristotelian consensus radically changed both science and religion, so, in the forging of a new, postmodern consensus, they will surely change once again. These changes will be difficult, as they have always been. But a world hungry for wholeness yearns for them.

NOTES

PROLOGUE
The Medieval Star-Gate

1. "Wisdom is knowledge about certain principles and causes." Aristotle, *Metaphysics*, W. D. Ross, trans., in *Works*, Vol. 1 (Chicago: Encyclopedia Britannica, 1952), 1.1, 982a36–37.
2. As the Catholic historian Étienne Gilson put it, "The origins of modern rationalism are commonly traced back to the intellectual revolution which took place early in Italy, when such men as Galileo made their first scientific discoveries. And I am very far from saying that there is nothing true in that assertion.... The fact remains, however, that there has been another rationalism, much older than that of the Renaissance, and wholly unrelated to any scientific discovery." *Reason and Revelation in the Middle Ages* (New York and London: Charles Scribner's Sons, 1950), p. 37.
3. See, for example, Fernand van Steenberghen, *Aristotle in the West: The Origins of Latin Aristotelianism*, Leonard Johnston, trans. (New York: Humanities Press, 1970), pp. 58–59: "The thirteenth century was to provide medieval Christianity with the decisive crisis of its development in the field of the intellectual life. For the first time Christian thinkers were to be confronted with Aristotle; his naturalistic view of the universe was to come face to face with the

Christian outlook so long familiar to the minds of men." R. W. Southern, the great historian of "medieval humanism" says much the same thing in *Medieval Humanism and Other Essays* (New York and Evanston: Harper & Row, 1970), p. 47: "Put in its very simplest terms medieval thought became a dialogue between Aristotle and the Bible." In *The Passion of the Western Mind* ([New York: Ballantine Books, 1991], p. 47), Richard Tarnas states that "the new [Aristotelian] attitudes were to transform drastically the nature and direction of European thought." He goes on to explain (p. 48) that the Aristotelians "prepared the way in the late medieval universities for the massive convulsion in the Western world view caused by the Scientific Revolution." Anthony Gottlieb, in *The Dream of Reason* ([New York and London: W. W. Norton, 2000], p. 399), says: "the conflict between faith and reason at the end of the thirteenth century generated ideas that eventually helped to undermine the whole medieval approach to knowledge."

4. David C. Lindberg, *The Beginnings of Western Science* (Chicago and London: University of Chicago Press, 1992), pp. 161–82, also discusses the claim of Pierre Duhem, now discredited, that Arab science was a mere copy of the Greek, "destitute of all originality."

5. On Galileo's respect for Aristotle and contempt for his seventeenth-century followers, see Edward Grant, *God & Reason in the Middle Ages* (Cambridge: Cambridge University Press, 2001), pp. 301–11. On Galileo's scholastic predecessors, see pp. 170–78.

6. Ibid., p. 355. Quoted by Grant: "Modern philosophy did not have to establish the rights of reason against the Middle Ages," remarks the historian Étienne Gilson. "It was, on the contrary, the Middle Ages which established them for it, and the very manner in which the seventeenth century imagined that it was abolishing the work of preceding centuries did nothing more than continue it."

7. Erasmus, *Praise of Folly,* rev. ed., Betty Radice, trans. (London: Penguin Books, 1993), p. 87.

8. Galileo Galilei, *Dialogue Concerning the Two Chief World Systems— Ptolemaic & Copernican,* Stillman Drake, trans. (Los Angeles: Uni-

versity of California Press, 1962), p. 110. And see the discussion infra, p. 303.

Chapter One
"The Master of Those Who Know"
Aristotle Rediscovered

1. Robert Fossier, ed., *Cambridge Illustrated History of the Middle Ages*, Vol. 2: *950–1250* (Cambridge: Cambridge University Press, 1997), p. 258.

2. See, for example, the materials collected in Olivie Remie Constable, ed., *Medieval Iberia: Readings from Christian, Muslim, and Jewish Sources* (Philadelphia: University of Pennsylvania Press, 1997).

3. David C. Lindberg, *The Beginnings of Western Science* (Chicago and London: University of Chicago Press, 1992), p. 176. For a summary of ancient science and Islamic adaptations and additions, see pp. 86–182.

4. Norman F. Cantor, *The Civilization of the Middle Ages*, rev. ed. (New York: HarperCollins, 1993), p. 358.

5. Friedrich Heer believes he was a converted Jew; see *The Medieval World: Europe 1100–1350*, Janet Sondheimer, trans. (Cleveland and New York: The World Publishing Company, 1962), p. 194.

6. John Marenbon, "Medieval Christian and Jewish Europe," in Seyyed Hossein Nasr and Oliver Leaman, eds., *History of Islamic Philosophy, Part II* (London and New York: Routledge, 1996), p. 1001.

7. Amable Jourdain, *Recherches: Critiques sur l'Age et l'Origine des Traductions Latines d'Aristote*, rev. and enl. by Charles Jourdain (Paris, 1843; New York: Burt Franklin, 1960), p. 111. See also Josef Pieper, *Scholasticism: Personalities and Problems of Medieval Philosophy*, Richard and Clara Winston, trans. (New York and Toronto: McGraw-Hill, 1964), p. 106. Michael Haren points out that this was not the usual modus operandi (*Medieval Thought: The Western Intellectual Tradition from Antiquity to the Thirteenth Century*, 2d ed. [Toronto and Buffalo: University of Toronto Press, 1992], p. 135).

8. Cantor, op. cit., p. 358.

9. Lindberg, op. cit., p. 205.

10. Heer, op. cit., p. 194.

11. Colin McEvedy, *The New Penguin Atlas of Medieval History* (London: Penguin Books, 1992), p. 66.

12. Charles Homer Haskins, *The Renaissance of the Twelfth Century* (New York: The World Publishing Company, 1957), pp. 292–93.

13. Lindberg, op. cit., pp. 325–26 et seq.

14. Roger French and Andrew Cunningham, *Before Science: The Invention of the Friars' Natural Philosophy* (Aldershot, U.K.: Scolar Press, 1996), p. 61.

15. Jourdain, *Recherches*, pp. 125–26.

16. The story of Plato's relationship with the aristocrat Dion, an old student of his, and the tyrants Dionysius I and Dionysius II is told by Plutarch in his life of Dion. *Plutarch's Lives*, Arthur H. Clough, ed. (Princeton: Princeton Review, 2001). Like much of Plutarch's material, it needs to be taken with a grain or more of salt.

17. W. D. Ross, *Aristotle*, 5th ed. (London: Methuen & Company, 1949), p. 2. Colloquially, we would say "brains" rather than "mind."

18. William Turner, "Aristotle," in *New Advent Catholic Encyclopedia* (2003), http://www.newadvent.org/cathen/01713a.htm (From 1907 *Catholic Encyclopedia*, Vol. 1).

19. Lindberg, op. cit., p. 113.

20. Ibid., pp. 115–16.

21. It is generally assumed that Aristotle went with his parents to the Macedonian court, but the evidence for this (as for most other events of his life) is based largely on hearsay. The chief authority for Aristotle's life is the third century C.E. writer Diogenes Laertius. See Ross, *Aristotle*, pp. 1–2.

22. Nobody seems to know whether Proxenus was Aristotle's uncle by blood or merely a good friend of the family. Considering the great efforts he made on behalf of the boy, I have opted for the uncle theory.

23. In the absence of reliable biographical data, we have theories like that of Werner Jaeger, who speculated in his famous *Aristotle: Fundamentals of His Development* (New York: AMS Books, 1999, reprint of 1923 ed.) that Aristotle moved from full-fledged Platonism to his own empiricism. Other scholars have expressed skepticism about this theory, especially given the difficulty of dating Aristotle's works. See, e.g., Jonathan Barnes, ed., *The Cambridge Companion to Aristotle* (Cambridge: Cambridge University Press, 1995), pp. 16–22.

24. George Gershwin and Ira Gershwin, "I Got Rhythm" from "Girl Crazy" (1930).

25. Corinthians I 13:12.

26. Quoted in W. D. Ross, "Biographical Note," in *The Works of Aristotle*, Vol. 1 (Chicago: Encyclopedia Britannica, Inc., 1952), p. v.

27. An inescapable analogy is the relationship of Karl Marx to his master, Hegel, which Friedrich Engels summarized by remarking that Marx "stood Hegel on his feet."

28. Aristotle, *Metaphysics*, W. D. Ross, trans., in *Works*, Vol. 1 (Chicago: Encyclopedia Britannica, 1952), 1.9, 991b9–14 and 992a32–34. Philosophers still argue about whether mathematical descriptions of the universe represent one language among others or whether they are privileged in some way.

29. See the discussion in Barnes, op. cit., pp. 10–15, and compare the older approach of Ross's (*Aristotle*, pp. 7–19), which attempts to date the works according to historical and logical inferences that Barnes considers suspect.

30. A catalog of Aristotle's works containing about 150 entries was compiled by Diogenes Laertius and is quoted in Barnes, op. cit., pp. 7–9.

31. Salo Wittmayer Baron, *A Social and Religious History of the Jews*, Vol. 8: *Philosophy and Science*, 2d ed.(New York: Columbia University Press; and Philadelphia: Jewish Publication Society of America, 1958), p. 64.

32. Dante Alighieri, *The Divine Comedy, Inferno*, Canto 4, line 131, H. W. Longfellow, trans. (New York: Modern Library), p. 22.

33. Barnes, op. cit., p. 6 (citing Aelian, *Varia Historia III*).

34. Ibid.

35. The story was first told by Strabo and repeated by Plutarch. See William Turner, "Aristotle," in *New Advent Catholic Encyclopedia*, op. cit.

36. Barnes, op. cit., p. 12.

37. Aristotle, *Politics*, Benjamin Jowett, trans., in *Works*, Vol. 2 (Chicago: Encyclopedia Britannica, 1952), 1.5, 1254b15–26.

38. Aristotle, *Nicomachean Ethics*, W. D. Ross, trans., in *Works*, Vol. 2 (Chicago: Encyclopedia Britannica, 1952), 10.6, 1177a12–18; and Aristotle, *On the Soul*, J. A. Smith, trans., in *Works*, Vol. 1 (Chicago: Encylopedia Britannica, 1952), 3.4, 429a10–28.

39. Aristotle, *On the Heavens*, J. L. Stocks, trans., in *Works*, Vol. 1 (Chicago: Encyclopedia Britannica, 1952), 2.14, 297b24–298a–20. Christopher Columbus was aware of this passage and these calculations; see the discussion infra at 311.

40. "Actual knowledge is identical with its object." Aristotle, *On the Soul*, 3.5, 430a20–26.

41. Aristotle, *Metaphysics*, 1.1, 981b10–35 and 982a1–2.

42. Ibid., 5.2, 1013a24–38 and 1013b1–3.

43. Aristotle did conceive of the heavenly bodies, which he thought were composed of a non-earthly element called aether, as having consciousness.

44. Aristotle, *Metaphysics*, 7.3, 1029a7–31 et seq.

45. Ibid, 12.7, 1072a23–27.

Chapter Two
The Murder of "Lady Philosophy"
How the Ancient Wisdom Was Lost,
and How It Was Found Again

1. Augustine of Hippo, *The City of God*, Marcus Dods, trans. (New York: Modern Library, 1950), p. 478.

2. Tertullian, *De praescriptione haereticorum, vii,* in Henry Bettenson,

ed., *Documents of the Christian Church*, 2d ed. (Oxford and London: Oxford University Press, 1963), p. 6.

3. Ibid.

4. Clement of Alexandria, *Stromateis*, in Bettenson, op. cit., p. 6.

5. Augustine of Hippo, *The Confessions of Saint Augustine*, Rex Warner, trans. (New York: Penguin Books, 1963), p. 149.

6. Augustine of Hippo, *Confessions*, pp. 135–59.

7. Ibid., p. 87.

8. Christ was pictured by the Manicheans as God's foremost archangel or Messenger. See Steven Runciman, *The Medieval Manichee: A Study of the Christian Dualist Heresy* (Cambridge: Cambridge University Press, 1947, reissued 1982), p. 14 et seq.

9. Peter Brown, *Augustine of Hippo: A Biography* (New York: Dorset Press, 1967), p. 93.

10. Neoplatonism was initially the invention of a group of third-century pagan philosophers led by the brilliant, if mystifying, Plotinus and his disciple, Porphyry. See W. T. Jones, *The Medieval Mind*, Vol. 2: *A History of Western Philosophy*, 2d ed. (New York: Harcourt, Brace & World, 1969), pp. 8–20.

11. Justin Martyr, an early Father of the Church, stated that Christ had been "known in part even by Socrates." Quoted in Jaroslav Pelikan, *The Christian Tradition: A History of the Development of Doctrine*, Vol. I: *The Emergence of the Catholic Tradition (100–600)* (Chicago and London: University of Chicago Press, 1971), p. 31.

12. Augustine of Hippo, *The Confessions of Saint Augustine*, p. 147. See also Richard Tarnas, *The Passion of the Western Mind: Understanding the Ideas That Have Shaped Our World View* (New York: Ballantine Books, 1991), p. 101: "the spiritually resonant Platonic philosophy not only harmonized with, it also elaborated and intellectually enhanced, the Christian conceptions derived from the revelations of the New Testament." Pelikan, however, emphasizes the limitations of this apparent "harmony" (op. cit., pp. 35–36).

13. "It was possible," the Neoplatonists taught, "to 'touch' by thought the concentrated center that had been sensed through the unrolled

beauty of all visible things." Peter Brown, *The World of Late Antiquity: AD 150–750* (New York and London: W. W. Norton, 1971), p. 74.

14. This Dionysius is known to scholars as the "pseudo-Dionysius" because his writings were wrongly attributed to Dionysius the Areopagite, a first-century Christian described by Saint Paul. Pelikan, op. cit., pp. 344–49.

15. Augustine recounts the story of the voice that he heard in his garden in *The Confessions of Saint Augustine,* pp. 182–83.

16. Ibid., pp. 150–52.

17. Jones, op. cit., p. 131.

18. Augustine of Hippo, *The City of God,* pp. 45–46.

19. Peter Brown points out that the so-called "barbarian invasions . . . were not perpetual destructive raids; still less were they organized campaigns of conquest. Rather, they were a 'gold rush' of immigrants from the underdeveloped countries of the north into the rich lands of the Mediterranean." Op. cit., p. 122.

20. See, for example, Norman F. Cantor, *The Civilization of the Middle Ages,* rev. ed. (New York: HarperCollins , 1993), p. 110. Cantor suggests that the eastern emperor (Anastasius) incited Theodoric to overthrow Odoacer in order to get the Ostrogoths to stop threatening his own territories (p. 106).

21. Brown, op. cit., p. 123. Josef Pieper cites a more pro-Goth version of the maxim: "a bad Goth wished to be a Roman, and a bad Roman a Goth" in *Scholasticism: Personalities and Problems of Medieval Philosophy,* Richard and Clara Winston, trans. (New York and Toronto: McGraw-Hill, 1964), p. 27.

22. Cantor, op. cit., pp. 107–8.

23. Pieper, op. cit., p. 30.

24. Boethius, *The Consolation of Philosophy,* S. J. Tester, trans. (Cambridge, Mass., and London: Harvard University Press, Loeb Classical Library, 1973).

25. H. F. Stewart and E. K. Rand, "Life of Boethius," in Boethius, *The Theological Tractates,* H. F. Stewart, E. K. Rand, and S. J. Tester,

trans. (Cambridge, Mass. and London: Harvard University Press, Loeb Classical Library, 1973), p. xii.

26. Ibid., p. 55.

27. Ibid., p. 5.

28. Ibid., p. 37. Emphasis added.

29. Mark Twain, *Following the Equator: A Journey Around the World* (Mineola, NY: Dover Publications), p. 232.

30. "It is agreed that a proof supported by firm reasoning must be drawn not from signs nor from arguments fetched from outside the subject, but from relevant and necessary causes." Boethius, *The Consolation of Philosophy*, p. 407.

31. Boethius, *"De Trinitate"* and *"Utrum Pater et Filius,"* in *The Theological Tractates*, pp. 3–37.

32. This version of the story is told by Cantor, op. cit., pp. 109–10.

33. These events are referred to by Boethius in *The Consolation of Philosophy*, pp. 149–57. The scattered references are all the more convincing in that they are not presented as a systematic "defense," but simply assume that a good man was victimized by evildoers.

34. Pieper, op. cit., pp. 41–42.

35. The Arian controversy is described at length in Richard E. Rubenstein, *When Jesus Became God: The Struggle Over Christ's Divinity in the Last Days of Rome* (New York, Harcourt, Brace, 1999).

36. The Goths and many other "barbarian" tribes outside the empire were converted to Arian Christianity and retained that faith for several centuries, until they were converted to Catholicism. See Henry Chadwick, *The Early Church*, rev. ed. (London: Penguin Books, 1993), pp. 247–52.

37. Brown, op. cit., p. 174. See also Heinrich Graetz, *History of the Jews*, Vol. 2 (Philadelphia: Jewish Publication Society, 1949), pp. 617–18.

38. Chadwick, op. cit., p. 167.

39. Graetz, op. cit., p. 618.

40. The official reason given for the pogrom was an alleged unprovoked "massacre" of Christians by Jews. See John Chapman,

"Saint Cyril of Alexandria," in *The New Advent Catholic Ency-clopedia,* (2003), http://www.newadvent.org/cathen/04592b.htm (From Vol. 4 of 1908 *Catholic Encyclopedia*). The report is singularly unconvincing. It is possible that there was religious competition between Christians and Jews, since many Christians were attracted to Jewish thought and practices during this period. In the same year, this sort of competition appears to have provoked Saint John Chrystostom, bishop of Antioch, to preach a series of anti-Semitic sermons that resulted in the destruction of Antioch's synagogue. See James Carroll, *Constantine's Sword: The Church and the Jews* (Boston: Houghton Mifflin, 2001), p. 213.

41. Ibid.

42. There are various versions of Hypatia's life and murder. Three selections from ancient historians are reprinted in the journal *Alexandria,* Vol. 2 (Phanes Press, 1993).

43. Chadwick, op. cit., p. 198.

44. Pelikan, op. cit., p. 227.

45. Chadwick, op. cit., p. 199.

46. Pelikan, op. cit., pp. 263–64.

47. Ferdinand B. Artz, *The Mind of the Middle Ages: An Historical Survey,* A.D. 200–1500, 3d ed. rev. (Chicago and London: University of Chicago Press, 1980), p. 111. There were exceptions; for example, the Alexandrian Neoplatonist John Philoponus, who was the first Christian director of the Platonic Academy, wrote an important critique of Aristotle's theory of motion. See David C. Lindberg, *The Beginnings of Western Science* (Chicago and London: University of Chicago Press, 1992), pp. 302–5.

48. Brown, op. cit., pp. 174 and 180.

49. On the movement of the Nestorians eastward and its effects, see Samuel Hugh Moffett, *A History of Christianity in Asia,* Vol. 1: *Beginnings to 1500* (San Francisco: HarperSanFrancisco, 1992), pp. 185–215.

50. On the Nestorian and Monophysite translators, see Majid Fakhry, *A History of Islamic Philosophy,* 2d ed. (New York and London: Columbia University Press and Longmans, 1993), pp. 4–19.

51. See Pieper, op. cit., p. 28, discussing the translations made by Boethius: "Strictly speaking...the translator...does not create new words, but establishes co-ordinates."

52. Fakhry, op. cit., pp. 155–57.

53. Roger French and Andrew Cunningham, *Before Science: The Invention of the Friars' Natural Philosophy* (Aldershot, U.K.: Scolar Press, 1996), p. 86. And see, more generally, pp. 81–88.

54. Ibid., p. 87.

55. See the discussion in Fakhry, op. cit., pp. 272–92; and, more generally, in Oliver Leaman, *Averroes and His Philosophy* (Oxford: Clarendon Press, 1988).

56. On Maimonides' critique of anthropomorphic language applied to God, see Oliver Leaman, *Moses Maimonides* (Richmond, Surrey: Curzon Press, 1997), pp. 24–36.

57. Averroës suggested that the immortal soul might not be the individual soul, but a collective "active intellect." For an extensive discussion, see Leaman, *Averroes and His Philosophy*, pp. 82–103.

58. This was the Ash'arite view, which Syyed Hossein Nasr analogizes to that of David Hume. Syyed Hossein Nasr, *Islamic Life and Thought* (Albany, N.Y.: State University of New York Press, 1981), p. 62.

59. Ibid., p. 72. For a more detailed analysis of al-Ghazali's work, see Fakhry, pp. 217–33. See also Pervez Amir Ali Hoodbhoy, "How Islam Lost Its Way," *The Washington Post Outlook*, December 30, 2001, B4.

60. Fakhry, op. cit., p. 315. There are authorities who believe that this characterization is unfair, and that Islamic philosophy developed in creative new directions (e.g., Sufism) after the decline of *falsafah*. See, e.g, Nasr, op. cit., pp. 63–64.

61. See Leaman, *Moses Maimonides*, pp. 6–7; and Cantor, op. cit., pp. 369–70.

62. Cantor, op. cit., p. 370. Cantor suggests that this was a defensive move made to prevent the Jewish community from being identified with heresy, but the effect is the same in either case. The author's attempt to picture the Jews as more liberal, in this respect, than the

Muslims (see p. 363) is qualified by his own account of their turn toward legalism and mysticism, which paralleled that of the Muslims (see pp. 366–73).

CHAPTER THREE
"His Books Have Wings"
PETER ABELARD AND THE REVIVAL OF REASON

1. "The Story of My Calamities," in *The Letters of Abelard and Heloise*, Betty Radice, trans. (London and New York: Penguin, 1974), p. 62.
2. Ibid., p. 58: "I preferred the weapons of dialectic to all the other teachings of philosophy, and armed with these I chose the conflicts of disputation instead of the trophies of war."
3. The question is one discussed by Abelard in *Scito Teipsum* (*Know Thyself*) and in *Christian Theology*. See J. G. Sikes, *Peter Abailard* (New York: Russell & Russell, 1965 reprint), p. 187; and Frederick C. Copleston, *Medieval Philosophy* (New York and Evanston: Harper & Row, 1961), pp. 51–52. I have taken the liberty of imagining Abelard addressing his class.
4. The first "blood libel" pogrom took place in Norwich, England. See James Carroll, *Constantine's Sword: The Church and the Jews* (Boston: Houghton Mifflin, 2001), pp. 272–73.
5. Blanche Boyer and Richard McKeon, eds., *Peter Abailard Sic et Non, A Critical Edition* (Chicago: University of Chicago Press, 1976).
6. The word for doubting, *dubitando*, is translated by several authors as "calling into question" or "raising questions." See, e.g., the translations cited by Michael Haren, *Medieval Thought: The Western Intellectual Tradition from Antiquity to the Thirteenth Century*, 2d ed. (Toronto and Buffalo: University of Toronto Press, 1992), p. 108; and Edward Grant, *God & Reason in the Middle Ages* (Cambridge: Cambridge University Press, 2001), pp. 60–61. This has the virtue of showing that Abelard was not advising his students to doubt the

basic doctrines of faith, but it understates the provocativeness of Abelard's language. Sikes's literal translation (in *Peter Abailard*, p. 82) seems preferable. (I have replaced his British spelling of "enquiry" with the American "inquiry.")

7. Augustine also warned Christians not to murder the Jews, since they still had a historic role to play in the drama of universal salvation. Carroll, op. cit., p. 215.

8. Ibid., p. 271, quoting Bernard of Clairvaux in "Letter to the People of England."

9. Abelard's doctrine of ethical intentionality has been widely discussed. Sikes, op. cit., pp. 179–90.

10. Ibid., pp. 179–90 and 200–208. These questions and answers are discussed in Abelard's *Scito Teipsum* (*Know Thyself*), analyzed in Sikes. On Abelard's view of salvation outside the Church, see Jaroslav Pelikan, *The Christian Tradition: A History of the Development of Doctrine*, Vol. 3: *The Growth of Medieval Theology (600–1300)* (Chicago and London: University of Chicago Press, 1978), p. 255; and Carroll, op. cit., pp. 290–300.

11. Copleston (op. cit., p. 52) notes that Abelard's view apparently changed. In *Scito Teipsum*, Abelard implies that non-Christians are damned because of their lack of faith, but in *Theologica Christiana* he takes the position ascribed to him in the text.

12. John of Salisbury called Abelard the "Peripatetic of Le Pallet" (Abelard's birthplace). See *The "Metalogicon" of John of Salisbury: A Twelfth-Century Defense of the Verbal and Logical Arts of the Trivium*, Daniel D. McGarry, trans. (Berkeley and Los Angeles: University of California Press, 1955), p. 95.

13. Ibid., p. 66.

14. "Letter 4. Abelard to Heloise," in *The Letters of Abelard and Heloise*, op. cit., p. 147.

15. Ibid., "History of My Calamities," pp. 67–68.

16. Ibid., p. 75.

17. Ibid., "Letter 3. Heloise to Abelard," p. 133: "Men call me chaste; they do not know the hypocrite that I am."

18. Ibid., "Letter 4. Abelard to Heloise," p. 143.

19. Ibid., "History of My Calamities," p. 58.

20. Friedrich Heer, *The Medieval World: Europe, 1100–1350,* Janet Sondheimer, trans. (Cleveland and New York: The World Publishing Company, 1961), pp. 261–66.

21. Jaroslav Pelikan, *Jesus Through the Centuries: His Place in the History of Culture* (New Haven: Yale University Press, 1985), pp. 122–32.

22. Norman F. Cantor, *The Civilization of the Middle Ages,* rev. ed. (New York: HarperCollins, 1993), p. 332.

23. Robert Fossier, ed., *The Cambridge Illustrated History of the Middle Ages,* Vol. 2: *950–1250,* Stuart Airlie and Robyn Marsack, trans. (Cambridge: Cambridge University Press, 1997), pp. 1–12 and 243–55.

24. Ibid., p. 2.

25. Bernard of Clairvaux, "Letter 239," quoted in Carroll, op. cit., p. 296.

26. Anselm of Canterbury, *Monologion and Proslogion, with the Replies of Gaunilo and Anselm,* Thomas Williams, trans. (Indianapolis and Cambridge: Hackett Publishing Company, 1995), p. 93.

27. Ibid., p. 10.

28. Ibid., p. 125.

29. Ibid., p. 131.

30. Ibid., p. 90.

31. Matthew 19:21.

32. David A. Luscombe, "Peter Abelard," in Peter Dronke, ed., *A History of Twelfth-Century Western Philosophy* (Cambridge: Cambridge University Press, 1992), p. 293.

33. Marcia L. Colish, *Medieval Foundations of the Western Intellectual Tradition, 400–1400* (New Haven and London: Yale University Press, 1997), p. 275.

34. Quoted in Sikes, op. cit., p. 48.

35. Aristotle, *Categories,* E. M. Edghill, trans., in *Works,* Vol. 1 (Chicago: Encyclopedia Britannica, 1952), 4, 2a11–2b7. See also Aris-

totle, *Topics*, W. A. Pickard-Cambridge, trans., in *Works*, Vol. 1 (Chicago: Encyclopedia Britannica, 1952), 1.9, 103b20 et seq.

36. Some modern religious thinkers do the same sort of thing today, for example, when they assert that the big bang theory of the astronomers is consistent with the doctrine of Creation. See Kenneth W. Kemp's thoughtful essay "The Possibility of Conflict Between Science and Christian Theology," in Jitse M. van der Meer, ed., *Facets of Faith and Science*, Vol. 1: *Historiography and Modes of Interaction* (Lanham, Md.; New York; and London: University Press of America, 1996), pp. 247–65.

37. Quoted in Grant, op. cit., p. 52.

38. Aristotle, *Metaphysics*, W. D. Ross, trans., in *Works*, Vol. 1 (Chicago: Encyclopedia Britannica, 1952). See especially 7.13, 1038b1–14.

39. Philippe Aries, *The Hour of Our Death*, Helen Weaver, trans. (New York: Oxford University Press, 1991).

40. See the discussion in G. E. Evans, *Philosophy and Theology in the Middle Ages* (London and New York: Routledge, 1993), pp. 55–60.

41. Dronke, op. cit., p. 293: Luscombe, "Peter Abelard."

42. There are still strong differences of opinion about the orthodoxy of this treatise. Sikes (op. cit., pp. 145–69) acquits him of most of the charges later brought against him, although he concedes that some phrases of his could be interpreted as Sabellian. Colish (op. cit., pp. 278–79) condemns him quite harshly for the opposite error— overemphasizing the separation and differences of the three Persons.

43. "History of My Calamities," in *The Letters of Abelard and Heloise*, op. cit., pp. 88–89.

44. Josef Pieper, *Scholasticism: Personalities and Problems of Medieval Philosophy*, Richard and Clara Winston, trans. (New York and Toronto: McGraw-Hill, 1964), p. 80.

45. Quoted in Grant, op. cit., p. 64.

46. Quoted in Josef Pieper, op. cit., pp. 82–83.

47. Quoted in Carroll, op. cit., p. 296.

48. Sikes, op. cit., pp. 226–27.

49. Ibid., p. 229.
50. *The Letters of Abelard and Heloise,* op. cit., p. 40, n. 1.
51. Ibid., p. 270.

Chapter Four
"He Who Strikes You Dead Will Earn a Blessing"
Aristotle Among the Heretics

1. "Abelard asked for a public discussion with Bernard; the latter showed his opponent's errors with such clearness and force of logic that he was unable to make any reply, and was obliged, after being condemned, to retire." M. Gildas, "St. Bernard of Clairvaux," in *The New Advent Catholic Encyclopedia,* (2003), http://www.newadvent.org/cathen/02498d.htm (Vol. 2 of 1907 *Catholic Encyclopedia*).
2. Norman F. Cantor, *The Civilization of the Middle Ages,* rev. ed. (New York: HarperCollins, 1993), p. 359.
3. See, e.g., John H. Mundy, *Europe in the High Middle Ages, 1150–1300,* 3d ed. (Harlow, U.K.: Longman, 2000), p. 177.
4. Cantor, op. cit., p. 251.
5. Malcolm Lambert, *Medieval Heresy: Popular Movements from the Gregorian Reform to the Reformation,* 2d ed. (Oxford, U.K., and Cambridge, Mass.: Blackwell, 1992), p. 44.
6. Ibid., p. 45.
7. Abelard believed in the necessity for confession to a priest, but denied that the latter could "gauge with any degree of certainty the sinfulness of a deed and the satisfaction necessary for its atonement." J. G. Sikes, *Peter Abailard* (New York: Russell & Russell, 1965, reprint), p. 197 and, more generally, pp. 193–204.
8. Ibid., Bernard of Clairvaux, "Letter 189," p. 227.
9. E. Vacandard, "Arnold of Brescia," in *The New Advent Catholic Encyclopedia,* (2003), http://www.newadvent.org/cathen/01747b.htm (From Vol. 1 of 1907 *Catholic Encyclopedia*).
10. Ibid.
11. Quoted in R. I. Moore, *The Birth of Popular Heresy* (Toronto, Buffalo, and London: University of Toronto Press, 1995), p. 69.

12. Ibid., p. 67.

13. Ibid.

14. E. Vacandard, "Arnold of Brescia," op. cit.

15. Moore, op. cit., p. 68.

16. Lambert, op. cit., p. 53.

17. E. Vacandard, "Arnold of Brescia," op. cit.

18. The letter is signed by "Wezel," but this is very likely a pseudonym for Arnold. See Moore, op. cit., pp. 68 and 69–71.

19. E. Vacandard, "Arnold of Brescia," op. cit.

20. Moore, op. cit., p. 75.

21. Ibid., pp. 76–77.

22. Lambert, op. cit., pp. 120–24.

23. Ibid., pp. 139–40.

24. Zoe Oldenbourg, *Massacre at Montsegur: A History of the Albigensian Crusade*, Peter Green, trans. (New York: Pantheon Books, 1961), pp. 62–70.

25. Ibid., pp. 90–91.

26. Ibid., p. 377.

27. Ibid., pp. 61–64. And see the discussion supra, p. 55.

28. See the useful discussion in W. T. Jones, *The Medieval Mind*, Vol. 2: *A History of Western Philosophy*, 2d ed. (New York: Harcourt, Brace & World, 1969), pp. 94–101.

29. See G. K. Chesterton's angry description of Catharism's "Easternness," *St. Thomas Aquinas* (New York: Sheed & Ward, 1954), pp. 110–41.

30. Job 1:1.

31. Roger French and Andrew Cunningham, *Before Science: The Invention of the Friars' Natural Philosophy* (Aldershot, U.K.: Scolar Press, 1996), p. 134. And see the useful discussion of *On the Two Principles* at pp. 132–35.

32. To say that the cause "draws" things from potency to actuality suggests that the commentator is thinking of Aristotle's "formal" and "final" causes as well as their "efficient" cause.

33. Quoted in Oldenbourg, op. cit., p. 2.

34. Ibid., p. 5.

35. Ibid., p. 116–17.

36. Robert Fossier, ed., *Cambridge Illustrated History of the Middle Ages*, Vol. 2: *950–1250* (Cambridge: Cambridge University Press, 1997), p. 196 et seq.

37. Innocent III did not make peace with all the evangelical movements. The Waldensians, most notably, remained outside the organized Church and ended by accepting the Protestant Reformation. See Lambert, op. cit., pp. 73–74, 92–93, and 360–67.

38. On the literary explosion and the Church's loss of its "cultural monopoly," see Fossier, op. cit., pp. 401–11.

39. There are many descriptions of the education offered by medieval universities. See, e.g., Hastings Rashdall, *The Universities of Europe in the Middle Ages*, Vol. 1: *Salerno-Bologna-Paris*, new ed., F. M. Powicke and A. B. Emden, eds. (Oxford: Oxford University Press, 1936); Friedrich Heer, *The Medieval World: Europe, 1100–1350*, Janet Sondheimer, trans. (Cleveland and New York: The World Publishing Company, 1961), pp. 190–212; Michael Haren, *Medieval Thought: The Western Intellectual Tradition from Antiquity to the Thirteenth Century*, 2d ed. (Toronto and Buffalo: University of Toronto Press, 1992), pp. 137–43; and Edward Grant, *God & Reason in the Middle Ages* (Cambridge: Cambridge University Press, 2001), pp. 98–114, passim.

40. Marcia L. Colish, *Medieval Foundations of the Western Intellectual Tradition, 400–1400* (New Haven and London: Yale University Press, 1997), p. 267.

41. "By 1362 there were 441 masters in the [Paris] faculty of arts as compared with 25 in theology, 25 in medicine and 11 in canon law." Heer, op. cit., p. 200.

42. Ibid.

43. Fernand van Steenberghen, *Aristotle in the West: The Origins of Latin Aristotelianism*, Leonard Johnston, trans. (New York: Humanities Press, 1970), p. 67 (my translation).

44. Ibid., p. 68.

45. Fernand van Steenberghen, *La Philosophie au XIIIe Siecle.* (Lou-

vain: Publications Universitaires, 1966; and Paris VIe: Vander-Oyez, S.A., 1977), pp. 88–91.

46. Rashdall, op. cit., p. 356.

47. Ibid., p. 354, states that Amalric "died of chagrin" after being forced to retract his heretical views. Heer, op. cit., p. 214, suggests that ten Amalricians were burned. Other historians have them sentenced to life imprisonment.

48. French and Cunningham, op. cit., pp. 99–100.

49. According to Heer, op. cit., p. 214, the Amalricians identified the Holy Spirit with the *intellectua agens* or activating intellect described in Aristotle's *On the Soul*.

50. "If the first age had been one of fear and servitude, and the second age one of faith and filial submission, the third age would be one of love, joy and freedom, when the knowledge of God would be revealed directly in the hearts of all men." Norman Cohn, *The Pursuit of the Millennium: Revolutionary Millenarians and Mystical Anarchists of the Middle Ages*, 3d. ed. (New York: Oxford University Press, 1970), p. 108.

51. The "Amalricians" are identified as proto-Joachimites by Heer, op. cit., p. 214, and by Mundy, op. cit., p. 307.

52. See, e.g., Lambert's discussion of the Brethren of the Free Spirit, op. cit., pp. 182–86.

CHAPTER FIVE
"Hark, Hark, the Dogs Do Bark"
ARISTOTLE AND THE TEACHING FRIARS

1. Hastings Rashdall, *The Universities of Europe in the Middle Ages*, Vol. 1: *Salerno-Bologna-Paris*, new ed., F. M. Powicke and A. B. Emden, eds. (Oxford: Oxford University Press, 1936), p. 334. I have based this account of the riot and strike of 1229–1231 on several sources, including Rashdall, pp. 334–43; Fernand van Steenberghen, *Aristotle in the West: The Origins of Latin Aristotelianism*, Leonard Johnston, trans. (New York: Humanities Press, 1970),

pp. 78–82; and Friedrich Heer, *The Medieval World: Europe, 1100–1350,* Janet Sondheimer, trans. (Cleveland and New York: The World Publishing Company, 1961), p. 202.

2. Rashdall, op. cit., p. 335.

3. Ibid.

4. Van Steenberghen, op. cit., p. 82, my translation.

5. Ibid., p. 78.

6. Ibid., p. 84.

7. The remark is M. De Wulf's, quoted in van Steenberghen, op. cit., p. 116.

8. Roger French and Andrew Cunningham, *Before Science: The Invention of the Friars' Natural Philosophy* (Aldershot, U.K.: Scolar Press, 1996), p. 161.

9. My reading of William of Auvergne's work follows that of French and Cunningham, op. cit., pp. 160–68, but is also influenced by W. T. Jones's distinction between events within a system and the system as a whole, made in connection with his discussion of Aquinas (*The Medieval Mind,* Vol. 2: *A History of Western Philosophy,* 2d ed. [New York: Harcourt, Brace & World, 1969], pp. 220–21 and 238–39).

10. "Clearly, then, the bad does not exist apart from bad things; for the bad is in its nature posterior to the potency. And therefore we may also say that in the things which are from the beginning, i.e. in eternal things, there is nothing bad, nothing defective, nothing perverted (for perversion is something bad)." Aristotle, *Metaphysics,* W. D. Ross, trans., in *Works,* Vol. 1 (Chicago: Encyclopedia Britannica, 1952), 9.9, 1051a17–21.

11. The most comprehensive discussion of this doctrine is that of Richard C. Dales, in *Medieval Discussions of the Eternity of the World* (Leiden and New York: E. J. Brill, 1990).

12. Aristotle, *Physics,* R. P. Hardie and R. K. Gaye., trans., in *Works,* Vol. 1 (Chicago: Encyclopedia Britannica, 1952), 8.1, 250b10 et seq.

13. Edward Grant, *God & Reason in the Middle Ages* (Cambridge: Cambridge University Press, 2001), p. 237.

14. French and Cunningham, op. cit., p. 167, paraphrasing William's words.

15. Ibid., p. 165.

16. Michael Haren, *Medieval Thought: The Western Intellectual Tradition from Antiquity to the Thirteenth Century*, 2d ed. (Toronto and Buffalo: University of Toronto Press, 1992), p. 172.

17. Josef Pieper, *Scholasticism: Personalities and Problems of Medieval Philosophy*, Richard and Clara Winston, trans. (New York and Toronto: McGraw-Hill, 1964), p. 109.

18. Ibid., p. 114. Pieper notes his "crude and noisy" attacks on ignorant critics (p. 109).

19. Vincent's work, described in French and Cunningham (op. cit., pp. 172–77), also included *Mirror of Doctrine* and *Mirror of History*.

20. Ibid., p. 115.

21. Pieper, op. cit., p. 116. The quote is from Albert's book on plants, *De Vegetabilibus*.

22. Ibid. From Albert's commentary on Aristotle's *Physics*. Pieper's discussion of the duty to understand things "as they are in themselves" is both brief and illuminating.

23. Grant, op. cit., p. 192.

24. Ibid., p. 197.

25. Ibid., pp. 193–94.

26. See the illuminating discussion by John Hedley Brooke, *Science and Religion: Some Historical Perspectives* (Cambridge: Cambridge University Press, 1991), pp. 275–317.

27. This, at least, is Marcia I. Colish's conclusion in *Medieval Foundations of the Western Intellectual Tradition, 400–1400* (New Haven and London: Yale University Press, 1997), p. 321.

28. Pieper, op. cit., p. 109.

29. Heer, op. cit., p. 247.

30. S. C. Easton, *Roger Bacon and His Search for a Universal Science: A Reconsideration of the Life and Work of Roger Bacon in the Light of His Own Stated Purposes* (Oxford: Oxford University Press, 1952), p. 126 et seq. According to Heer (op. cit., p. 244), "Bacon was wholly dominated by the historical vision of the Franciscan Spirituals, on which he explicitly based himself."

31. See the description of Francis's vision and stigmata in Michael

Robson, *St. Francis of Assisi: The Legend and the Life* (London: Geoffrey Chapman, 1997), pp. 262–64.

32. Quoted in French and Cunningham, op cit., p. 241.

33. Bacon based his theory of sight by "intromission" on the work of the Arab scientist Alhazen. See David C. Lindberg, *The Beginnings of Western Science* (Chicago and London: University of Chicago Press, 1992), pp. 309–13.

34. Ibid., pp. 226–27; on Bacon's optics, see pp. 312–15. French and Cunningham, who offer enlightening explanations of Bacon's work and Franciscan science in general, take the position that "Bacon could not of course have been a 'scientist' because he lived in the wrong age for this" (op. cit., p. 238). What they mean by this is that it is anachronistic to consider a thinker like Bacon an odd combination of religious mystic and modern (or proto-modern) scientist, since "there was no scientific tradition (in the modern sense of the term 'scientific') of looking at nature in the thirteenth century, only a religio-political way of doing so" (p. 273). While sympathizing with this attempt to avoid the anachronism current in some histories of medieval science, one cannot help feeling that French and Cunningham run to the other extreme of denying the connections between medieval and modern science on the basis of "essentialist" definitions of each.

35. French and Cunningham, op. cit., p. 230. See also Lindberg, op. cit., p. 313: "Bacon accepted the Neoplatonic conception of the universe as a vast network of forces, in which every object acts on objects within its vicinity through the radiation of a force or likeness of itself."

36. Heer, op. cit., p. 247.

37. G. K. Chesterton, *St. Thomas Aquinas* (New York: Sheed & Ward, 1954), p. 31.

38. Chesterton, op. cit., p. 74.

39. There has been considerable recent discussion of Bonaventure's work, emphasizing his originality as a systematic theologian. Haren's summary (op. cit., pp. 161–71) is particularly useful. And

see the appreciative discussion of Bonaventure's views on the eternity of the world in Dales, op. cit., pp. 86–97.

40. *Summa Theologica*, I.1.8, in *Essential Writings of Saint Thomas Aquinas*, Anton C. Pegis, ed. (New York: Random House, 1945), p. 62. For useful summaries of Saint Thomas's work, see also Jones, op. cit., pp. 208–86; and Haren, op. cit., pp. 176–206. I have also relied on Étienne Gilson's discussion of Thomism (*The Spirit of Medieval Philosophy*, A.H.C. Downes, trans. [Notre Dame and London: University of Notre Dame Press, 1991; orig. ed., 1936]) and other works cited below.

41. Thomas denied that the existence of God is self-evident, as Bonaventure had maintained. See especially Thomas Aquinas, *Summa Contra Gentiles, Book One: God*, Anton C. Pegis, trans. (Notre Dame and London: University of Notre Dame Press, 1975), pp. 79–123.

42. Thomas Aquinas, *Summa Contra Gentiles, Book Three: Providence*, Part I, Vernon J. Bourke, trans. (Notre Dame and London: University of Notre Dame Press, 1975), p. 97.

43. Van Steenberghen, op. cit., p. 166.

44. Robert Fossier, ed., *Cambridge Illustrated History of the Middle Ages*, Vol. 2: *950–1250* (Cambridge: Cambridge University Press, 1997), pp. 326–29.

45. There are conflicting theories about the origins of this rhyme, but Chesterton attributes it to the period under discussion in his biography (op. cit., p. 41). "Jags" are tattered garments, very likely those of the Franciscan friars; "velvet gown" (an alternative version is "silken gown") probably refers to the academic dress of the Dominicans.

46. Timothy 2:3, 1–5.

CHAPTER SIX
"*This* Man Understands"
THE GREAT DEBATE AT THE UNIVERSITY OF PARIS

1. Fernand van Steenberghen, *Aristotle in the West: The Origins of Latin Aristotelianism*, Leonard Johnston, trans. (New York: Humanities

Press, 1970), pp. 220–21. See also van Steenberghen, *Maitre Siger de Brabant* (Louvain: Publications Universitaires, 1966; and Paris VIe: Vander-Oyez, S.A., 1977).

2. Dante Alighieri, *The Divine Comedy, Paradise*, Canto 10, lines 133–38. Italian version, http://www.divinecomedy.org/divine_comedy.html (Author's translation).

3. According to Richard C. Dales, Siger was "a very acute independent philosopher, as well as a devout Christian," as was his colleague, Boethius of Dacia (*Medieval Discussions of the Eternity of the World* [Leiden and New York: E. J. Brill, 1990], pp. 140–53).

4. Quoted in Dales, *Medieval Discussions*, p. 144.

5. Ibid.

6. Ibid., pp. 145–46.

7. Van Steenberghen, op. cit., p. 231. The author estimates Siger's "party" as "probably numbering less than a quarter of the members of the faculty, masters and students."

8. Quoted in Ralph McInerny, *Aquinas Against the Averroists: On There Being Only One Intellect* (West Lafayette, Ind.: Purdue University Press, 1993), p. 11.

9. Quoted in Michael Haren, *Medieval Thought: The Western Intellectual Tradition from Antiquity to the Thirteenth Century*, 2d ed. (Toronto and Buffalo: University of Toronto Press, 1992), p. 203.

10. See Chapter 8, infra.

11. Friedrich Heer, *The Medieval World: Europe, 1100–1350*, Janet Sondheimer, trans. (Cleveland and New York: The World Publishing Company, 1961), p. 216. The view of Siger as an early rationalist was initially developed by Pierre Mondonnet, *Siger de Brabant et l'averroisme latin au XIIIe siecle*, Vols. 1 and 2, 2d ed. (Louvain: Institut supérieur de philosophie de l'Université, 1911).

12. Étienne Gilson, *Reason and Revelation in the Middle Ages* (New York and London: Charles Scribner's Sons, 1950), p. 58.

13. Translated in McInerny, op. cit., p. 143; see also the discussion at pp. 212–13.

14. See David Caute, *The Great Fear: The Anti-Communist Purge under Truman and Eisenhower* (London: Secker and Warburg, 1979).
15. The translation is from Haren, op. cit., p. 198.
16. The translations below are from McInerny, op. cit., p. 9. I have added words in brackets for clarity.
17. Ibid. The additional proposition relating to monopsychism was "That the soul, which is the form of the human being insofar as the human being is human, corrupts when the body corrupts."
18. Ibid. The three propositions relating to necessity were "That a human being's will necessarily wills or chooses"; "That all things here below come under the necessary control of the heavenly bodies"; and "That free will is a passive not an active power, and that it is moved necessarily by the desired object."
19. "External riches are necessary for the good of virtue: since by them we support the body, and help others . . . the possession of riches is good for some who use them for virtue: while to others it is an evil, because they are withdrawn thereby from virtue." Thomas Aquinas, *Summa Contra Gentiles, Book Three: Providence*, op. cit., pp. cxxxiii and cxxxv.
20. Aristotle, *Nicomachean Ethics*, W. D. Ross, trans., in *Works*, Vol. 2 (Chicago: Encyclopedia Britannica, 1952), 10.7, 1177a11 et seq.
21. Aquinas, op. cit., pp. xxxvii–xxxviii and lxi–lxii.
22. Some commentators believe that Thomas's rationalist, voluntarist ethics conflict with his own affirmation of the Christian dogmas of predestination and grace. See, e.g., W. T. Jones, *The Medieval Mind*, Vol. 2: *A History of Western Philosophy*, 2d ed. (New York: Harcourt, Brace & World, 1969), pp. 278–85.
23. Aristotle, *Politics*, Benjamin Jowett, trans., in *Works*, Vol. 2 (Chicago: Encyclopedia Britannica, 1952), 1.2, 1253a2–3.
24. McInerny, op. cit., p. 175, summarizing Aristotle, *On the Soul.*
25. The differences between Aquinas and Bonaventure had already produced a "polarization of views" in the 1250s (Richard C. Dales, *The Problem of the Rational Soul in the Thirteenth Century* [Leiden and New York: E. J. Brill, 1995], pp. 99–112).

26. The text of this tract, a translation, and a useful commentary are to be found in McInerny, op. cit.
27. Aristotle, *On the Soul*, J. A. Smith, trans., in *Works*, Vol. 1 (Chicago: Encyclopedia Britannica, 1952), 1.4, 408b18–19.
28. Ibid., 1.4, 408b13–14.
29. Another implication of Siger's monopsychism is that the resurrection of the body becomes impossible, since there is no individual soul to reanimate it. For a useful discussion of Averroës's original monopsychism, see Oliver Leaman, *Averroes and His Philosophy* (Oxford: Clarendon Press, 1988) pp. 90–96.
30. Averroës grappled inconclusively with this problem. See Leaman, op. cit., pp. 93–94.
31. Thomas Aquinas, *On There Being Only One Intellect*, I, quoted in McInerny, op. cit., p. 19. See also IV, p. 11; and McInerny's discussion, p. 205 et seq. Thomas argued generally that Aristotle's concept of the "active intellect" did not have the meaning ascribed to it by Averroës.
32. See Arthur Koestler, *The Ghost in the Machine* (New York: Random House, 1982).
33. Étienne Gilson, *The Spirit of Medieval Philosophy*, A.H.C. Downes, trans. (Notre Dame and London: University of Notre Dame Press, 1991; orig. ed., 1936), pp. 180–88.
34. See van Steenberghen, op. cit., pp. 377–83; Ralph McInerny, op. cit., p. 12; and Haren, op. cit., pp. 201–2.
35. Josef Pieper, *Scholasticism: Personalities and Problems of Medieval Philosophy*, Richard and Clara Winston, trans. (New York and Toronto: McGraw-Hill, 1964), p. 121.
36. G. K. Chesterton (*St. Thomas Aquinas* [New York: Sheed & Ward, 1954], p. 140) connects Thomas's "materialism" with the doctrine of the Incarnation: "After the Incarnation had become the idea that is central in our civilization, it was inevitable that there should be a return to materialism, in the sense of the serious value of matter and the making of the body. When once Christ had risen, it was inevitable that Aristotle should rise again."

37. Siger de Brabant, *On the Eternity of the World*, quoted in Dales, *Medieval Discussions*, p. 141.

38. Ibid., p. 143.

39. For example, Bonaventure argued that positing an endless series of events is illogical, because it involves adding new items to an already infinite series, which was then considered a mathematical impossibility; ibid., pp. 91–93. See also Edward Grant, *God & Reason in the Middle Ages* (Cambridge: Cambridge University Press, 2001), pp. 237–52, which also discusses Gregory of Rimini's (d. 1358) solution to the problem of the "absolute infinite." Bonaventure distinguished "eternal," referring to an infinite duration of time, from "eternal" in the sense of something existing outside time and space altogether.

40. Thomas's essay "On the Eternity of the World" is discussed in Dales, *Medieval Discussions*, pp. 134–40. Thomas's major point was that, since there is no "before" or "after" in eternity, God could have made the world co-eternal with himself if he had wanted to.

41. Haren, op. cit., p. 180.

42. "In the sight of those who could not understand the deeper meaning of his philosophical innovations, Thomas Aquinas was bound to appear, if not as an Averroist, at least as a fellow traveller." Étienne Gilson wrote this line in 1955. See his *History of Christian Philosophy in the Middle Ages* (New York and London: Charles Scribner's Sons, 1955), p. 409.

43. Considering his generally moderate temper, Aquinas is frequently compared to a liberal or Whig, but in some ways he resembles radical figures like Leon Trotsky, who argued that what was wrong with Stalinism was that it was insufficiently Marxist. (Trotsky was not, of course, a moderate by temperament.)

44. See, e.g., van Steenberghen, op. cit., pp. 80–88.

45. Rashdall, op. cit., pp. 328–30.

46. Haren, op. cit., p. 204.

47. See, e.g., van Steenberghen, op. cit., p. 144 et seq.

48. This conclusion is the result of recent research by Rene Gauthier

summarized by J.M.M.H. Thijssen, *Censure and Heresy at the University of Paris, 1200–1400* (Philadelphia: University of Pennsylvania Press, 1998), pp. 47–48.

49. Pieper, op. cit., pp. 123–24.

50. See Thijssen's discussion of older and newer theories as to the letters of Pope John XXI, *Censure and Heresy,* pp. 43–47.

51. Ibid., p. 49. Other references to this letter are on pp. 49–52.

52. Quoted in Haren, op. cit., p. 194.

53. Translated and discussed by Grant, op. cit., pp. 215–17. See also John F. Wippel, "The Condemnations of 1270 and 1277 at Paris," in *Journal of Medieval and Renassiance Studies* 7 (1977), pp. 169–201.

54. Dales, *Medieval Discussions,* p. 176.

55. Grant, op. cit., p. 214.

56. This has been a subject of dispute among scholars, with Wippel arguing, persuasively, in my view, that Thomas was a target of the condemnations ("Thomas Aquinas and the Condemnations of 1277," in *The Modern Schoolman* 72 [1995].) See also Henry F. Nardone, *St. Thomas Aquinas and the Condemnations of 1277,* doctoral dissertation (Washington, D.C.: The Catholic University of America Philosophical Studies No. 209, 1963). Thijssen and some others disagree (Thijssen, *Censure and Heresy at the University of Paris, 1200–1400,* pp. 52–56).

57. The Thomist propositions censured by Kilwardby included the unicity of substantial form, the uniting of the soul directly with matter, and the absence of "seminal reasons" in prime matter, all doctrines developed by Thomas in his debates with Bonaventure and Peckham on the nature of the soul. See Haren, op. cit., p. 206.

58. Quoted in Thijssen, op. cit., pp. 55–56.

59. See, e.g., Fernand van Steenberghen, *La Philosophie au XIIIe Siecle* (Paris: Louvain, 1966), p. 304.

60. The apt "glancing blow" is a phrase of Haren's, op. cit., p. 208.

61. See Heer, op. cit., p. 284.

62. Ibid., p. 239.

63. Gilson, *History of Christian Philosophy*, p. 405.
64. Van Steenberghen, *Maitre Siger de Brabant*, p. 405.

CHAPTER SEVEN
"Ockham's Razor"
THE DIVORCE OF FAITH AND REASON

1. Friedrich Heer, *The Medieval World: Europe, 1100–1350*, Janet Sondheimer, trans. (Cleveland and New York: The World Publishing Company, 1961), p. 274.
2. Karl Marx, *The Eighteenth Brumaire of Louis Bonaparte* (New York: International Publishers, 1963), p. 15.
3. Norman F. Cantor, *The Civilization of the Middle Ages*, rev. ed. (New York: HarperCollins, 1993), p. 495.
4. Malcolm Lambert, *Medieval Heresy: Popular Movements from the Gregorian Reform to the Reformation*, 2d ed. (Oxford, U.K., and Cambridge, Mass.: Blackwell, 1992), p. 180.
5. Quoted in Heer, op. cit., p. 196.
6. Cantor, op. cit., p. 481.
7. Colin McEvedy, *The New Penguin Atlas of Medieval History* (London: Penguin Books, 1992), p. 86.
8. Cantor, op. cit., p. 495.
9. See, e.g., Barbara Tuchman, *A Distant Mirror: The Calamitous Fourteenth Century* (New York: Ballantine Books, 1987).
10. See, e.g., Lambert, op. cit., pp. 189–214.
11. David Burr, "The Persecution of Peter Olivi," in *Transactions of the American Philosophical Society* 66 (1976), pp. 3–98.
12. A modern parallel is Marx's critique of Hegel, which Engels termed "standing Hegel on his feet."
13. Richard Cross, *Duns Scotus* (New York and Oxford: Oxford University Press, 1999), pp. 3–6. On Scotus's philosophy, see also Allan B. Wolter, *The Philosophical Theology of John Duns Scotus* (Ithaca and London: Cornell University Press, 1990). W. T. Jones offers a useful short summary of Duns Scotus's ideas in *The Medieval*

Mind, Vol. 2: *A History of Western Philosophy*, 2d ed. (New York: Harcourt, Brace & World, 1969), pp. 299–316.

14. Josef Pieper, *Scholasticism: Personalities and Problems of Medieval Philosophy*, Richard and Clara Winston, trans. (New York and Toronto: McGraw-Hill, 1964), p. 139. See also Pieper's respectfully critical (pro-Thomist) commentary at pp. 139–46.

15. The controversies about how we know what we know are thoroughly discussed in Robert Pasnau, *Theories of Cognition in the Later Middle Ages* (Cambridge: Cambridge University Press, 1997).

16. For an extended discussion of Aquinas's views on being, see Philipp W. Rosemann, *Understanding Scholastic Thought with Foucault* (New York: St. Martin's Press, 1999), pp. 133–81.

17. For Duns Scotus's discussion of our ability to reach conclusions that are certain, see Jones, op. cit., pp. 305–9. See also Pieper (op. cit., p. 145), in which the author accuses Duns Scotus of demanding "an argument so absolutely evident as to be almost beyond human powers," while on the other hand preaching "a resignation almost equivalent to renunciation when it came to making 'reasons' intelligible."

18. Very little is known of Ockham's life. In all likelihood, he was too young to have studied directly with Duns Scotus either at Oxford or at Paris. See, e.g., Gordon Leff, *William of Ockham: The Metamorphosis of Scholastic Discourse* (Manchester: Manchester University Press, and Totawa, N.J.: Rowman and Littlefield, 1975), pp. xvi–xvii; and William Courtenay, *Schools and Scholars in Fourteenth-Century England* (Princeton, N.J.: Princeton University Press, 1987), pp. 193–96.

19. Gordon Leff, op. cit., pp. 42–44.

20. For a good short discussion of Ockham's "terminism," see Marcia L. Colish, *Medieval Foundations of the Western Intellectual Tradition, 400–1400* (New Haven and London: Yale University Press, 1997), pp. 311–15. It is worth noting that Aristotle's own position on the subject of the reality of universals was somewhat ambiguous; according to him, universals exist, but their existence is purely

derivative. See the discussion in Jonathan Barnes, ed., *The Cambridge Companion to Aristotle* (Cambridge: Cambridge University Press, 1995), pp. 96–98.

21. Leff (op. cit., p. 35, n.141) points out that the principle is much older than Ockham, going all the way back to Aristotle, and that Duns Scotus employed it as well, although not so extensively as Ockham.

22. On Scotus's individuation theory, see Wolter, op. cit., pp. 68–97. For Ockham's views, see Leff, op. cit, pp. 62–77. An interesting recent discussion of the medieval debate from the point of view of modern philosophy is in Richard A. Lee, Jr., *Science, the Singular, and the Question of Theology* (New York: Palgrave, 2002).

23. For Ockham's views, see Leff, op. cit., pp. 62–77.

24. Lee, op. cit., p. 104.

25. Ibid.

26. See the discussion supra at pp. 116–18.

27. See Oliver Leaman, *Moses Maimonides* (Richmond, Surrey: Curzon Press, 1997), pp. 18–38.

28. Thomas Aquinas took this as his starting point: "For, by its immensity, the divine substance surpasses every form that our intellect reaches. Thus we are unable to apprehend it by knowing *what it is*. Yet we are able to have some knowledge of it by knowing *what it is not*." *Summa Contra Gentiles; Book One: God*, Anton C. Pegis, trans. (Notre Dame and London: University of Notre Dame Press, 1975), p. 96.

29. Oliver Leaman, *Moses Maimonides*, op. cit., p. 26. William of Ockham reached a similar conclusion (see Leff, op. cit., p. 370 et seq.).

30. Ibid., p. 19.

31. Ibid., pp. 29 (2) and 30 (2).

32. Leff, op. cit., p. 159; and see the discussion at pp. 159–63.

33. An example is Duns Scotus's concept of the "formal distinction," which he had used to avoid taking a clearly nominalist position on the issue of individuals and universals. See Leff, op. cit., pp. 111–20.

34. Cited and discussed in Pieper, op. cit., pp. 148–49.

35. Leff, op. cit., xvi.

36. See the cases discussed in J.M.M.H. Thijssen, *Censure and Heresy at the University of Paris, 1200–1400* (Philadelphia: University of Pennsylvania Press, 1998).

37. Richard Tarnas, *The Passion of the Western Mind: Understanding the Ideas That Have Shaped Our World View* (New York: Ballantine Books, 1991), p. 201.

38. Frank Tobin, *Meister Eckhart: Thought and Language* (Philadelphia: University of Pennsylvania Press, 1986), p. 11.

39. The mystical experience, of course, moves beyond sensory knowledge to the "ground of being." But, like sensory knowledge, it does not require reasoning. Colish describes Eckhart as a "Christian Aristotelian and . . . an essentially cognitive and analytic mystic" (op. cit., p. 240).

40. Tobin, op. cit., p. 70.

41. Jeanne Ancelet-Hustache, *Master Eckhart and the Rhineland Mystics*, Hilda Graef, trans. (New York and London: Harper Torchbooks and Longmans, 1957), p. 121. And see Ancelet-Hustache's description of the trial at pp. 120–38.

42. It has been suggested that this investigation may have been undertaken at Eckhart's request in order to clear his reputation before more hostile inquisitors appeared. See Tobin, op. cit., p. 9. Eckhart later argued (fruitlessly) that since he had been found innocent of heresy by a papal investigator, he could not be tried a second time on the same charge.

43. Ancelet-Hustache, op. cit., p. 125.

44. Meister Eckhart, "See What Love," quoted in Reiner Schurmann, *Meister Eckhart: Mystic and Philosopher* (Bloomington, Ind., and London: University of Indiana Press, 1978), pp. 133–34. See also Schurmann's commentary on the sermon at pp. 137–71.

45. Tobin, op. cit., pp. 129–30.

46. Ibid., p. 92. See also Ancelet-Hustache, op. cit., p. 128.

47. Ancelet-Hustache, op. cit., pp. 139–71. The author points out that this revival may also have been a response to the appearance of the Black Death beginning in the 1340s.

48. See the discussion infra at p. 273 et seq. The term "Ockhamist" was used in a general way to designate scholars whose work was inspired, to some extent, by William of Ockham's approach to natural philosophy. Ockham's theological teachings at the Paris faculty of arts were restricted by a series of statutes passed by the masters in the 1340s, and some latter-day "Ockhamists" had their work condemned, but there was no "wholesale clearing out of entrenched Ockhamist opinions" at the University of Paris. See David A. Luscombe, *Medieval Thought* (Oxford: Oxford University Press, 1997), p. 161.

Chapter Eight
"God Does Not Have to Move These Circles Anymore"
Aristotle and the Modern World

1. Aristotle, *On the Heavens* (*De Caelo*), J. L. Stocks, trans., in *Works*, Vol. 1 (Chicago: Encyclopedia Britannica, 1952), 2.14, 297b.24–298a.20.
2. Edward Grant, *God & Reason in the Middle Ages* (Cambridge: Cambridge University Press, 2001), pp. 339–40. See also Jeffrey Burton Russell, *Inventing the Flat Earth: Columbus and Modern Historians* (New York: Praeger, 1991).
3. According to Rabbi Stephen S. Wise, a leader of American Reform Judaism, Freudian psychoanalytic theory was "a digging down into the sewage of our moods and appetites, dreams and passions." Peter Gay, *Freud: A Life for Our Time* (New York and London: W. W. Norton, 1988), p. 451.
4. The current battle between "Right to Life" activists and scientists wishing to do research on embryonic stem cells is a current example of the genre.
5. Although known as "Ockhamists," many members of the Parisian school differed with William of Ockham on theological matters. The theological writings of certain latter-day "Ockhamists" were censured by the university authorities.
6. Buridan's philosophical work is famous, among other things, for "Buridan's ass," an image provoked by his idea that people's free

will is limited by the strength of their motivation. If the intellect presents one alternative as better than another, he maintained, that judgment dictates the choice that people will make, while if all alternatives are considered equally worthwhile, people will make no choice at all. "Buridan's ass" (an idea concocted by one of his philosophical opponents) is a hungry donkey tempted by two equally desirable, equidistant bales of hay. Unable to choose between them, the poor creature dies of starvation.

7. See Thomas S. Kuhn's discussion of science as a series of paradigmatic "revolutions" in *The Structure of Scientific Revolutions* (Chicago: University of Chicago Press, 1962).

8. Aristotle and the ancients considered the heavenly bodies intelligent beings that were "moved," not in the sense of being pushed but in the sense of being impelled to change in the way that a lover is impelled to unite with the beloved. See the discussion by Jonathan Barnes, ed., *The Cambridge Companion to Aristotle* (Cambridge: Cambridge University Press, 1995), pp. 104–5.

9. Quoted in Harold P. Nebelsick, *The Renaissance, the Reformation, and the Rise of Science* (Edinburgh: T & T Clark, 1992), p. 63.

10. Grant, op. cit., p. 167.

11. David C. Lindberg, *The Beginnings of Western Science* (Chicago and London: University of Chicago Press, 1992), p. 305.

12. Lindberg, op. cit., pp. 296–301; Grant, op. cit., pp. 172–74.

13. Pierre Duhem, "Nicole Oresme," in *The New Advent Catholic Encyclopedia*, http://www.newadvent.org/cathen/11296a.htm (From Vol 11 of 1911 *Catholic Encyclopedia*).

14. Quoted in Grant, op. cit., p. 200. Grant says "experience," not "experiment," but this may be a mistranslation of the French word "expérience" (Oresme's book was written in French).

15. Quoted in Lindberg, op. cit., p. 260.

16. Ibid.

17. Ibid., p. 261.

18. Ibid., pp. 361–62.

19. "Strictly speaking, it was impossible to effect a fusion of Aristotle with Christianity—as Aquinas was well aware." John Hedley

Brooke, *Science and Religion: Some Historical Perspectives* (Cambridge: Cambridge University Press, 1991), pp. 60–61. Brooke points out that Aquinas therefore shifted the central emphasis in metaphysics from Aristotle's doctrines of motion and becoming to "the problem of existence."

20. By requiring "that one pay attention to God's creative will, rather than God's knowing and creative intellect," the condemnations probably accelerated the split between methods of understanding the material universe and methods of relating to God. See Richard A. Lee, Jr., *Science, the Singular, and the Question of Theology* (New York: Palgrave, 2002), pp. 59–60.

21. For a useful short summary of the period, see Eugene F. Rice, Jr., *The Foundations of Early Modern Europe, 1460–1559* (New York: W. W. Norton, 1970).

22. An excellent summary of the "continuity debate" is to be found in Lindberg, op. cit., pp. 355–68.

23. See Pierre Duhem, *To Save the Phenomena: An Essay on the Idea of Physical Theory from Plato to Galileo*, Edmund Doland and Chaninah Maschler, trans. (Chicago: University of Chicago Press, 1969).

24. Albert Einstein, "Physics and Reality," in *Ideas and Opinions*, Sonja Bargmann, trans. (New York: Dell, 1954), p. 286.

25. Grant, op. cit., p. 364.

26. Francis Bacon, *The Physical and Metaphysical Works of Lord Bacon, Including "The Advancement of Learning" and "Novum Organum,"* Joseph Devey, ed. (London: George Bell and Sons, 1904), pp. 384–414.

27. Francis Bacon, *The Advancement of Learning*, B. W. Kitchin, ed. (London: Dent, 1965), 1.4.2, 24.

28. Galileo Galilei, *Dialogue Concerning the Two Chief World Systems—Ptolemaic & Copernican*, Stillman Drake, trans. (Los Angeles: University of California Press, 1962), p. 110.

29. Martin Luther, *Against Pelagianism*, quoted in J. H. Merle d'Aubigné, *The Life and Times of Martin Luther*, H. White, trans. (Chicago: Moody Press, 1953), p. 85.

30. Martin Luther, "Against Scholastic Theology," in *Luther's Works,*

Vol. 31: *Career of the Reformer: I,* Harold J. Grimm, ed. (Philadelphia: Muhlenberg Press, 1957), p. 12.

31. Thomas Hobbes, *Leviathan,* J.C.A. Gaskin, ed. (New York: Oxford University Press, 1998), p. 445.

32. See the discussion supra, at pp. 6–7.

33. Hobbes, op. cit., p. 86 ex. seq.

34. Ibid., pp. 183, 189–90, 192–93, 235.

35. See Thomas Aquinas, "On Law," in *Selected Writings of Saint Thomas Aquinas,* Anton C. Pegis, ed. (New York: Random House, 1945), p. 362.

36. Aristotle, *Politics,* Benjamin Jowett, trans., in *Works,* Vol. 2 (Chicago: Encyclopedia Britannica, 1952), and see the important discussion of Hobbes's conflict with Aristotle in Pierre Manent, *The City of Man,* Marc A. LePain, trans. (Princeton: Princeton University Press, 1998), pp. 169–77.

37. In *Against Pelagianism* (quoted in Aubigné, op. cit., p. 85), Luther declared: "Every work of the law appears good outwardly, but inwardly it is sin. This will, when it turns toward the law without the grace of God, does so in its own interest alone. Cursed are all those who perform the works of the law. Blessed are all those who perform the works of God's grace."

38. Luther was, in fact, a graduate of the Ockhamist University of Erfurt.

39. Epistle of Paul to the Romans 1:17. The quotation from the Book of Habakkuk (2:4) is also translated as "The righteous shall live by faith."

40. Aubigné, op. cit., p. 46.

41. The discrediting of Marxism after the Cold War provides an interesting parallel. Karl Marx's ideas had become so identified with the practices of Soviet and Chinese Communism that most people could not be bothered to disentangle them.

42. Richard Tarnas, *The Passion of the Western Mind: Understanding the Ideas That Have Shaped Our World View* (New York: Ballantine Books, 1991), p. 286.

43. Ibid.

44. See John Hedley Brooke, op. cit., p. 29.

45. "With war in Iraq looming, and much of the world opposed to his position, the president in recent weeks has adopted a strongly devotional tone. In a series of speeches... Bush has far more openly embraced Christian theology." *The Washington Post,* February 11, 2003, A2.

46. See, for example, René Descartes, *Discourse on Method and Meditation* (New York: Liberal Arts Press, 1976).

47. This does not mean, of course, that such conflicts are impossible. See Kenneth W. Kemp, "The Possibility of Conflict between Science and Christian Theology," in Jitse M. ven der Meer, ed., *Facets of Faith and Science,* Vol. 1: *Historiography and Modes of Interaction* (Lanham, Md.; New York; and London: University Press of America, 1996), pp. 247–65.

48. Ibid., pp. 275–309.

49. For a general discussion, see James Davison Hunter, *Culture Wars: The Struggle to Define America* (New York: Basic Books, 1992).

Select Bibliography

Abelard, Peter. *A Dialogue of a Philosopher with a Jew and a Christian.* Translated by Pierre J. Payer. Toronto: The Pontifical Institute of Mediaeval Studies, 1979.

————. *The Story of Abelard's Adversities: A Translation with Notes of the "Historia Calamitatum."* Translated by J. T. Muckle. Toronto: The Pontifical Institute of Mediaeval Studies, 1964.

Abrahams, Israel. *Jewish Life in the Middle Ages.* New York: Atheneum, 1975.

Abulafia, David. *Frederick II: A Medieval Emperor.* London: Allen Lane, The Penguin Press, 1988.

Abulafia, D., M. Franklin, and M. Rubin, editors. *Church and City, 1000–1500: Essays in Honour of Christopher Brooke.* Cambridge: Cambridge University Press, 1992.

Afnan, Soheil M. *Avicenna: His Life and Works.* London: George Allen & Unwin, 1958.

Agius, Dionisius A., and Richard Hitchcock, editors. *The Arab Influence in Medieval Europe.* Reading, U.K.: Ithaca Press, 1994.

Ancelet-Hustache, Jeanne. *Master Eckhart and the Rhineland Mystics.* Translated by Hilda Graef. New York and London: Harper Torchbooks and Longmans, 1957.

Anselm of Canterbury. *Monologion and Proslogion, with the Replies of*

Gaunilo and Anselm. Translated by Thomas Williams. Indianapolis and Cambridge: Hackett Publishing Company, 1995.

Aquinas, Thomas. *Summa Contra Gentiles, Book One: God.* Translated by Anton C. Pegis. Notre Dame, Indiana, and London: University of Notre Dame Press, 1975.

————. *Summa Contra Gentiles, Book Three: Providence, Part I.* Translated by Vernon J. Bourke. Notre Dame, Indiana, and London: University of Notre Dame Press, 1975.

Archer-Hind, R. D. *The Timaeus of Plato.* London and New York: Macmillan and Co., 1888.

Aristotle, *Works, Vols. 1 and 2.* Chicago: Encyclopedia Britannica, 1952.

Armstrong, Karen. *A History of God: The 4000-Year Quest of Judaism, Christianity, and Islam.* New York: Ballantine Books, 1993.

————. *Islam: A Short History.* New York: Modern Library, 2000.

Artz, Ferdinand B. *The Mind of the Middle Ages: An Historical Survey, A.D. 200–1500.* 3d ed. rev. Chicago and London: University of Chicago Press, 1980.

d'Aubigné, J. H. Merle. *The Life and Times of Martin Luther.* Translated by H. White. Chicago: Moody Press, 1953.

Augustine of Hippo. *The City of God.* Translated by Marcus Dods. New York: Modern Library, 1950.

————. *The Confessions of Saint Augustine.* Translated by Rex Warner. New York: Penguin Books, 1963.

Bacon, Francis. *The Advancement of Learning.* Edited by B. W. Kitchin. London: Dent, 1965.

————. *The Physical and Metaphysical Works of Lord Bacon, Including "The Advancement of Learning" and "Novum Organum."* Edited by Joseph Devey. London: George Bell and Sons, 1904.

Barber, Malcolm. *The Two Cities: Medieval Europe, 1050–1320.* London and New York: Routledge, 1992.

Barnes, J., M. Schofield, and R. Sorabji, editors. *Articles on Aristotle.* Vol. 2: *Ethics and Politics.* New York: St. Martin's Press, 1977.

————. *Articles on Aristotle.* Vol. 3: *Metaphysics.* New York: St. Martin's Press, 1979.

Barnes, Jonathan. *Aristotle: A Very Short Introduction*. Oxford and New York: Oxford University Press, 2000.

Barnes, Jonathan, editor. *The Cambridge Companion to Aristotle*. Cambridge: Cambridge University Press, 1995.

Barnes, Michael Horace. *Stages of Thought: The Co-Evolution of Religious Thought and Science*. Oxford and New York: Oxford University Press, 2000.

Baron, Salo Wittmayer. *A Social and Religious History of the Jews, High Middle Ages, 500–1200*. Vol. 8: *Philosophy and Science*, 2d ed. New York: Columbia University Press; Philadelphia: Jewish Publication Society of America, 1958.

Berman, Harold J. *Law and Revolution*. Cambridge, Mass.: Harvard University Press, 1985.

Bettenson, Henry, editor. *Documents of the Christian Church*. 2d ed. Oxford and London: Oxford University Press, 1963.

Biller, Peter, and Anne Hudson, editors. *Heresy and Literacy, 1000–1530*. Cambridge: Cambridge University Press, 1994.

Boethius. *The Consolation of Philosophy*. Translated by S. J. Tester. Cambridge, Mass., and London: Harvard University Press (Loeb Classical Library), 1973.

———. *The Theological Tractates*. Translated by H. F. Stewart, E. K. Rand, and S. J. Tester. Cambridge, Mass., and London: Harvard University Press (Loeb Classical Library), 1973.

Boyer, Blanche, and Richard McKeon, editors. *Peter Abailard Sic et Non, A Critical Edition*. Chicago: University of Chicago Press, 1976.

Braudel, Fernand. *A History of Civilizations*. Translated by Richard Mayne. New York and London: Allen Lane, The Penguin Press, 1994.

Bredero, Adriaan H. *Bernard of Clairvaux: Between Cult and History*. Grand Rapids, Mich.: William B. Eerdmans, 1993.

Brentano, Franz. *Aristotle and His World View*. Edited and translated by Rolf George and Roderick M. Chisholm. Berkeley and Los Angeles: University of California Press, 1978.

Brooke, John, and Geoffrey Cantor. *Reconstructing Nature: The Engagement of Science and Religion.* Edinburgh: T & T Clark, 1998.

Brooke, John Hedley. *Science and Religion: Some Historical Perspectives.* Cambridge: Cambridge University Press, 1991.

Brown, Peter. *Augustine of Hippo: A Biography.* New York: Dorset Press, 1967.

———. *Power and Persuasian in Late Antiquity: Towards a Christian Empire.* Madison, Wis.: University of Wisconsin Press, 1992.

———. *The World of Late Antiquity: AD 150–750.* New York and London: W. W. Norton, 1971.

Burr, David. "The Persecution of Peter Olivi," in *Transactions of the American Philosophical Society,* 66, 1976, 3–98.

Butterworth, Charles E., and Black Andree Kessel, editors. *The Introduction of Arabic Philosophy into Europe.* Leiden, New York, Koln: E. J. Brill, 1994.

Campbell, Joseph. *The Masks of God: Creative Mythology.* New York: Viking Press, 1968.

Cantor, Norman F. *The Civilization of the Middle Ages.* Rev. ed. New York: HarperCollins, 1993.

———. *Inventing the Middle Ages: The Lives, Works, and Ideas of the Great Medievalists of the Twentieth Century.* New York: William Morrow, 1991.

Cantor, Norman F., editor. *The Medieval World, 300–1300.* 2d ed. New York and London: Macmillan and Collier Macmillan, 1968.

Caputo, John D. *Heidegger and Aquinas: An Essay on Overcoming Metaphysics.* New York: Fordham University Press, 1982.

Carroll, James. *Constantine's Sword: The Church and the Jews.* Boston: Houghton Mifflin, 2001.

Chadwick, Henry. *The Early Church.* Rev. ed. London: Penguin Books, 1993.

Chenu, M. D. *Nature, Man, and Society in the Twelfth Century: Essays on New Theological Perspectives in the Latin West.* Translated by Jerome Taylor and Lester K. Little. Chicago and London: University of Chicago Press, 1968.

Chesteron, G. K. *St. Thomas Aquinas.* New York: Sheed & Ward, 1954.

Clark, Mary T., editor. *An Aquinas Reader.* Garden City, New York: Image Books, 1972.

Cohen, Mark R. *Under Crescent and Cross: The Jews in the Middle Ages.* Princeton, N.J.: Princeton University Press, 1994.

Cohn, Norman. *The Pursuit of the Millennium: Revolutionary Millenarians and Mystical Anarchists of the Middle Ages.* 3d. ed. New York: Oxford University Press, 1970.

Colish, Marcia L. *Medieval Foundations of the Western Intellectual Tradition, 400–1400.* New Haven and London: Yale University Press, 1997.

Copleston, Frederick C. *Medieval Philosophy.* New York and Evanston: Harper & Row, 1961.

Courtenay, William. *Schools and Scholars in Fourteenth-Century England.* Princeton, N.J.: Princeton University Press, 1987.

Cross, Richard. *Duns Scotus.* New York and Oxford: Oxford University Press, 1999.

Dales, Richard C. *Medieval Discussions of the Eternity of the World.* Leiden and New York: E. J. Brill, 1990.

———. *The Problem of the Rational Soul in the Thirteenth Century.* Leiden and New York: E. J. Brill, 1995.

Davidson, Herbert A. *Alfarabi, Avicenna, and Averroës on Intellect.* New York and Oxford: Oxford University Press, 1992.

Devey, Joseph, editor. *The Physical and Metaphysical Works of Lord Bacon, Including "The Advancement of Learning" and "Novum Organum."* London: George Bell and Sons, 1904.

Dodd, Tony. *The Life and Thought of Siger of Brabant, Thirteenth-Century Parisian Philosopher: An Examination of His Views on the Relationship of Philosophy and Theology.* Lewiston, N.Y.: Edwin Mellen Press, 1998.

Douie, Decima L. *The Conflict Between the Seculars and the Mendicants at the University of Paris in the Thirteenth Century.* New York: AMS Press, 1954.

Dronke, Peter, editor. *A History of Twelfth-Century Philosophy*. Cambridge: Cambridge University Press, 1992.

Duhem, Pierre. *To Save the Phenomena: An Essay on the Idea of Physical Theory from Plato to Galileo*. Translated by Edmund Doland and Chaninah Maschler. Chicago: University of Chicago Press, 1969.

Easton, S. C. *Roger Bacon and His Search for a Universal Science: A Reconsideration of the Life and Work of Roger Bacon in the Light of His Own Stated Purposes*. Oxford: Oxford University Press, 1952.

Eco, Umberto. *Art and Beauty in the Middle Ages*. Translated by Hugh Bredin. New Haven, Conn.: Yale University Press, 1986.

———. *The Name of the Rose*. Translated by William Weaver. New York: Warner Books, 1983.

Einstein, Albert. *Ideas and Opinions*. Translated by Sonja Bargmann. New York: Dell, 1954.

Emhardt, W. C., and G. M. Lamsa. *The Oldest Christian People: A Brief Account of the History and Traditions of the Assyrian People and the Fateful History of the Nestorian Church*. New York: AMS Press, 1926.

Erasmus. *Praise of Folly*. Translated by Betty Radice. Rev. ed. London: Penguin Books, 1993.

Evans, G. R. *Philosophy and Theology in the Middle Ages*. London and New York: Routledge, 1993.

Fakhry, Majid. *A History of Islamic Philosophy*. 2d ed. New York and London: Columbia University Press and Longmans, 1993.

Fichtenau, Heinrich. *Heretics and Scholars in the High Middle Ages, 1000–1200*. Translated by Kenise A. Kaiser. University Park, Penn.: Pennsylvania State University Press, 1998.

Fossier, Robert, editor. *The Cambridge Illustrated History of the Middle Ages*. Vol. 2: *950–1250*. Translated by Stuart Airlie and Robyn Marsack. Cambridge: Cambridge University Press, 1997.

French, Roger, and Andrew Cunningham. *Before Science: The Invention of the Friars' Natural Philosophy*. Aldershot, U.K.: Scolar Press, 1996.

Frend, W.H.C. *The Rise of Christianity*. Philadelphia: Fortress Press, 1984.

Galilei, Galileo. *Dialogue Concerning the Two Chief World Systems—Ptolemaic & Copernican*. Translated by Stillman Drake. Los Angeles: University of California Press, 1962.

Geremek, Bronislaw. *The Margins of Society in Late Medieval Paris*. Translated by Jean Birrell. Cambridge: Cambridge University Press, 1987.

Gilson, Étienne. *History of Christian Philosophy in the Middle Ages*. New York and London: Charles Scribner's Sons, 1955.

———. *Reason and Revelation in the Middle Ages*. New York and London: Charles Scribner's Sons, 1950.

———. *The Spirit of Medieval Philosophy*. Translated by A.H.C. Downes (1936). Notre Dame and London: University of Notre Dame Press, 1991.

Given, James. *State and Society in Medieval Europe: Gwynedd and Languedoc under Outside Rule*. Ithaca and London: Cornell University Press, 1990.

Gottlieb, Anthony. *The Dream of Reason: A History of Philosophy from the Greeks to the Renaissance*. New York and London: W. W. Norton, 2000.

Grant, Edward. *God & Reason in the Middle Ages*. Cambridge: Cambridge University Press, 2001.

Grant, Michael. *Dawn of the Middle Ages*. New York: Bonanza Books, 1981.

———. *From Rome to Byzantium: The Fifth Century A.D.* London and New York: Routledge, 1998.

Hanson, R.P.C. *The Search for the Christian Doctrine of God: The Arian Controversy, 318–381*. Edinburgh: T & T Clark, 1988.

Haren, Michael. *Medieval Thought: The Western Intellectual Tradition from Antiquity to the Thirteenth Century*. 2d ed. Toronto and Buffalo: University of Toronto Press, 1992.

Haskins, Charles Homer. *The Renaissance of the Twelfth Century*. New York: The World Publishing Company, 1957.

Havinghurst, Alfred F., editor. *The Pirenne Thesis*. Boston: Little, Brown, 1958.

Heer, Friedrich. *The Medieval World: Europe, 1100–1350.* Translated by Janet Sondheimer. Cleveland and New York: The World Publishing Company, 1961.

Hobbes, Thomas. *Leviathan.* Edited by J.C.A. Gaskin. New York: Oxford University Press, 1998.

Hunter, James Davison. *Culture Wars: The Struggle to Define America.* New York: Basic Books, 1992.

Illich, Ivan. *In the Vineyard of the Text: A Commentary to Hugh's Didascalion.* Chicago and London: University of Chicago Press, 1993.

James, Bruno Scott. *Saint Bernard of Clairvaux: An Essay in Biography.* New York: Harper & Brothers, 1957.

John of Salisbury. *The "Metalogicon" of John of Salisbury: A Twelfth-Century Defense of the Verbal and Logical Arts of the Trivium.* Translated by Daniel D. McGarry. Berkeley and Los Angeles: University of California Press, 1955.

Johnson, Paul. *A History of Christianity.* New York: Atheneum, 1976.

Jones, W. T. *The Medieval Mind.* Vol. 2: *A History of Western Philosophy.* 2d ed. New York: Harcourt, Brace & World, 1969.

Jourdain, Amable. *Recherches: Critiques sur l'Age et l'Origine des Traductions Latines d'Aristote.* Revised and enlarged by Charles Jourdain. New York: Burt Franklin, 1960.

Kaiser, Christopher B. *Creation and the History of Science.* Grand Rapids, Mich.: William B. Eerdmans, 1991.

Keen, Maurice. *The Penguin History of Medieval Europe.* London: Penguin Books, 1968.

Koestler, Arthur. *The Ghost in the Machine.* New York: Random House, 1982.

Kretzman, Norman, and Eleonore Stump, editors. *The Cambridge Companion to Aquinas.* Cambridge: Cambridge University Press, 1993.

Kuhn, Thomas S. *The Structure of Scientific Revolutions.* Chicago: University of Chicago Press, 1962.

Ladurie, Emmanuel Le Roy. *Montaillou: The Promised Land of Error.* Translated by Barbara Bray. New York: Vintage Books, 1979.

Lambert, Malcolm. *The Cathars.* Oxford and Malden, Mass.: Blackwell Publishers, 1998.

————. *Medieval Heresy: Popular Movements from the Gregorian Reform to the Reformation.* 2d ed. Oxford and Cambridge, Mass.: Blackwell, 1992.

Landes, Richard. *Relics, Apocalypse, and the Deceits of History: Ademar of Chabannes, 989–1034.* Cambridge, Mass., and London: Harvard University Press, 1995.

Leaman, Oliver. *Averroes and His Philosophy.* Oxford: Clarendon Press, 1988.

————. *Moses Maimonides.* Richmond, Surrey: Curzon Press, 1997.

Lee, Richard A., Jr. *Science, the Singular, and the Question of Theology.* New York: Palgrave, 2002.

Leff, Gordon. *William of Ockham: The Metamorphosis of Scholastic Discourse.* Manchester: Manchester University Press; and Totawa, N.J.: Rowman and Littlefield, 1975.

Letters of Abelard and Heloise, The. Translated by Betty Radice. London: Penguin Books, 1974.

Lewis, Archibald R. *Nomads and Crusaders, A.D. 1000–1368.* Bloomington and Indianapolis: University of Indiana Press, 1988.

Lewis, Archibald R., editor. *The Islamic World and the West, A.D. 622–1492.* New York and London: John Wiley & Sons, 1970.

Lindberg, David C. *The Beginnings of Western Science: The European Scientific Tradition in Philosophical, Religious, and Institutional Context, 600 B.C. to A.D. 1450.* Chicago and London: University of Chicago Press, 1992.

Luscombe, David A. *Medieval Thought.* Oxford: Oxford University Press, 1997.

————. "Peter Abelard," in Peter Dronke, editor, *A History of Twelfth-Century Western Philosophy.* Cambridge: Cambridge University Press, 1988.

Luther, Martin. *Luther's Works,* Vol. 31: *Career of the Reformer: I.* Edited by Harold J. Grimm. Philadelphia: Muhlenberg Press, 1957.

Malloy, Michael P. *Civil Authority in Medieval Philosophy: Lombard,*

Aquinas and Bonaventure. Lanham, N.Y., and London: University Press of America, 1985.

Manent, Pierre. *The City of Man.* Translated by Marc A. LePain. Princeton: Princeton University Press, 1998.

Marcolongo, Francis Jeremiah. *Aristotle-Aquinas-Ockham: A Comparative Study of Three Approaches in Metaphysics and Their Philosophical Significance for Understanding the Medieval Contribution to the Scientific Revolution.* Ph.D. dissertation in philosophy, University of California, San Diego. Ann Arbor, Mich.: University Microfilms, 1971.

Marcus, Jacob R. *The Jew in the Medieval World: A Source Book: 315–1791.* New York: Atheneum, 1969.

Marenbon, John. *Early Medieval Philosophy (480–1150): An Introduction.* London: Routledge & Kegan Paul, 1983.

McEvedy, Colin. *The New Penguin Atlas of Medieval History.* London: Penguin Books, 1992.

McInerny, Ralph. *Aquinas Against the Averroists: On There Being Only One Intellect.* West Lafayette, Ind.: Purdue University Press, 1993.

McNeill, William H., and Schuyler Houser, editors. *Medieval Europe.* New York: Oxford University Press, 1971.

Moffett, Samuel Hugh. *A History of Christianity in Asia,* Vol. 1: *Beginnings to 1500.* San Francisco: HarperSanFrancisco, 1992.

Moore, R. I. *The Birth of Popular Heresy.* Toronto, Buffalo, and London: University of Toronto Press, 1995.

Mundy, John H. *Europe in the High Middle Ages, 1150–1300,* 3d ed. Harlow, U.K.: Longman, 2000.

Nardone, Henry F. *St. Thomas Aquinas and the Condemnations of 1277.* Doctoral dissertation. Washington, D.C.: The Catholic University of America Philosophical Studies no. 209, 1963.

Nasr, Syyed Hossein. *Islamic Life and Thought.* Albany, N.Y.: State University of New York Press, 1981.

Nebelsick, Harold P. *The Renaissance, the Reformation, and the Rise of Science.* Edinburgh: T & T Clark, 1992.

New Advent Catholic Encyclopedia. http://www.newadvent.org/cathen (2003).

O'Brien, John A. *The Inquisition*. New York and London: Macmillan and Collier Macmillan, 1973.

Oldenbourg, Zoe. *Massacre at Montsegur: A History of the Albigensian Crusade*. Translated by Peter Green. New York: Pantheon Books, 1961.

Ormsby, Eric L., editor. *Moses Maimonides and His Time*. Washington, D.C.: Catholic University of America Press, 1989.

Pasnau, Robert. *Theories of Cognition in the Later Middle Ages*. Cambridge: Cambridge University Press, 1997.

Pegis, Anton, editor. *Essential Writings of Saint Thomas Aquinas*. New York: Random House, 1945.

Pelikan, Jaroslav. *The Christian Tradition: A History of the Development of Doctrine*. Vol. 1: *The Emergence of the Catholic Tradition (100–600)*. Chicago and London: University of Chicago Press, 1971.

———. *The Christian Tradition: A History of the Development of Doctrine*. Vol. 3: *The Growth of Medieval Theology (600–1300)*. Chicago and London: University of Chicago Press, 1978.

———. *Jesus Through the Centuries: His Place in the History of Culture*. New Haven: Yale University Press, 1985.

Peters, F. E. *Aristotle and the Arabs: The Aristotelian Tradition in Islam*. New York: New York University Press; and London: University of London Press, 1968.

Pieper, Josef. *Scholasticism: Personalities and Problems of Medieval Philosophy*. Translated by Richard and Clara Winston. New York and Toronto: McGraw-Hill, 1964.

Pirenne, Henri. *Mohamed and Charlemagne*. Translated by B. Miall. Garden City, NY: Dover Publications, 2001.

Quinn, John Francis. *The Historical Constitution of St. Bonaventure's Philosophy*. Toronto: Pontifical Institute of Medieval Studies, 1973.

Rashdall, Hastings. *The Universities of Europe in the Middle Ages*. Vol. 1: *Salerno-Bologna-Paris* (1895). New edition edited by F. M. Powicke and A. B. Emden. Oxford: Oxford University Press, 1936.

Robson, Michael. *St. Francis of Assisi: The Legend and the Life*. London: Geoffrey Chapman, 1997.

Rosemann, Philipp W. *Understanding Scholastic Thought with Foucault.* New York: St. Martin's Press, 1999.

Ross, W. D. *Aristotle*, 5th ed. London: Methuen & Company, 1949.

————. *The Works of Aristotle*, Vols. 1 and 2. Chicago: Encyclopedia Britannica, Inc., 1952.

Roth, Norman. *Jews, Visigoths, and Muslims in Medieval Spain: Cooperation and Conflict.* Leiden, New York, and Koln: E. J. Brill, 1994.

————. *Maimonides: Essays and Texts.* Madison: Hispanic Seminary of Medieval Studies, 1985.

Rougement, Denis de. *Love in the Western World.* Rev. ed. Translated by Montgomery Belgion. New York: Pantheon, 1956.

Rubenstein, Richard E. *When Jesus Became God: The Epic Struggle over Christ's Divinity in the Last Days of Rome.* New York: Harcourt Brace, 1999.

Runciman, Steven. *The Medieval Manichee: A Study of the Christian Dualist Heresy.* Cambridge: Cambridge University Press, 1947 (reissued 1982).

Russell, Jeffrey Burton. *Dissent and Order in the Middle Ages: The Search for Legitimate Authority.* New York: Twayne Publishers, 1992.

————. *Inventing the Flat Earth: Columbus and Modern Historians.* New York: Praeger, 1991.

————. *Lucifer: The Devil in the Middle Ages.* Ithaca, N.Y., and London: Cornell University Press, 1984.

Schurmann, Reiner. *Meister Eckhart: Mystic and Philosopher.* Bloomington, Ind., and London: University of Indiana Press, 1978.

Secondo, Louis J. *The Relation of Human Reason to God's Nature and Existence in the Philosophy of St. Bonaventure.* Ph.D. dissertation. Rome: Pontificium Athenaeum Internationale "Angelicum," 1961.

Sikes, J. G. *Peter Abailard.* New York: Russell & Russell, 1965 (original edition, 1932).

Smith, Charles Edward. *Innocent III: Church Defender.* Baton Rouge: Louisiana State University Press, 1951.

Southern, R. W. *The Making of the Middle Ages.* New Haven and London: Yale University Press, 1953.

————. *Medieval Humanism and Other Essays*. New York and Evanston: Harper & Row, 1970.

Stiefel, Tina. *The Intellectual Revolution in Twelfth-Century Europe*. New York: St. Martin's Press, 1985.

Tarnas, Richard. *The Passion of the Western Mind: Understanding the Ideas That Have Shaped Our World View*. New York: Ballantine Books, 1991.

Thijssen, J.M.M.H. *Censure and Heresy at the University of Paris, 1200–1400*. Philadelphia: University of Pennsylvania Press, 1998.

Tobin, Frank. *Meister Eckhart: Thought and Language*. Philadelphia: University of Pennsylvania Press, 1986.

Trevor-Roper, Hugh. *The Rise of Christian Europe*. San Diego, Cal.: Harcourt Brace Jovanovich, 1965.

Tuchman, Barbara. *A Distant Mirror: The Calamitous Fourteenth Century*. New York: Ballantine Books, 1987.

Tugwell, Simon, editor. *Albert & Thomas: Selected Writings*. New York: Paulist Press, 1988.

van der Meer, Jitse M., editor. *Facets of Faith and Science*. Vol. 1: *Historiography and Modes of Interaction*. Lanham, New York, and London: University Press of America, 1996.

van Steenberghen, Fernand. *Aristotle in the West: The Origins of Latin Aristotelianism*. Translated by Leonard Johnston. New York: Humanities Press, 1970.

————. *Maitre Siger de Brabant*. Louvain: Publications Universitaires, 1966; and Paris VIe: Vander-Oyez, S.A., 1977.

————. *La Philosophie au XIIIe Siecle*. Paris and Louvain: Publications Universitaires, 1966.

————. *Thomas Aquinas and Radical Aristotelianism*. Washington, D.C.: Catholic University of America Press, 1980.

Wahba, Mourad, and Mona Abousenna, editors. *Averroës and the Enlightenment*. Amherst, N.Y.: Prometheus Books, 1996.

Watt, W. Montgomery. *Islamic Philosophy and Theology: An Extended Survey*. Edinburgh: Edinburgh University Press, 1987.

Wippel, John F. "The Condemnations of 1270 and 1277 at Paris," in *Journal of Medieval and Renassiance Studies* 7 (1977).

———. *Medieval Reactions to the Encounter Between Faith and Reason.* Milwaukee: Pontifical Institute for Theological Studies, 1995.

———. "Thomas Aquinas and the Condemnations of 1277," in *The Modern Schoolman* 72 (1995).

Wolter, Allan B. *The Philosophical Theology of John Duns Scotus.* Ithaca and London: Cornell University Press, 1990.

Wood, Charles T. *The Quest for Eternity: Manners and Morals in the Age of Chivalry.* Hanover, N.H., and London: University Press of New England, 1983.

ACKNOWLEDGMENTS

A LARGE NUMBER OF friends and associates helped me make this journey into previously unknown territory. Terry Beitzel read an early draft of the manuscript and made many useful suggestions. Martin J. de Nys brought a philosopher's insight and precision to his extensive and valuable comments on a later draft. Dean Pruitt talked with me about the social psychology of medieval intellectuals and their theories of knowledge. Jonathan Macy and Rabbi Bruce Aft supplied reading materials and food for thought about religion and conflict. Elham Atashi, Victoria J. Barnett, John Hammang, Talha Kose, Manal Radwan, Alex Scheinman, and Zheng Wang provided valuable research assistance. Maureen Connors of the George Mason University Fenwick Library was, as ever, a source of technical aid and moral support. I am most grateful to the students, faculty, and staff of the Institute for Conflict Analysis and Resolution, and to the institute's working group on religion and conflict, for allowing me to present the ideas discussed in *Aristotle's Children* and discussing them with me at length. Dr. Sara Cobb, director of the institute, provided the institutional support, personal encouragement, and protection against bureaucratic slings and arrows that every author needs, but few obtain.

I owe a special debt of gratitude to those who, in important ways, made this book their own. Jane Isay, editor in chief of Harcourt, encouraged me to undertake the work, sustained my spirits during the hard times, made galvanizing editorial suggestions, and was unfailingly patient, insightful, enthusiastic, and helpful. We will need to invent a new word to describe the sort of partnership that an editor like Jane establishes with authors lucky enough to count themselves among her colleagues and friends. Thanks, too, to David Hough, Harcourt's managing editor, and to Gail Ross, my skillful and dedicated literary agent, for giving this project such creative and energetic attention.

Shana and Hannah Rubenstein deserve special recognition for allowing their dad to pay so much attention for so long a time to so many dead philosophers. Thank you, dear ones, for your helpfulness and patience. Thanks also to my sons, Matthew and Alec Rubenstein, for listening to me rant at long distance about the relevance of Aristotelian thought to burning contemporary issues. I have dedicated this book to Susan Ryerson, a loving comrade whose support makes the most challenging enterprises possible.

INDEX